True Experiences
The Sins That Brought Me to My Knees

by

Raymond A. Francis

DORRANCE PUBLISHING CO., INC.
PITTSBURGH, PENNSYLVANIA 15222

All Rights Reserved
Copyright © 2010 by Raymond A. Francis
No part of this book may be reproduced or transmitted
in any form or by any means, electronic or mechanical,
including photocopying, recording, or by any information
storage and retrieval system without permission in
writing from the publisher.

ISBN: 978-1-4349-0611-3
Printed in the United States of America

First Printing

For more information or to order additional books, please contact:
Dorrance Publishing Co., Inc.
701 Smithfield Street
Pittsburgh, Pennsylvania 15222
U.S.A.
1-800-788-7654
www.dorrancebookstore.com

Warning:

Note to the readers: If you are under eighteen years old and are suffering from any form of mental illness, I do not suggest this book for your reading pleasure. The reason is that, to some people, the contents of this book may cause stress, depression, and may drive the sane *insane!* Nevertheless, read at your own peril! You have been warned. Enjoy the read, and I do hope that when you reach the end, you will be stress-free.

If you can relate to this story, I do wish you all the best, and I would like to help you to understand when you dry your tears as I did mine. *Enjoy the read…*

…The content of this book is true. The name of one of the big four food stores in which Carol works is changed to Sudbury's Super Store, purely to protect myself from prosecution and also to protect Rochelle from losing her mother to the prison system and nothing else! If you are clever, you will know which one of the big four. Have a guess! Read between the lines.

My Wonderful Family
Chapter One

My dear friends, if I may call you that, before I get into the real story, I must introduce you to *my wonderful family* comprised of myself (Raymond), my two brothers, Malcolm and Rupert, my two sisters, Jane and Judy, and of course, my parents, Vincent and Betty. There were also my cousin, Velma, Aunt Pam, Aunt Agnes, and Grandma Elsie. I would not be forgetting Aunt Louise and her husband, David, whom I regard as my true parents.

I was asked not to write this chapter, but I do believe you should know, so you would have more understanding of the whole shebang!

To begin with, my grandmother on my father's side had seven children, believe it or not, from six different fathers (Is this not disgraceful even in today's society?). My biological father and his brother were fortunate enough to have the same father.

In today's society, my grandmother would be branded a whore! Nonetheless, what puzzled me was how my father met my mother because in those days, people were very class conscious.

My mother, on the other hand, came from a family which, in my opinion, would be a decent and close-knit family in today's society. My grandma and grandpa from my mother's side had six children, all from the same parents and none outside of their marriage. My grandma was from a mixed race, but her skin tone was more on the white side. My mother and her sisters had a light brown complexion. In those days, it appeared to me that the lighter skinned people are in a class of their own and found themselves a cut above the darker ones. As far as I could see in today's society, not much had changed.

My mother's family appeared to be slightly wealthy. Now, my mother had gotten herself involved with a man—my biological father! He was from a totally different background. Here we had two people: one from a wealthy home and the other from a one-parent, seven children, and six different fathers' background, living in a single-roomed apartment, with no sanitary facilities and no support from their fathers. I thought my mother was slipping into darkness at this point, and indeed, she was.

However, she ignored the wishes of her loving parents and went with this rascal. My granddad on my mother's side was quite a decent old chap, in my opinion. When I was a mere lad, he always read Bible stories to me and tried to teach me Spanish. He was a person who travelled extensively because of his job, hence, his wealthy lifestyle.

In my opinion, my mum and dad should not have been together, but she was totally enchanted by the love coming from the lower end of society; fooled I guessed, just like myself when I thought Mrs. Woodburn was projecting love to the upper end of society. How unfortunate! Mother dear, as well as myself, sought love from the wrong end of society—the bottom! However, she tried her utmost best to keep what she had as a family together. Unfortunately, due to the hard life that she faced when she was cast out from under the family umbrella, she decided to follow my so-called father to come to England to seek a better life. My brother, Malcolm, and I were left in Jamaica and cared for by my Aunt Louise and her husband, David. They eventually had seven children of their own, all girls. The childhood was not of suffering or pain. In fact, it was rather a happy childhood. Although we walked to school barefooted, it was just the tradition of the lower-middle class, even though some children did wear shoes.

My mother gave me up at the age of one year old. My brother, Malcolm, was approximately three years old at the time. My aunt took us with the promise of payment once my biological parents reached the streets of London that were known to be paved with *gold*. I could tell you to date that the streets were not paved with gold, but, occasionally, with *dog shit*. This mentality of third world countries was the same as it is today—in year 2006, not much has changed!

I met my mother and father when I was eleven years old. My aunt always told me about my mother to keep me in touch with who I was. When my parents descended from England, I was under the impression that my whole life would change for the better. But my blessing was a curse because my dad had turned out to be the worst nightmare a child could ever experience. My brother, Malcolm, and I were taken over by our biological parents whom we were both unfamiliar with. We moved into a very large house in a residential area. We also had to change school. I believed we were placed into a society different from the one we knew. We also began to wear shoes to school; that was very strange indeed. My father bought a car—I remember it as if it were yesterday—a gold coloured Ford Cortina MKII with registration BV953. I would never forget that car, and I don't think his victim would forget that car either.

My father found himself a job with the local taxi company, United Cars, but unfortunately, he found himself in a sticky situation where he was arrested for raping a female teenage passenger on her way home from school.

The day after the arrest, the news was all over the school like a wild fire! I was mocked, jeered, and spat upon at the time I was attending Mandeville all-age school.

The police cell that became home for my dad, were across the road from my school. I was devastated: What did I do at the age of eleven to deserve this? I wished, at that point, that my parents did not come to Jamaica to live there; it was an embarrassing experience. Fortunately, for my dad, due to family and close friends, bail surety was raised. I remember well going home from school, seeing my distressed mother whom I was just getting familiar with. Believe it or not, my dad fled Jamaica after three days on bail awaiting trial. After a while, things began to calm down. My dad obviously did not attend trial. That in itself proved his guilt.

One year later, my mother mentioned that she was leaving Jamaica. I was now twelve years old, and indeed, she left with her three British-born children, Rupert, Jane, and Judy. My brother Malcolm and I were placed with Aunt Linda (from my mother's side). She did her best with what God had provided for her. She also had children of her own to care for. Living with Aunt Linda and her children were very different from the life I had had up to that point, but one had no complaint due to the fact that Mother dear had promised that she would never let my brother and I down. One day, she promised we would get to England to join the rest of this family, and indeed, she kept her promise.

One year after her departure from Jamaica, she had managed to send for my brother Malcolm, and believe it or not, one year after Malcolm's departure, yes, it was my turn. I left Jamaica at age fourteen in 1974, and I never returned until that disastrous year in 1993.

In 1992, my parents decided to return to Jamaica after the collapse of the family business. The family business was a pub in the East End of London. I worked there as a barman and a disk jockey. I also had a girlfriend who worked there as a barmaid. Unfortunately, my girlfriend, Jennifer, at the time, was attacked. Her clothes were ripped from her body. This attack happened in the basement of our pub where she went to fetch a crate of drinks. Believe it or not—*shall I ask you, my dear friends,* who did you think the attacker was? *I dare say it was my one and only loving father!*

Jennifer rang me one evening, crying hysterically. I managed to calm her down in order to ascertain the incident that took place. She then made a serious allegation; at least I thought it was an allegation. Her exact words were, "Your dad ripped off my clothes and tried to rape me."

I asked her, "Are you sure about this?"

She replied, giving graphic detail of her ordeal.

She said, "I was in the cellar of the pub, looking for a crate of orange juice. I heard footsteps coming down the stairs, but I ignored them. I was suddenly grabbed from behind. My skirt was ripped off, and I felt a hand holding on to my pussy. I managed to break free from my attacker. At this point, I was on the floor, looking up. The face of my attacker was your father. His underwear was down, and he was fully aroused. I could not believe what was happening to me."

I replied, "Let us meet up to discuss this."

On my journey to meet to her, I rang my dad, literally fuming with anger. I asked, "What did you do to Jennifer?"

He replied, "I did nothing to her; she left the job."

I met Jennifer, and we discussed the allegation. She showed me her ripped skirt and underwear. I advised her to call the police. In fact, I took her to the station myself. She was interviewed by the police, but due to the fact that there was no penetration, just an attempt, and there were no forensic evidence to prove the allegation, the police had no power to make an arrest. The next day, I went to the pub. My dad said to me, "How could you take this cheap woman's word over mine?" I did believe that he forgot he was referring to my girlfriend—*that's my wonderful dad!*

During the planning of their return to Jamaica, my beloved parents had ordered approximately £20,000 worth of top quality furniture using the existing business at the time as collateral. Unknown to the creditors, the so-called-business was literally on its face heading for liquidation, and it came to pass. This quantity of furniture was shipped to Jamaica, but unfortunately, for the furniture stores they were not paid. The business premises were closed down, and the poor suppliers had nowhere to go for their money. Nevertheless, all that lovely furniture was safe at home, in the freshly built mansion that was built from the extraction of £80,000 from the property situated at Hawstead Road, the same property that was handed to me verbally by Father dear in order for me to pay the remortgage of £1,000 per month. On reflection, if I knew then what I know now, I would have had all the documentation in black and white and not verbally. Back then, I was a fool. To date, Father sought forgiveness. *Just like Jesus, I forgave the bastard, but just like the elephant, I would never fucking forget!* An investigation was carried out. However, it came to a dead end because the building used for the business was demolished. Oftentimes, when I visited East London, I always bumped into ex-punters who never failed to remind me that my father was an evil man. I would always reply, "I know that," but what goes around would come around!

In 1992, before they went to Jamaica, the family home was up for repossession due to non-payment of the mortgage. My sister, Judy, was living there alone. In fact, she was pregnant, but luckily, for her, she managed to get herself an apartment.

Having made a decision to return to Jamaica, my dear dad had propositioned for the other four children to take on the property and pay the arrears on the mortgage. Unfortunately, for him, none of them was in a position to take on such a huge financial burden. My brother, Malcolm, had discussed this with me in confidence due to the fact that time was running short, and my parents had to make a run. Although I was the most hated child *(You may call me the prodigal son.)*, I was approached at the last minute to save the family home from repossession, and indeed, I did. My dear father and I had a meeting with the bank manager to discuss methods of saving the property. The bank manager liked my strategy. I had put the ideas into operation; it was working very well. I was paying the mortgage and the arrears simultaneously. I was doing very well. I had turned the family home into a hostel for homeless people. I had furnished the property. I also registered myself as a business called Francis Properties Services. I was fully tenanted. The rent for my tenants was paid by Lewisham Council. The bank manager was very happy because he was paid each month in advance before the due date for payment. We had a good working relationship although it was illegal to rent the property.

Ten years later, my dear dad came back to England. The money that was borrowed fifteen years ago to set up the business and to build a mansion in Jamaica was borrowed against the family home, and that money had been paid back by myself. My dear dad, coupled with three of my siblings, Rupert, Judy and Jane, had the audacity to fight against me for the family house that I saved. I decided, after paying the arrears and the mortgage for ten years, that I was no longer prepared to be a pushover.

This was on reflection of the collapse of my small business known as Francis Property Services at the hands of Father dear. At this point, the house was again getting ready to be repossessed by the bank. Due to the extreme pressure from all the members of the family, especially Father alongside my sisters, Jane and Judy, all my tenants had vacated the premises.

One day, I was at the property known as 4 Hawstead Road. I was, in fact, doing some repairs on some damaged furniture I had put up "for sale." To my utmost shock, I heard a key being inserted into the front door. At this point, I ran all the way to the top floor of the building. I then heard voices of whoever entered the building. I also heard footsteps coming up the stairs. I then hid behind the cupboard in the attic room. I covered myself, leaving only my eyes exposed. My sisters, Jane and Judy, and Father appeared clearly in my view. I watched them stare from the window, looking down into the garden. They stood in my view for approximately thirty minutes. I then got a bit restless and changed my position of seating. Sister Jane saw something moved and screamed at the top of her voice. She shouted, "There's someone behind the cupboard. I swear I saw movement." I then banged the side of the cupboard to scare them off, and they all ran down the stairs as if they were being chased by a ghost. I remained behind the cupboard because I thought I had frightened them away! But to my unpleasant surprise, thirty minutes later, I heard footsteps again coming up the stairs in abundance. It was Father, coupled with the two so-called sisters, and yes, you guessed it, an army of police! I was escorted off the premises by the police, although I have tried to explain that I had been the mortgage payer for the past ten years. They had no interest in what I had to say because Father dear had already claimed ownership of the property. But then, I asked myself, "What was the point of his visit?" Two weeks later, the bank came along and boarded it up because it was now their property—repossessed, of course! What I really wanted to do was to clear the property of everything, leaving just the walls standing, but all I got was some rather dishy fireplaces which I sold for a reasonable price. Much to my regret, I gave Carol half of the money. What a fool I was.

Believe it or not, my dear friends, as I stood in 2008, the family were still questioning whether or not the mortgage repayments were really £1000 per month. I could assure them that all the payments were £1000, and I still had the repayment book as proof, but then, to add salt to the wound, I dared to say the money I was paying back to the bank was simply the payment for the remortgage that Father took out for the building of the mansion in Jamaica. Theoretically, distant family members always said to me, "In actual fact, you paid for the house in Jamaica by paying the remortgage in England." But I said, "Looking at the present situation, we all know who the house belongs to. Think about it, my wonderful family."

The deal I had with my dad verbally was that upon the sale of the house, he would receive £10,000. I had a meeting with my dad to discuss this payment to get him off my back because I had a power of attorney that stated I could do whatever I like with the house. However, due to the fact that there was a court battle between myself and my dad, I was unable to do anything to regain my financial losses. During the two-year battle with my family over my money that was tied up in the house, I decided not to take any rent from the tenants. The mortgage had not been paid, and the property drifted back into the same position it was in 1992. At this point, I began to rehouse the tenants with friends I had in the same line of business. I also went to see the bank manager whom I had been dealing with for the past twelve years. He had enlightened me as to what would take place and that repossession of the property was now inevitable.

He shook my hand and said, "Mr Francis, you happened to be the best customer I have ever had." I then left the bank. By this time, all the tenants were rehoused. The rent for two years that I did not collect was given to the tenants by the council in order to pay me. I instructed the tenants to keep every penny for themselves. The house was repossessed and sold at an auction—all because my dad was avaricious. At the time, I had arranged to borrow £10,000 against the house to pay my father, but he refused this offer. He wanted the sum of £20,000. I told him that this was impossible, but nonetheless, I offered £20,000 against the house to pay him. This offer was rejected. He had now changed his mind.

He no longer wanted the money; he wanted the house. Because of his avariciousness, he wanted it all, and through the process, he lost everything. However, the biggest loss was mine. Ten years of laboriously paying the mortgage and arrears had gained me nothing except disdain.

I had the most bitter experience in meeting the first alleged rape victim of my dad, the same young lady who was raped at the time I was a school boy. I met this young lady in 1993 when I retuned to Jamaica to visit Mrs. Woodburn whom I unfortunately married. At the time, Carol knew the story of the rape case, but she had kept it quiet until one day, she introduced me to the lady who was raped by my father. I was rather astonished by that meeting, but there was nothing I could do at that point except to apologise, of course. The young lady relived that day when she was thirteen years old, as she told me of her horrifying experience of being raped as a child and had had the pregnancy terminated in order to continue with her education. Mrs. Woodburn stared at me with her jaws dropped, waiting for my reaction. Unfortunately, I did not react to the news because I knew this allegation was true.

Although I pretended to be calm, when I left the presence of Mrs. Woodburn and the rape victim, what was said to me simply ate me inside. That night, I went out of town trying to bury the shame that was brought upon me. I visited several bars. The last bar I visited had go-go dancers, and they were all over me when they heard my accent. However, all I was interested in was getting as much drink inside me as possible. I could not get over the shame no matter what I did. I was stoned drunk, I did not know what was happening.

The next morning, I woke up in a strange place that had been catered for by a beautiful Indian woman with a strong Jamaican accent who I have never seen before. I asked for her name, and she replied, "Angie."

I said to her, "What am I doing here with you?"

She said, "We met in the club where I was working as a dancer, but you don't remember—or you were too drunk to remember."

I had a delicious West Indian breakfast, and I felt strong—almost like a lion.

Angie asked what's my plan for the day.

I told her I have to go because I have business in town.

She asked, "do you drive?"

I said, "Yes."

"Aren't you going to tell me what to call you?"

I made a joke and said, "Call me what you like." She then handed me her car keys. As I walked towards the car, she mumbled, "*Super grine*. That's what I will call you," in a Jamaican accent. I guessed she enjoyed the night to say that the morning after!

I drove to the business premises owned by my parents enraged with the previous days' thoughts still fresh in my mind. I was also very upset about the revelation of the chef that he saw my dear father having sex with a waitress whilst Mother dear was away, having treatment for her terminal illness. I got out of the car and started to swear at my dad in front of his staff about the allegation. He denied all knowledge of this. He then shouted, "Go pack your bags, and go back to England where you belong." As the argument became more heated, the spectators gathered around for their free entertainment like a pack of hungry hyenas that had not eaten a meal in days over a dead carcass. My dad called the police, and six of them came to the scene. Believe it or not, my dear friends, they were pointing their guns at me, but I had no fear.

One officer shouted, "Hey, bwoy, what kind a trouble yuh a cause here?" pointing his gun at me.

I replied, "I beg your pardon." Then another of his colleague shouted, "English man." One of them went into the business premises. On his return, he said, "English family problem." They ordered me to go away from the scene. I left, went to my dad's mansion, collected my clothes, and spent the last few days of my holiday with Angie who I should have married.

In 2005, the notorious past of my dearly beloved father had raised its ugly head once more, as a teenager the name Velma had been mentioned several times. Apparently, it was an unknown cousin who I never had the pleasure of meeting until Christmas of 2005. Meeting her was an extremely shocking experience because the name had appeared several times throughout my life, and I never took any notice of who this person might be. Velma happened to be a cousin from my mother's side. She was the daughter of my Aunt Pricilla. Unfortunately, for this fifty-year old woman, a part of her childhood had a disturbing twist that would take her to her grave. This was not a fault of her parents or herself but the fault of the monster who raped her when she was thirteen. Cousin Velma got the blame for seducing the monster at age thirteen. Believe it or not, she was still being blamed today for this despicable crime committed upon her. My Aunt Pricilla begged me not to write about this event, but the pain I felt drove me to do so, as this was one way of healing the pain I felt inside me.

When I met Cousin Velma, I had no idea who she was or what she was about. My aunt Agnes took on the painful job of filling me in with the story, from start to finish. During the telling of this horrific story, my poor aunt and I were reduced to tears of shame. After hearing this, I had to face my cousin. This experience was almost like having a nail driven through the palm of your hand. My cousin gave birth to a son just before her fourteenth birthday. The child was taken into care because of the family scandal. Velma told me that due to the emotional turmoil of her life caused by the rape and the unwanted pregnancy, she had not been able to love as she would like to; as a result of this, she has had several broken relationships because of her childhood reflections. As she spoke to me, I had focussed on her eyes, and the tears flowed like rain.

Barrened by the trauma she suffered as a child and unable to conceive, she went in search of the child she gave birth to when she was still a child. She had tried for another child several times but failed. She had traced the couple whom her son was given to through an adoption agency. The agency had kindly provided her with an address for him. Unfortunately, after several attempts to contact him, her son refused to have anything to do with her. He had left words with the agency—words to this effect, "You gave me away at birth, what do you want with me now? Leave me alone. I don't need you." When Velma's son refused to see her, it gave her a devastating blow to the heart. I must say that, for a woman in her position, I could only imagine her pain of rejection. Somewhere out there was an angry young man who was rejected as a child. However, no one had the opportunity to explain to him the truth about his situation. I did wonder how he would receive me and what I would call him—brother or cousin? I guessed I was both! I wondered what my cousin would think. Or should I say my dear brother, if he knew his existence was due to a rape! I guess I myself would be rather disgusted, and it would sure drive me to suicide personally.

Believe it or not, my dear friends, when I met Mrs. Woodburn, she was ashamed of who I was and where I came from. However, she could not believe that the man who was my father could have produced such an offspring. To this day (in 2006), I stood tall and looked them all in their eyes because I knew I was the last of a dying breed - *my wonderful family.* Upon the demise of my dearest mother, she tried to prove to all her children that she had some form of love for them, although this was quite hard to prove, especially to me, due to the fact of how I was treated as a teenager. If you asked me if I had loved Mother dear, I would find it hard to give you a straight answer as lying was not one of my specialty. However, during the time of her passing, she had asked for me personally. I was told that one of her last request was to talk to me before she dies. She had left word with my other siblings of a gift she had left for me. This gift was a piece of land left to her by her dear father, but this could have as well not been said. In today's society, if it was not written in black and white, it meant nothing. At the same time, my other siblings were heading for a great fight for when Father dear passed away. Brother Rupert, in his mighty character, had said that he would fight to the death to get Mother's name honoured. He was her favourite son, I may add, but that I would like to see! It was said by a family member in brief that they looked upon me as a *nobody* simply because I did not own a property. But believe it or not, *my dear friends,* I was, in fact, working my way up to being on the property ladder. I had a mortgage approved by the Royal Bank of Scotland through Gray Fox Estate Agent in Sittingbourne. I was on the hunt for a property around the time of my arrest in 2002, but my imprisonment had stopped me in my tracks *(Thanks to Carol and D. C. Duffus who tried to destroy me but failed.)*. When you really think about it, I was already paying a mortgage for the family home, but due to my so-called father's avariciousness, I lost it all.

Dear Sister Jane told Carol that she was too good for me, but looking back, Carol was the pit who was not good enough for any man to call "wife." Seeing that Zora was better than Carol, even my daughter wished she was her mother. I wondered if Jane also thought Zora was too good for me. The big question was, "Did God take her husband away because he thinks he was too good for her?" Only God knows. I guess they all think I am somebody now! Several weeks before my second marriage, family members had borrowed sums of money from me that was meant to be paid back on or near the date of the wedding, but in fact, it was repaid way past the wedding date. So who were they to look down on me as if I was a *nobody* when in fact, they had no idea who was the better one. I saw them all at my wedding, stuffing their faces, wishing they were as happy as I was. *My wonderful family!*

THIS WAS THE MORTGAGE APPROVAL CERTIFICATE

A.I.P CERTIFICATE

A mortgage has been agreed in principle for :

Mr Raymond Francis

Maximum borrowing £81250

An agreement in principle does not guarantee a mortgage offer

REGISTERED ADDRESS 11 WEST STREET SITTINGBOURNE KENT ME10 1AJ   REGISTERED NO. 3528232

ZURICH

Unfortunately, for those who are waiting for Father dear to pass away, they will have a long wait. He was now with a thirty-year old woman who was carrying his child (At least that was what they say, but I am sure DNA would prove different). At his age, he should be preparing himself for heaven, but he was too busy still sowing his seed. I recently spoke to my aunt Louise, and she had informed me that my father was now married to the woman he had during Mother's illness (which unfortunately took her life). She had now given birth to their child.

I must take this opportunity to say to my brother, Rupert, "You were born and bred in England. Do not go to Jamaica and fight for something you know nothing about. I know you want the eight-bedroom mansion you claimed Mother dear had left for you upon Father's death. Forget it. His woman, her child, and her family will send you back to England in a body bag, failing that the plot next to Mother dear in the cemetery is available." *My wonderful family.*

In 1996, I went through an extremely difficult situation with the property that was left for me. I was having difficulty with the repayment of the mortgage because I had a shortage of tenants. I was not getting sufficient revenue to pay the mortgage. I approached my other siblings for help, but unfortunately, they declined.

My brother, Rupert, had advised me to let the property go because at that time, his property was repossessed, and also, there were a lot of repossessing taking place during this period. However, I stuck to my guns. I began to put my own income from my nine-to-five job into the property. This was only a temporary setback because I soon overcame this. After six months, I was fully tenanted once more, and I was back on top. Shortly after my miraculous recovery, my siblings who had rejected me when I was down they all had the audacity, with the exception of my brother, Malcolm, to want to share my success. However, I refused to let them. As a refusal to incorporate them in my venture, they joined forces against me with my dear father, and, believe it or not, came to fight me for the property. Hence, I had no option but to let it get repossessed. After the repossession, the bank sold the property. Fifteen thousand pounds (£15,000) was left over, which was paid to my dear mother who at the time was terminally ill. I believed Mother dear knew she was on her way to meet her creator. She gave the money to my dear Sister Judy in order to give her a good send off when she died.

Unfortunately, for my dear mother whom we loved dearly, she was taken away by cancer. How sad. I always thought she was Aquarius; I am Scorpio. How unfortunate for her!

She had a low budget "send off," and the money left with my dear sister, Judy, was used for her own personal gains. Believe it or not, she furnished her apartment, imported a man from Jamaica, and also got wed whilst Mother dear was crying out for a decent tomb. Two years later, there was a collection for the building of a tomb, and believe it or not, I also made a contribution to this misadventure.

The marriage of my dear sister, Judy, did not last five minutes. As soon as the British papers were in hand and permission to stay in the United Kingdom was granted, her husband flew the nest, leaving her a single parent (What was new? I guess we were both in the same boat). Regardless of all they did to me, I had found it in my heart to forgive them because "they know not what they do," *my wonderful family.*

Sister Jane had brought it to my attention that whilst Mother dear was on her deathbed, a will was forced upon her to be signed. Although she was nearly gone, her brain seemed to be working perfectly. She managed to read the contents of the will where she discovered one of her children's names was missing. I was told she asked my dear father, "Why is Raymond's name not on the will?"

He replied, "I do not have a son by that name."

Jane never failed to remind me of the love Mother had for me. She did not sign the will because my name was absent from it. I guess the pain of giving birth is always remembered by a woman. *I dared to say rest in peace, old girl!*

This put her in a state of shock, although she was already on her deathbed. I was told that when Mother dear died, her last words were "I want to see my son, Raymond." Though I had sent my estranged wife, Carol, to represent me, that was not good enough. Mother dear had now been dead for a while. I dared say her soul was not rested. I owed her a visit at some point in the future, although this might seem a little morbid!

Family members were extremely annoyed with me, especially Jane's husband when he was alive. He said if it was his father behaving in such a manner, he would definitely put him in his place. However, knowing myself and my bad temper, I took the easy option: I stood back and looked from the outside to save my soul from the devil. They all claimed that I should have participated in the fight against Father for bringing a *much younger* woman into the home during Mother's passing. Mother dear went to her grave carrying vengeance against Cousin Velma for what had happened. Was it her fault, I ask? I don't think so.

Apparently, it was alleged that my dear father and his floozy were the ones who shortened Mother's time because she was not ready to meet Jesus so soon (metaphorically speaking).

My dear brother, Rupert, was still insisting in 2006 that he would go to Jamaica and preserve his mother's honour. Good luck to him, I dared say. My sister Jane's husband had mentioned that if it was with his father, the woman that was brought in the home would have to get past him first. Although John spoke like a dangerous cold-hearted person like myself, he happened to be the best person who had ever left the soil of Jamaica. I dared say John was an example of what all men should be like; he was a blessing for my sister. I am certain if Mother was alive, she would have seconded my opinion.

My brother, Rupert, was going through tremendous turbulence in his marriage. Looking from the outside, I did not know of any man apart from him who would tolerate such a poor lifestyle and disrespect from his wife. I had given him my advice repeatedly over the last two years. He had not listened to me, and so, his situation became worse. The last time I visited him, the drink of water offered to me ended up in the flowerpot, if you know what I mean.

In 1998, my dear father came up from Jamaica. He went to the unemployment office where he signed on for financial assistant. Two weeks later, he returned to Jamaica, leaving his payment book as he tricked the government, claiming he was sick and was unable to sign on in person. He had elected another family member whom I dared not name to sign on his behalf and send the money to him whilst he was living in his eight-bedroom mansion, and the joke was on the British government. This lasted for two years until he returned back to England.

Believe it or not, *my dear friends,* this was even more shocking in 2006. My dear father managed to wangle himself a council apartment from the government because he was now a pensioner; a small amount of his pension was deducted for the rent of the apartment, but my father had once again pulled it off! He returned to his mansion, and the apartment was rented for eighty pounds per week to a close friend of the family. This money was sent directly to him, rubbing his palms with glee. The joke was on Tony Blair! Who at the time was Prime Minister of the United Kingdom.

My dearest friends and readers, this particular section had caused me great pain to write. My sister's husband, John, was very ill for approximately nine months. He was diagnosed with the killer disease that took Mother's life (*cancer*). This caused great heartache and pain for the family. John was very much loved by all the family members, both at home and abroad. Unfortunately, he had to take up residence in the Royal Marsden Hospital for cancer patients because the local hospital could not facilitate his medical needs. I had personally visited John for almost seven months. One day, I believed that John felt as if his time had come. I was leaving on that day I said to him, "I am going to leave you now. I will see you tomorrow." He looked at me in great depths with tears flowing from his eyes. I was deeply touched and disturbed by this that I pretended as if I wanted to use the toilet and went inside to compose myself. I did not want to cry in front of John although I felt his pain.

He said to me, "You are a very strong person because you have experienced hardcore prison. I don't think I would be strong enough to go through that. What I am going through is nothing compared to what you went through."

I said, "What you are going through is much greater than what I went through because if given the choice, I would not have chosen cancer over prison." I guess he was trying to justify his death sentence because it was inevitable. Not many people beat the killer disease, but many like myself had left prison. The insensitive doctor had said to me in the presence of John, "Has there been any preparation for organ donation?" At this point, John and I looked at each other in horror, and we both looked at the doctor. The expression on his face was "game over" or words to that effect.

February 10, 2007. John was sent home by the doctors because at that point, there was nothing else they could do for my dear brother-in-law. It was clear to me that the doctors sent him home to say good-bye to his family. They gave him two weeks to live. During those two weeks, I visited John almost everyday. Family and friends joined in prayer for him. I always tried to be humorous in his presence, to take his mind off his inevitable destiny. I remember clearly that the last time I saw him laugh was when Rochelle refused to go home to her mother. All family members found her extremely hilarious; as usual, she refused to go. I guess time spent with me was always too short for Rochelle. I said to her, "What are you going to do when D. C. Duffus take your daddy? Can't you see that I have to get you home?" At this point, John started chuckling. He really had a good laugh that day. However, little did we know it was going to be his last. *The man who laughs last laughs best.* After two weeks, to the date of the doctors' prediction, Dear John left us all broken hearted and tearful. The night before he died, I visited him. When I was about to leave, I said good-bye to my sister, Jane, and her daughter. At this point, he had lost the use of speech. He could barely breathe. He used all the strength he had left in his dying body to wave to me his final farewell. I would always remember that moment until the day I join him. At that point, I was almost like a river that burst its bank; I just could not help it. I loved John as a brother. The pain of losing him was almost unbearable.

When I reflected back on what the disease had done to John, it always brought tears to my eyes. He was transformed from a twelve-stone healthy young man to something unrecognisable—a skeleton covered with skin. I wished I had not seen him at this stage because I believed it had left a terrible scar in my mind, but I loved him just the same. You could imagine, *my dear friends,* the pain that my sister Jane went through and was still going through. His last words to his wife were a request to be buried next to his brother and his past family members in their family plot in Jamaica. She had granted his request, and his body was brought to Jamaica. In fact, we were all on the same flight on the eight of March 2007. On the plane, I was deeply touched when John's two-year old daughter cried, "I want my daddy. I want to see my daddy." I sat there in my seat, fighting the tears once again. The poor child did not know her daddy was on the same plane, going home to his final resting place. That was very painful for me to experience because I was told that my daughter, Rochelle, was crying just the same when I was in prison. He was buried on March 11, 2007 at his requested place of rest. The day he was buried, a strange thing happened. All the family went back to my father's mansion where we all stayed. The atmosphere was very tense upon our arrival. There were tension between Sister Judy and Father's new wife due to the fact that during Mother's illness, our dear father was having an affair with the young lady whom he had now married. Although we all promised to keep our cool when we were all in England, when we got to Jamaica, it was almost like a time bomb waiting to explode, and indeed, it did. Judy was in the kitchen with Doris (dad's new wife) when there came an outburst. Sister Judy threatened to slash Doris's throat and screamed at her, "Get out of my mother's house. You don't belong here. If you don't leave, I will cut your fucking throat!"

At this point, Doris left the kitchen and went into hiding in another part of the house. Unfortunately, Doris's daughter, Susan, had entered the kitchen unaware of what was happening. She was also given the same message by my sister, Judy. The poor child was in a great state of panic. She rushed towards me for help, but unfortunately, I did not want to get involved. Father dear was in his room when all this commotion was taking place. He heard Susan crying and came to investigate. He asked me what was going on. I said, "I do not want to get involved." I asked Susan to explain to him, and she did. At this point, Dad rushed up the stairs as if there were no steps. He grabbed Judy around the neck, and pulled a bottle as if he wanted to smash it over her head. Judy's two children, aged fourteen and seven, and Jane's child, aged two, all looked at the action; their facial expressions were horrific. Brother Malcolm pulled Father dear away from Judy. There was a huge argument. Judy and Jane went into one room followed by my brother, Malcolm. Dad screamed at them and said, "You two better be careful or else *I will cut your fucking throats.*" I was blown away by the outrageous argument and the threat he made to them. Judy was screaming, "You killed my mom. You killed my mom." But I do recall that Mother dear died from cancer! Perhaps, what she really meant was that Mother was not treated very well in her last days on earth because during her illness, my dear father was having an affair with his present wife. I did believe that a broken heart also contributed to the cause of Mother's death. However, the question was, "What did she really die of?" I believed it was a broken heart.

That same night, at 2:00 A.M., Judy asked me to take her to her in-laws; she could not stay in Father's house after her behaviour. She asked me to take her to a place called Cross Key. That night in the pitch black, I tried to find my way to this forbidden place. I got lost several times, but I did find my way eventually. When I got there, I was told that Tom, Judy's husband (You might remember him, my dear friends. He was the male version of my first wife, a good-for-nothing has been) was out on the town with a woman. My sister was very angry to see that she went all that way for some comfort, but instead, she got a blast in the heart like a bullet. She started screaming at me as if it was all my fault, but I was only trying to help. Her two children were also crying in the back of the car, and I must say I was so exhausted, I felt as if I was dead. So at that point, I said to Judy, "I want to go to sleep, so tell me what you want because I need to go."

"Take me to a hotel. All I want to do is to go back to England," she screamed.

I said, "At this time of the night, you will not get a hotel room."

She screamed at me again to take her to the airport. She said, "I just want to get out of here."

I said to her, "It would be best if you come back to Mandeville with me."

She said, "Go back to Mandeville and sleep, you bastard. Just leave me here to sleep on the street." She was crying hysterically. I removed her luggage from the car and the children.

I then asked her, "What do you want me to do?"

She screamed at me again. "Leave me alone. Go and get your beauty sleep." I drove off. I had not seen her since, but I knew she was okay.

The next day, Father's dear wife, Doris, did something quite remarkable: She apologised to the family for having an affair with Dad that contributed to Mother's death. Rather noble of her, I might say, but forgiveness was not from me! Brother Malcolm and Sister Jane seemed to be sucked in by this woman's charms. She made food on a regular basis, and I watched brother Malcolm eating like a pig, but not me. Jamaicans have a way of mixing food with other ingredients to make you do what they want you to do. This is practiced in other West Indian Islands. This behaviour has got to be out of desperation! I would not be caught that way again! I always eat out breakfast, lunch, and dinner. I went to Jamaica purely to support my sister, Jane, on the death of her husband. I did not wish to overstay. Although I had rented a car, after the funeral, I started to feel restless and homesick. I decided to go to Ocho Rios for a few days. Although there were several routes to go there, my travelling companions wanted to go to Spanish Town to visit a few friends en route to Ocho. After we visited our friends from the United Kingdom, we decided to continue to Ocho Rios. Unfortunately, for me, the car I was driving died on me in the middle of a place named by the locals as Zinc City. This was a place where if nightfall caught you, you would not live to see the next day. The locals were afraid of this place, and the car chose to break down at this point! I myself, a man of no fear, for the first time, must confess that I became paranoid with fear. Down a slope, near the side of the road, a bear-footed Rasta man was working on a motorcycle. I went and asked for help using the local lingo as I always did. He tried his best to get the car going but came up with embarrassing failure. It did not take him long to figure out that my colleagues and I were not from Jamaica, and he did mention this. I guessed, during conversation, he had his ears peeled to our lips. He was simply analysing every word we said without our knowledge. Although he failed to fix the car, he still mentioned a charge of $1000 for his failed effort. (In Jamaica, money talks). On reflection, Sister Judy had a swollen finger. The ring was getting tighter and tighter. I rushed her to the hospital. There was a charge of $3000 that came with a full medical report from the doctor, justifying the charge. I watched him removed the ring with a pair of clippers. I wonder how much those clippers cost him. No matter what level of society, avariciousness is always extreme. It appears to me that hearing an English accent spells money. We towed the car along the road to a garage that was capable of fixing it further and left it there to be repaired. "This will take a couple of days," we were told. We continued our journey to Ocho Rios, an extremely beautiful place. We stayed for a few days at my friend Tony's father's guesthouse. The nightlife was excellent and so was the beach. There were women on the street naming their price! However, I had no interest. Brother Malcolm and Tony made a meal of the situation. Believe it or not, the girl Tony was with did something in front of me which I found quite unladylike. She mentioned she wanted to pee, and without any warning, her skirt was up above her waist. She had no underwear on, and all I saw was a big hairy nest squirting like a fountain! I could not believe my eyes. For a moment, I thought I was on the set of a blue movie from *seehersquirt.com*. The next day, we all got up bright and early to go to the local market to buy food to make breakfast. We got back to the guesthouse, and the woman, the same woman that squirted in front of me who appeared to be coughing with weeping eyes, offered her services to make breakfast! Could you believe it? I was horrified! At this point, I was riddled with disbelief because there was no way under the sun that I would eat from such a woman! I cooked breakfast myself: ackees, saltfish, dumplings, callaloo, bananas, and the whole shebang. I felt proud of myself because breakfast had disappeared, and there was not even a scrap for the dog! After breakfast, we went to the beach and had a wonderful day. The next day, we went to Spanish Town to collect the car *en route* to Mandeville. When we arrived in Mandeville, I just could not get into the swing of things. My brother, Malcolm, started to boss me around by telling me to pick up this woman and that woman and chauffer them around at my expense to his benefit. I was rather pissed off by this. Although the car was rented for two weeks, paid in full, it was not my wish to jump to my brother's commands; every move I made for him was costing me financially. At that point, I stood my ground and refused to do as he said. This happened at the restaurant owned by my dear father. On that day, there were a lot of customers who, unfortunately, witnessed my brother talking down to me. I was rather upset, not to mention embarrassed. He also shouted that if I died, he would not attend my funeral, as if he would be doing me a favour. To be totally honest with you, my dear friends, Malcolm was my brother!

During my short visit to Jamaica, brother Malcolm and I visited our childhood home where we were brought up by Aunt Louise. There was a special feeling because my childhood memories came rushing back, but my Aunt Louise was not present. She was away in America, but it was still a special day.

I went to a travel agent and bought my flight forward. I was due to leave Jamaica on Saturday, March 17. On that day, I did something rather strange and dangerous to my own well-being. I decided to drive to alligator pond on my own, just to have my last supper in Jamaica. I was on my way. I have never driven to this place myself, but that day, I just had the urge to do it. So I did. On my way to alligator pond, I happened to try a shortcut which was one straight road. I was going back into my memory bank. I had been through it many, many years ago, but then, I was with someone who knew that part of the world like the back of her hand. The shortcut that I took turned out to be disastrous on my part. I happened to end up in a place I would call "no man's land." To tell the honest truth, I was dead scared, but I did not panic. I drove and drove, but I saw no signposts or anything to point me in the direction I wanted to go. You could say I was lost! In the distance, I saw a young man walking towards me. I stopped the car in all my braveness to ask for direction, but at the same time, I never dared to let out the facts that I was not a local, so you could imagine I was trying to speak the local lingo once more. I said to this young man, talking in Jamaican style, "Do you know the way to alligator pond?"

He looked at me with a strange frown upon his face, as if to say everybody knows alligator pond. He responded in the local lingo, "Yes, I do know where it is."

"Is it far from here?" I asked.

He said, "Not far from here. I can show you." Each time he spoke, I responded in the local lingo. He asked "Where are you from?"

"Mandeville," I said. "It had been a long time since I travelled these parts." Although we were deep in conversation, as we drove along, my heartbeat was somewhat racing with the fear of this young man. I was thinking he could have had a weapon in his pocket to take my life in an instant. I guess he would if he knew I was a foreigner.

He said, "You look really clean and unusual." At this point, the sweat began to pour. His statement of my appearance was rather strange. Strange enough, we got to a road that was not far from alligator pond. He asked if I could let him off at that point, and so I did. He said, "Thanks for the ride and have a nice day, Sir."

I replied, "Yeh, man, respect due." I drove my way off to alligator pond with a sigh of relief. You know why? He did not suspect I was a foreigner because he did not ask me for anything; asking for something was standard. My local lingo must be good. *I dared say, "old chap."* Whilst at alligator pond, I walked along the beach, got my feet wet, ate bammy and fried fish, and downed a few bottle of ice-cold Red Stripe Beer! The waitress who served me, believe it or not, was an old friend of Carol and myself, or should I say, Mrs. Woodburn! Her name was Marcia, she said to me

"How come you are by yourself? Where is your wife? Didn't she come with you?" At this point, I began to laugh because the mention of Carol's name came to me as a joke. I told Marcia the story, and she was horrified to know that Carol could do such a thing to me.

I said to her, "Don't worry, my dear, I am rather happy. The past is dead. I am happily married." I showed her a picture of my current wife that I carry in my wallet. Marcia was indeed very happy for me. It was time to return to Mandeville and prepare myself for my pleasurable flight on Air Jamaica back to England. I gave Marcia a huge tip with thanks and left. I did the same thing I did on my way down—I picked up a passenger. This time, it was a lovely long-legged beauty as I pulled up the car next to her on this lonely stretch of the road. I asked, "Where are you going?" in Jamaican style. She looked at me with no reply. I then repeated the same question to her. She grumbled an answer from the depths of her throat. "Mandeville," she said.

I replied, "Hop in then," and so she did. As we drove along, we engaged in deep conversation. She was a rather ambitious young lady studying to be a teacher. As we approached Mandeville, she asked whether she would see me later. At this point, I began to chuckle. She said, "Why are you laughing?"

I said, "It is now 1:00 P.M. A taxi is meant to pick me up at 3:00 P.M."

She said, "A taxi? But you are driving."

I said, "My dear, I just went down to alligator pond to have my last supper in Jamaica! Two hours from now, I will be sitting in a taxi that will take me to Kingston Airport. I will be on my way back to England. I brought my flight forward due to my brother's impertinence."

She said, "Why can't you change it? We could spend some time together."

I said, "My dear, so many people ask me to do the same thing, but my mind is made up, and the wheels are turning."

She looked at me, almost tearful, "I always have bad luck."

"Why do you say that?" I asked.

She said, "I will never see you again, will I?" I said the chance of that is slimmer than winning the lotto. "You never know," she said, and we said good-bye.

I went into the market to buy myself some goodies to take back to England. I went home, packed my case, and drove round to families and friends to say good-bye. I went back home where I waited for the taxi. As I waited, my sister, Jane, called. She said she wanted to say good-bye in person, and she came by the house with her deceased husband's sister. She said good-bye. She would be returning to England in a month's time. Her sister-in-law was on the same vibes as the young lady I picked up on the way from alligator pond. She said, "Please change your mind. We have not spent any time together. There are a lot of things I want to show you, and also, there are a lot of things we can do together." I looked at her and mumbled to myself, "Not another one!" My taxi came and off I went. Thank God for that. I was once again free as a bird on my way back to England, back to work, and back to everything I missed. I was away from all things that spelt *STRESS!* Or should that be *distress?*

I wondered what brother Malcolm was going to do now. He had no driving licence. He had been driving using my name since 1980, twenty years ago! What would he do now when the police stop him, I wondered! At last, I was free of him. On the subject of police, father dear, I said if I might, owe his life to the Jamaican police. I believed it was the same lot that pointed the gun at me at his request. Hooray! They saved Father's life. Apparently, Father went to visit his mother-in-law in the same district he was brought up as a boy, and apparently, the ex-boyfriend of his dearly beloved spotted his Jaguar. The guy rounded up all his friends, and they all went for the kill! Father dear drove his Jaguar as fast as he could to save his life. He was chased by three cars with drugged up young men who was hungry for his head. He drove to Mandeville Police Station through the gates, and rested his hands on the horn. His car was surrounded by the police, astounded by his action.

I dared say, my dear friends, for one minute, I would not say that Father dear was not happy. His only problem that I can see was financial, but I did believe he was a very happy man. He had rebuilt his life, he had a lovely young wife and a new family, and in fact, he was doing quite well. I would never have thought at my tender age of forty-seven, not to mention brother Malcolm at the tender age of fifty-one, that I would meet a half-sister at the age of four months! Sister Judy with her angry self mentioned the child as "it." Nevertheless, the little girl was also a half-sister to every Francis born from the previous marriage, including the son of Cousin Velma that she gave birth to at the age of thirteen after being raped by dear Father. The children of his present wife are stepbrothers and sisters to all of his present siblings born from Mother dear who was now turning in her grave due to the present situation—accept it or not, it was a fact! I dared say, "Well done, old boy. Still strong, I can see!"

My wonderful family.

My dear friend, I must say that a deep feeling of regret had thrown itself upon me. I knew this would happen but not so early after the death of my dearly departed brother-in-law who was the cause of my visit to Jamaica. The visit to Jamaica, as you saw for yourself, had changed a lot of things. Family! So-called family members who had joined in the fury of my destruction had seen me in a different light, as if I was walking with a great tag on my forehead displaying a sign of forgiveness. It was because I was sweet-talked by brother Malcolm to stay at the family mansion, although I am not a person who was destitute. He also talked me into buying a gift for Father dear with a hidden agenda, but little did they know that one thing I did not do was look for friends and force myself upon family. I came alone in this world, and I would leave alone. That's the will of God. Could you believe it? In June 2007, Father dear became ill, and the bucket was going around for a collection for the plane fare to England. Sister Jane had the audacity of contacting me several times. In fact, you could say she was harassing me for money. Dear brother Malcolm and Sister Judy had declined and showed no interest in this collection. I was informed of this by Sister Jane. My dear friends, please take one step forward and five steps back and look into what they had done to me. Would it be fair for me to contribute to this distasteful venture although, to Father dear, it was a matter of life and death! The question that I asked myself was, "I live in a rented apartment. Father dear lives in a six-bedroom mansion in the Caribbean, with a beautiful young wife; he drives an air-conditioned Jaguar, and also has his *own* business. Is he not better off than me?" What do you think? It had crossed my mind to put a large sum of money in the bucket as an insult for what they had done to me. I had not forgotten, although I might have forgiven.

It came to pass that I did put money into the bucket with a heavy heart. Why do returnees come back to England for medical treatment? I was certain that the air fare cost more than paying a local doctor. *God bless the National Health Service (NHS) for free medical treatment in the United Kingdom!* The amount to pay for Father's flight was reached. I made it clear to Sister Jane that this was a loan that should be repaid as soon as possible. Father dear had arrived in England thinking all was well and his family was finally back where he wanted them—in the palm of his hands in order to live off their pockets. He was invited to my apartment for dinner along with the rest of the family. I cooked a meal that they all enjoyed along with my hospitality of drinks. More guests than I have estimated arrived, but I still managed to cater for them all; I must say it was a wonderful evening.

One week later, I had an e-mail from Sister Jane; it was a photo of the latest addition to the family. *Could you guess? It was my baby sister, my dear father's latest offspring!* I printed the picture off and took it with me when I went to visit Aunt Agnes. I sat down with Aunt Agnes and her son, and we chatted about the family. Then, I remembered the photo of the offspring in my pocked. As I presented it, there was a deafening silence in the room, and the atmosphere almost felt gothic. I said, "Have a look at this photo, and tell me who it is." The silence continued. My cousin, Basil, was using the computer at the time. As I glanced at the computer screen, he wrote *your sister*! I looked at Aunt Agnes's face. She appeared to be very upset as she was reduced to tears.

She said, "How could you bring a photo of the enemy in my house? How could you?"

I told her that Father dear was in the country. Aunt Agnes also revealed that Father dear had sexually assaulted her eldest daughter. At this point, her behaviour was somewhat aggressive. She had illustrated her hatred for my dear father due to what he did to her loving sister, not to mention Cousin Velma. She cried as she spoke, then she apologised for her behaviour.

I said, "No need to apologise, Auntie. I feel your pain." I tried to change the subject to get a better atmosphere in the room. Aunt Agnes looked at Zora and said "You look like my cousin."

I said, "Of course, she does, your cousin came back to life." We all laughed, but I could still see the pain written on her face. Zora was shocked to see the animation that Aunt Agnes projected. She has mentioned the fear and anger that she felt, and then we left her house.

When I looked at my cousins and saw how well their parents treated them, for the first time in my life, I felt a tinge of envy because all my parents ever did for me, especially my dear father, was to kick me in the fucking balls. If I had parents like Aunt Agnes and her husband, I would have had a better start in life. Aunt Agnes and her husband always looked out for their children and made sure they were financially stable. With me, it was the opposite. I tried to make it, but my dear father, with his avariciousness, sank the boat.

By taking on the property at Hawstead Road, I trusted my father, and after six years of paying a mortgage of £1,000 per month, he returned to reclaim the property, and I was devastated; all my efforts and energy was wasted.

After I released myself from the property at Hawstead Road, it was on its way to repossession once more. This time, it would not be saved. The property was repossessed by Halifax as it was sold to the highest bidder at the auction. There was money left over after the bank took what was owed to them. That money was given to Sister Judy by Mother dear for safe keeping. After Mother dear had gone to spend the rest of her time with Jesus, Father dear took Sister Judy to court, claiming the money was rightfully his. *What a joke!*

Six months later, I visited Jane's house. Father dear was present. We spoke about many things as if the gory past had not existed. During the conversation, Father tried his best to get Brother Malcolm and I to make-up for the incident in Jamaica, to forgive and forget. He also mentioned the pain family members had caused him but he had forgiven them. How convenient, I dared to say! He then asked me if I had heard from Aunt Louise. Aunt Louise was the person who raised me from age one to fourteen. She was the sister of my dear father. She now lived in Ohio, United States of America, but she visited Jamaica frequently. She had two homes not far from where Father resided in his mansion with his new family. Believe it or not, Aunt Louise was in Jamaica at the time when Father dear made a fool of himself by marrying the floozy. I couldn't say I blame my dear aunt for not attending this pathetic mockery of a wedding!

My dear friends, don't you think it was rather strange for my father to ask about his sister who did not live very far from him when she visited Jamaica? I believed Aunt Louise felt the same as Aunt Agnes. What do you think? The question is, why?

Sister Jane revealed that Father dear was wearing her dead husband's shoes. Father was very upset due to his pride. If only he could take one step into the life the dead man had lived, he would have been a better man. I was under the impression that Father dear came to England not for medical reasons, but looking at him, he did look rather under-nourished, and believe it or not, he had actually gone down two sizes since I saw him in March. From what I could see, I guess he was about nine stones in weight.

It was revealed to me that the real reason for Father's visit was to have a word with the *goose that laid the golden egg!* Apparently, Father dear did not want anyone to know he has worn the man with the goose's shoes. He was after something more precious than the shoes, that was! Sister Jane had made a huge mistake, in my opinion. She revealed to our dear father the amount that was paid out for the life insurance of her deceased husband. *That was the golden egg.* It was a huge mistake. Sister Jane's business was all over Brockley at the Gossip Shop owned by Brother Malcolm. Now, she lived in fear of being robbed. Father dear wanted his cut, could you believe it? Sister Jane was in a state of depression, if you asked me. It appeared she was cracking up not over the loss of her dear husband but the stresses of people trying to get what was not theirs. It appeared that Father was extremely upset by the sheer thought, and I mean the thought of Sister Jane giving what was due to her dead husband's family. Our dear father was insisting as if she owed him something. All I would like to say to Father dear was: "Go back to your mansion in Jamaica because the days when you get financial support from your children who did not know what you were and what you stood for are over!" I would love to say this to his face.

I do believe that Sister Jane was a fool with a capital "F." Could you imagine: Father was sixty-seven years old with a thirty-year old bride and a six-month old baby pouncing off his siblings, not to mention the British Government to support his young bride. One day, when his eyes are closed, it would be all over.

Who is going to take up the tab? I asked myself. I guess Sister Jane would always be there to the rescue! On our dear father's return to the United Kingdom, Sister Jane went all-out. I had never seen her in such abrasive action before. She went to Father's apartment/holiday home and cleaned it from top to bottom, but not only that, she also furnished it, putting in all personal comforts. The bed alone cost a small fortune of £1200. I asked her, "Why pay so much for a bed that will hardly be used?"

She replied, "Dad's health is of utmost importance." However, she did live to tell me that she regretted doing this. I said to her, "You have more money than sense, but if you feel to throw it away, my bin is empty." It was said that on Father's return to Jamaica, I would be able to reclaim the money I contributed for his airfare. I learnt that the money was in the same boat as Sister Jane's husband (*dead*). I simply gritted my teeth when I had to reveal my losses to Zora. She had no idea that I actually contributed to this misadventure! At this point, looking at Father's financial situation, I did believe that he was being hit with retribution. They all thought that the long-term family feud was over, but they were so wrong. How could I forget what they had done to me? There was an old proverb that goes, *"The man who laughs last, laughs best."*

It was said that during a telephone conversation with Sister Jane, Judy was made an executive of Francis Property Services, my company. I had no idea of this occurrence. Apparently, Judy had been made into the sole controller. It was now all clear to me why she was given the money after the repossession of the property. She was a true snake, if you asked me—slippery and slimy as they went. Jane claimed she had nothing to do with the fight against me over the property, and suddenly, horses started to fly or was it pigs that fly? Think about it!

Unfortunately, Sister Judy was taken to court by Father for the remains of the money that was left over after the repossession, but Father dear ended up with sweet *fa* because all the money was gone. It was proven that the dead had no power whatsoever because if it was not so, Mother dear would have smashed the face of that floozy who was sleeping in the bed in which she died. During the fight for the property that was left verbally to me by Father, it was alleged by his solicitor that the property was rented to me by himself and I took it upon myself to sub-let it without his consent. My dear friends, I beg you, do not laugh too much. The apartment that was given to Father dear and paid for by the government was now rented to another party whilst Father relaxed in the Caribbean, having the money sent direct to him. The question I ask, my friends, was this not sub-letting? Or was it fraud? You be the judge! There is another question I might ask. I learnt that the rent was £90 per week, but it was paid monthly at the exchange rate, I presume, of $130 to a pound. That was a tidy sum, plus the pension and income from the business. At this point, I dared say if I might, I would like to trade places with Father. *Ooops!* I better not! He was always broke! I wonder what he did with all that money? My dear friends, I know the burning question in your minds as you've just finished reading this chapter: Do I have love for my father? The day when I say yes to that, George Bush, Gordon Brown, and Osama Bin Laden would be sitting at the same table, having a good drink and a laugh, or should I say when hell freezes over! There is an old saying that said, "*The sins of the parents fall on the children.*" I refused to carry that of my father. We all have our own cross to carry; trust me, mine is damn heavy.

Father told me that what happened in the past was due to ignorance. I said to myself, "Pull the other one!" Father was forever putting great effort in getting his previous offspring to bond with his floozy of a wife. My dear friends, there is a burning question that you may be able to answer because I don't think I could. Why does Caribbean parents treat their Caribbean offspring differently from those who were born on British soil? Can you answer that? *My wonderful family.*

I also discovered recently that Sister Jane wanted to return to work. She had located a childminder through an agency but to her horrific discovery, the childminder had a husband. I understood that she declined from giving the childminder the job because she was married. The question was: If this woman was a single parent, would she had got the job? I believe that what happened to Cousin Velma was still carrying a huge impact on her childhood reflections. I think Sister Jane was terrified of the past repeating itself. *Think about it.*

My Wonderful Family.

It was said by Sister Jane's in-laws that she killed her husband. In my opinion, this was an extremely huge allegation, as I personally knew that he died of cancer.

The in-laws were extremely upset due to the fact that the life insurance had matured, and their share was not paid out! In my opinion, they didn't deserve shit!

I do believe that the allegation was a damn cheek! How dare those low class vagabonds to make such an allegation about my dear sister? Sister Jane cared so much for her husband, John, during the last three years of his life in his battle against death on this forbidden planet. I watched her nursed him with the highest degree of care. I must say, my dear friends, for someone to put up with bathing and cleaning toxic vomit, that person must really care. I dare say that must have been true love at its highest degree. To date, she still talked about him, and she had a burning desire to have his baby. For the in-laws to say that she killed him, that was punching way below the belt! But now, I knew he was somewhere else getting pampered daily by Angels. One day we will meet again, I dare say.

I remember clearly the day Brother John used his last breath to say farewell to me. The next day, I saw him being put into a body bag, being prepared for embalmment and transportation to his place of rest in Jamaica. On reflection, we were all on the same flight, although he was classified as cargo.

Just before Christmas 2008, Sister Jane had visited me. We started a discussion about Cousin Velma. My interpretation of Sister Jane's thoughts was somewhat horrific. I learnt that Cousin Velma was, in fact, Father dear's lover for quite a long time. Jane and I argued the fact: was Cousin Velma raped? Or was it purely consensual sex between two adults? Knowing that Cousin Velma was only thirteen years old at the time, that, in itself, told me that the poor child was raped. My opinion might not count, but I truly believed that a thirteen-year old was not capable of making decisions of such volume. Jane claimed that Mother dear, before she passed on, had filled her in on the information that she called facts! Cousin Velma tried to destroy the marriage of my so-called parents by getting herself pregnant. I found it almost impossible that Mother dear would come out with such garbage. It appeared that Mother dear was fully aware of the situation but kept silent in order to keep her turbulent marriage intact.

The knowledge of mathematics told me that Cousin Velma was in fact raped at age thirteen. She was now fifty-one years old. This incident happened thirty-eight years ago—in 1971, to be precise! I estimated that Father dear was approximately thirty-two years of age when this incident occurred. That told me that Cousin Velma, at the age of thirteen, was actually in love with a thirty-year old adult! Deep within my heart of hearts, I found it virtually impossible to believe. My dear friends, what do you think? I was personally horrified by Sister Jane's mind. A few days later, we spoke on the phone, and I mentioned how horrified I was. She then stated that she did not condone the event, but in my mind, it appeared to be normal, what she was thinking. I do hope, for her daughter's sake, that she did not condone what she said. My daughter, Rochelle, was now eleven years old, and if I heard anything similar to Cousin Velma's story from her, I would be afraid that this time around, the reason for imprisonment would be justified. Every night I went to sleep, I always keep watch with one eye on my little girl. Unfortunately, for Cousin Velma, her father who was a good friend of mine was a softie. If that was me, brother-in-law or not, his blood would be all over my hands!

It was Christmas day of 2008. The Christmas family get-together was at my home as usual. Although I hate to boast, my culinary skills are somewhat to be desired. On that day, I had prepared smoked salmon served with lettuce and avocado paste. This was the starter. The avocado paste was made from whisked avocado, crushed garlic, a touch of olive oil, and a pinch of salt and pepper whisked until fluffy. For the main course, there was traditional rice and peas with roast potatoes, a leg of New Zealand's finest lamb, and a selection of mixed vegetables including Brussels sprouts. These were followed by traditional Christmas pudding, and then came the best part, champagne, Baileys or brandy, you name it, I had it flowing like tap water! This was my secret recipe. It went down a treat. In fact, the whole meal went down a treat!

It was just like back in the day in 2001 and 2002 when it was not paid for! It was when Carol, my ex-wife, and her friends were working on the tills at good old Sudbury's supermarket; those were the days, my dear friends. But today, everything had to be paid for by myself. I dare say Christmas did cost me a small fortune. As the evening winded itself forward into night, a snigger of frustration raised its ugly head. The children started reading extracts from the Bible. This had somewhat changed the whole atmosphere as they passed the Holy Book around. Sister Judy had appeared to be upset due to the fact that her son could not read as well as the other children. At that point, believe it or not, the whole place had changed into what I would describe as the clash of the titans. There were screaming children, saying inappropriate things way above expectation. Sisters Jane and Judy were standing face-to-face like two angry grizzly bears, fighting for territory. As Jane advanced towards Judy, breathing, in my opinion, fire, I rushed towards the middle of the two towering inferno. I grabbed Judy by the waist as she continued to advance toward Jane. I was pulled along almost like a mini with its handbrakes on, being pulled by a bulldozer. I could not believe the strength that Judy had. In fact, I didn't even think Judy saw me. Jane was dragged off by Zora to the main bedroom where my two sisters exchanged grievous words of pain behind closed door. My dear friends, listening to the exchange of words simply told me that there was some deep-seated childhood bitterness that still remained unresolved between the two. The reading of the Bible by the children, coupled with the consumption of alcohol, brought on a strange atmosphere, *I dare say.*

Coincidentally, at that point, the phone rang. Who was it? You guessed it right—Father dear, of course, calling from Jamaica, wishing us a happy Christmas. I guessed it was the end of Christmas at that point. It was time for everyone to go home after speaking to Father dear. Almost a week later, I spoke to Sister Jane. She claimed she would never speak to Judy again. I reminded her that she needed her sister. She responded by saying, "I have lost my husband, and if I could live with that, not having my sister is nothing. I don't really need her anyway." However, I knew it was all talk. Two weeks later, Sisters Jane and Judy were best of friends again. This forbidden planet, as I always seemed to call it, was a lonely place when you stood alone. It is even worse when you were standing alone and penniless as I myself experienced on my release from Belmarsh prison.

My dear friends, in January 2009, several days after work, to my greatest horror, I received words from my other siblings that Father dear was in desperate need to communicate with me. The urgency was too much. As he insisted desperately, I left words to the effect that I was not at home. I simply did not wish to talk to him because I knew what the conversation would be about. My wife insisted that I speak to him because it sounded urgent. She handed me the phone. I spoke unwillingly as he pleaded poverty once more As I listened to his words of plea, I grew angry inside. I could hardly speak. His words came out with a slight stutter as I listened to his cry. Same old, same old.

"My electricity and my phone has been disconnected," he said. "I am in need of help. What can you do for me?" I thought to myself, *Here we go again.* The begging bowl was once more empty. On the two occasions, I bailed him out with a heavy heart. This money was simply a loan. Also, Sister Jane granted him the sum of £1,000 at Christmas. That made $110,000. An ordinary person in Jamaica would not see that kind of money. Now, the begging bucket was empty once more. Was the joke on me this time? He must be having a laugh! Personally, I worked very hard, but I lived within my means. To publish this book, who was going to help me? I wonder. Think about it.

My dear friends, in 2009, the word was out, circulating the ears of the public, that Father dear would be on his own very soon. In fact, the floozy that he married was threatening to leave him. I guess she had just found out, after all those years of marriage, that he had no money. Indeed, all he had was useless assets, i.e. a Jaguar car with no engine, a house that was worth six million Jamaican dollars on paper only, and the gift of the gab.

It was extremely ironic from where I was standing, observing the situation. On reflection, my dear mother, peace be upon her, was confronted by the same floozy that was now, unfortunately for me, my stepmother. She uttered these words to my dear mother, "You are finished. If you were any good, your husband would not be with me." Fifteen years later, the words she uttered to Mother dear came back and slapped the bitch right in the face! A young woman who was now the mistress had said almost the same words. It was said that the young woman, in her highest prime, shouted to Father dear in front of his floozy, *"This pussy is yours whenever you want it."* When I heard this, it took me all the way back to how Mother dear felt at that time. It also made me see clearly that the world was like a round table rotating slowly. What goes around always comes back around. Think about it. *Could you imagine the laughter that echoed from the grave of Mother dear when she looked down on the father of her children whilst sipping from a honeycomb!*

Personally, the day when Doris leaves my dear father, I would expect to hear that it is freezing in hell! Although the going was tough at the moment, I believe that if she hadn't walked yet, she never would.

My wonderful family.

CHAPTER Two
Lady X and the Mystery Woman

The names of the characters had been changed in order to not to expose them.

In 1993, I went to Jamaica because I thought I was getting old, and the desire to settle down was upon me.

Upon my arrival, I came upon a different world, far from the one I had known. It was a total shock to my system. I sought something that I could not find in the world I know, but it was extremely horrific. I met a young lady whom I thought I was in love with. We made love everywhere possible. *However, upon reflection,* I realized it was all about sex; *it was all about lust*! Yes, I was fooled by good sex! In fact, you might call me a fool, but at the time, I had no clue of what I was doing. I *was infatuated. Some might even say I was obsessed.* Don't forget that I said upon reflection, good sex and love were two separate entities but very close. When the charm of a woman is turned on, good sex is love in the eyes of British in a foreign land.

Believe it or not, on the day of my departure, I almost missed my flight because Lady X, whom I had not named, wanted sex to last her until I see her again.

I returned to the United Kingdom, but I came back with only the clothes on my back. Lady X had the same size of clothes as myself, so she begged me to leave them to remind her of me. It really did not matter because clothes in the United Kingdom were cheap.

One week later, after arriving in the United Kingdom, I used my first pay salary and simply replaced my clothes. I rang Jamaica several times. Lady X always encouraged me to have telephone sex. It was a strange concept for me, but I suppose it was the result of a long distance relationship. I got fed-up of that, and believe it or not, my phone bill was £1,500 (per quarter! Living in a studio apartment, I found it hard to pay such excessive bills, but I had to pay it regardless. I decided to give Lady X a trip over. I did believe she had a shock to see where someone of my calibre lived. In Jamaica, $70 to a pound made me into a king in my own right. However, as you know, in the United Kingdom, a pound was a pound!

I found it very hard to keep this young lady due to my income. Unfortunately, months after her arrival, I lost my job (At the time, John Major, the then prime minister, was not paying me enough for the two of us). Lady X left and met up with a former boyfriend from Jamaica who now resided in the United Kingdom.

She disappeared for a period of two months; there were no phone call, no contact, nothing. I sat in my studio apartment night after night, wondering what had happened to her.

I went job-hunting as usual, with huge success. To be totally honest, I was not exactly an unqualified person in my field (engineering, that is). I had a job working for Elmec Engineering Company as an engineer. I was doing very well. My life was gradually getting back on track, sorting my head out, etc. Two months later, Lady X returned with her expired Visa. A fool would always be a fool. She asked me to marry her. I thought about it but did not.

The night she asked me to marry her, we had great sex, and I said, "Yes, I will marry you."

At three in the *morning,* my phone rang. I was so tired, I thought I was having a dream. I answered it and said, "Hello."

A male voice spoke and uttered these words: "Who are you, mother fucker? Where is my wife?"

I said, "You have the wrong number."

He said, "Get my wife, and get her now before I get really mad."

I said, "Calm down. What is your wife's name?"

He said, "Nadine."

I said, "There is a Nadine here, but she is my girlfriend."

He said, "Put her on the phone, and if I find out that you have fucked her, I will rip your head off."

I did not know Nadine was married. Apparently, her husband was in America where he resided. She began speaking to him over the phone. The angry young man was indeed her husband! They spoke for an hour or two, and I just sat on the bed and stared. Obviously, I could never marry her after that.

I must admit I still felt something. Was it lust, love, or *confusion?* Or was I simply a fool for having these feelings? The following day, I had to make a decision. I had, in fact, decided to send her back to Jamaica. I had to stick to this decision for my own sanity. I told her I had to send her home because I was not happy with this situation. She cried for an hour or two. I went to work that day. I did very little as my mind was unsettled, unable to concentrate, and lacked focus.

I worked as a precision engineer that required maximum concentration. In fact, at that time, I was machining pistons for a train engine, so you could imagine what I was going through.

On my return home from work, I entered the front door. Nadine always came to the door when she heard the inserting of the key *into the lock.* This time, however, she did not come to the door.

I entered into the living area of the studio apartment. I then discovered that she was gone. I had no idea where she had gone because to my knowledge, she knew no one in England. But I was wrong.

I rang the Home Office and informed them of the situation. I did this to clear myself of any responsibility of her, although in my heart of hearts, I still had strong feelings for her. I took a week off work because I was becoming an emotional wreck. I stood by the window, wondering day after day, watching and waiting for her to return, though I had no knowledge as to whether or not she was dead or alive.

Early one morning, as I stood by the window, a car drove up very slowly. I looked closely at the occupants: a male and a female. They began kissing. The female got out, and believe it or not, it was her! I was shocked! I began to shake with fear, but was it really fear? Or was it the thoughts in my head? There was no need to ask what I was thinking. I kept my cool and went into the kitchen. She came into the apartment because she thought I was at work.

As I left the kitchen and entered the living area, I said, "Hello." She dropped her bags, covered her mouth, and stared at me as if she had seen a ghost. I told her not to look so shocked *(I do live here)* but to explain herself. She began by saying she panicked when her husband rang, and she was terrified when she saw how upset I was.

The man that drove her home was an old friend from Jamaica. He used to be her boyfriend.

"I spent some time with him at his place, but I had to leave because his girlfriend had suspicions that we slept together, but we did not," she said.

"His girlfriend kept arguing with him, so I had no choice but to leave. I came back to you because I have nowhere else to go. I have no money. I am destitute, so here I am again."

I then said to her at that point, "It is best if you go back to Jamaica because you are now an illegal immigrant." I made an arrangement with the British Airway to send her home with the promise that I would follow shortly, *and indeed, I did.* Six months went by, and we had constant communication by telephone almost every night. I recalled receiving a telephone bill that exceeded £1,500.

I went to Jamaica, a journey I remember very clearly. In 1994, strange events happened. I met her mom, and she greeted me in a way that made me feel as if she knew me for years. We became good friends.

One day, I visited Nadine's home, and she brought me a drink without asking me if I was thirsty. It was the drink of doom—good old carrot juice. Never ever drink carrot juice from a woman in the Caribbean, lads beware! I knew this before I went to Jamaica, so that put me one step ahead.

I told her that I do not drink carrot juice and told her to drink it herself. The look in her eyes was of terror and fear. She took it back to the kitchen, but I don't know what she did with it after that. Her mother enquired as to why I did not drink it. I told her it was not one of my favourite drinks. She appeared upset. I then proceeded to the shop to buy drinks which we all shared while sitting on the veranda.

After having a few drinks, I left and went back to Mandeville where I had lunch. After lunch, I went for a walk into the market place. I heard voices called out several times "Englishman."

I replied, "I am not an Englishman. I am the same as you, a born Jamaican." The two guys looked at me and laughed. They asked me if I had any pound in exchange for dollars. I did not trust them so I said, "None."

They then asked if I had any dollars to buy them a drink. I did not have a large amount of cash on me at the time, which I think was a lucky thing. The two lads went into my pockets and took $1,000. That was the equivalent of £20. I did not regard this as mugging because they placed a large bundle of marijuana inside my top pocket. I looked at this as a simple exchange. Although I was not a heavy smoker, my cousin and I smoked it and found it rather mind-blowing.

The next day, I took a taxi from my cousin's house back to Mandeville. I saw the same two guys. They asked, "How was the weed?"

I replied, "Very good," and gave them $500 to buy drinks for themselves.

I took a taxi back to Nadine's house. She was not at home, but her mother was. She invited me in. We sat down and chatted. We spoke of the unhappiness in Nadine's life, and the conversation became quite emotional. I said to her mother, "I should leave her to sort her life out."

To my greatest horror, her mother put her arms around me and pulled me close to her enormous bosom. Her breasts were very soft against my chest. She pushed my head down as if she wanted me to suffocate against them. She then pushed her pubic bone hard against me. At this point, I was aroused. She unzipped my trousers. Her hands reached down into my boxers, stroking my genital. I then suddenly remembered that this was the mother of my girlfriend!

I asked her, "What on earth are you doing?"

She replied, "Don't you want me?"

I said, "I can't do this; it is not right!"

I left and took a taxi to the KFC in Mandeville. That was the worst thing I had ever done in my life. *I was served by a woman with long brown hair and hazel coloured eyes.* I took the food back to my cousin's house in Hatfield where I was staying.

I said to my cousin, "A woman in the KFC served me, and *I have to have her.*"

The next day, my cousin and I went back to the KFC to investigate this mystery woman. My cousin looked at her and said she was nice but looked dangerous. Indeed, she was, but I had no care in the world. I just had to have her. My cousin and I went to see Nadine at work. I told her it was not possible to see her anymore. At this point, I closed the door that was leading to hell, but I opened another door that was hell unknowingly! I became infatuated with the mystery lady at KFC. I kept going back to the shop everyday for two weeks, hoping to see her, until one day, I was walking towards the shop and saw her walking towards me. Immediately, I froze, although the temperature was sweltering so much that the tarmac on the road was melting. I froze, speechless. She went past me with a grin on her face, which I will never forget. I managed to utter these words: "Excuse me, I have been looking for you."

She looked at me and laughed then replied, "I know. My friends at work told me that an English man is coming everyday, looking for me.'

At the time, I thought I was in heaven. But was I?

At that moment, I spoke to her using the fluency of the Queen's English. I was accompanied by my cousin, Claudette. Claudette spoke very well, but to me, it was a fake. Obviously, when she was around me she felt British. However, the mystery lady truly believed that my cousin was British. She asked me when *we* are going back to England.

I set a few dates for an excursion, with me driving, of course; I had a rented car. The island was at my fingertips. My mystery lady, after one whole week of travelling around the island, became my lover! But still, she remained a mystery to me. I was rather intrigued by this woman, but I was also very excited. The sex was good, but I would not call it great.

We explored the more renowned hot spots of the island such as Negril, Dunns River, YS Falls, the Rolling River, etc., to name but a few. She was truly ecstatic because she had never travelled around her own *country. It took someone from* England to show her the finer things in life. I was certain I made a huge impact on her well-being.

Now it came to the crunch to solve the rest of the mystery. This woman was too easy. I could see that there might be a catch. But in spite of my suspicions, I ignored my instincts. The thoughts came to my mind because I found myself developing feelings for her. It scared me half to death due to the fact that somewhere in my mind, this woman was still a mystery, and believe it or not, I was damn right!

We went to a processing plant where ackees were canned for exporting. For those of you who do not know what an ackee is, it is a vegetable that grows on a huge tree. It is almost a heart shape with a red pod. When it is ready for harvesting, it will open naturally whilst still on the tree, revealing three black seeds attached to a yellow flesh. It is picked from the tree and prepared for cooking. The seeds and the pink membrane inside the yellow flesh are removed then boiled for a few minutes *(as these are very delicate and must not be overcooked)* with some salt fish added, along with other seasoning, etc. It is very delicious, but with the wrong preparation, you are dead, especially if it is forced open before it is ready to open naturally whilst still on the tree.

Whilst I was at the factory, a strange thing happened. A beautiful young lady approached us.

She said, "Hello, Mrs. Woodburn. What brought you to this side of St. Elizabeth?"

My girlfriend looked at the young lady and asked, "What are you talking about? Do I know you?"

The young lady insisted that she knew the mystery lady who was my girlfriend.

At this point, I said, "Sorry, I do not think my girlfriend knows you, and there is nothing I can do." We then both walked away. I glanced back at the young lady, and she stood there as if she was in a state of shock. On reflection, Carol denied knowing Mr. Woodburn, just like Judas disowned knowing Jesus. Indeed, Mr. Woodburn was Carol's husband at that time.

I drove back to Mandeville to my mystery lady's house. I then discovered that she had a five-year old daughter whom I became acquainted with. The daughter was sent to visit her aunt a few blocks away so that we could have some quality time together. As soon as the child went, she ripped off my clothes, pushed me on the bed, then she started to blow—and I don't mean my trumpet! She claimed she had not done this before; it was her first time. However, her performance was like that of a professional. It was the best blow I had ever had in Jamaica. She made *Deep Throat* looked like a story for children, and I should know because I had had a few, I dare say. I think she was giving me something to remember her by! I was told that Jamaicans do not do this (*oral sex*) as they deemed this as a depraved act. Quite frankly, it was a load of bull.

After three hours of intense passion, I left and went back to my parents' mansion a few blocks away. I had a much-needed cold shower after such a heated session. I then went upstairs to see my beloved mother who was extremely upset with me. She was told by someone that I was having an affair with a married woman.

I told her, "This was an allegation. Mother dear, there is no truth in this. Where did you get this rubbish? I don't believe it."

She said, "Okay, my son, I want you to go to Super plus Supermarket and ask for Mr. Woodburn, the manager. He has a five-year-old daughter. I am certain you are seeing his wife. It is the wrong woman you are chasing, my son, it is the wrong woman." Indeed, Mother was right, but that did not stop me from *the sin that brought me to my knees.*

At this point, she wept *that made me feel rather uncomfortable.*

The next day, I went to the supermarket. It was extremely busy. *I approached the cashier at one of the cash register and enquired if Mr. Woodburn was there. She asked if it was important as they were very busy and he did not wish to be disturbed.* At that point, Mr. Woodburn came walking towards the cashier whom I was speaking to. Looking at him, indirectly she said, "*See im deh.*" (There he is.)

I looked at him but did not approach him because the information I wanted was confirmed there and then. I was troubled because no matter how I added 2+2, it still came to 6! I found this unacceptable, although the facts stared at me in the face. Mr. Woodburn appeared to be twice the age of my father, a frail old man with silver hair, slightly shaky hands, and a wrinkled face. I really couldn't understand why a young girl like Carol would be with such an old man three times her age! I could not believe she was married to him but, apparently, it was true. The whole story was true, as it was proven. I rang Carol and asked her what were her plans for the day. She had none. She had a free day, so I asked her if she would like to go for a drive down to the Dunns River waterfalls in Ocho Rios. We made a pleasurable day of it. I had not revealed to her my knowledge of her husband because I am certain that would spoil the fun. It was a splendid day indeed. We drove back to Mandeville and we had a meal at Bamboo Village, a very posh Chinese restaurant. It was rather amusing to the workers in the restaurant who were not of Chinese origin but of Caribbean origin. They did not know who I was or where I came from. All they could see was someone who resembled them in appearance. They crowded around my table giggling as I ate my meal using chopsticks. They had never seen this before, I was told. I thought it was rather funny.

Carol and I went back to my parents' home. She decided to stay for the night. In my thoughts, she had disregarded her family, but I truly believed she had forgotten due to the fun she was having with me.

The next morning, my parents went to open the business premises. I woke my girlfriend up at around 9:00 A.M. She was astonished to see what time it was. She dashed out the door like Cinderella. I watched her heading toward the shortcut from the window. Apparently, the shortcut went straight past my parents' business premises. At this point, I assumed she was on her way home. I had a cold shower, got dressed, and made my way to her house. I also took a shortcut that led directly into the town of Mandeville, five minutes from her marital home. To my utmost surprise, Mr. Woodburn was walking towards me. I stopped. He approached me in distress and then said to me, "What kind of a man are you? Don't you know my wife have a child to look after?"

He then reached into his pocket and presented me with a picture of myself. Then he uttered these words.

"I am on my way to the police station to report my wife missing. The last person she was seen with was this English man in the picture," he said to me.

I could not believe the trouble I had caused this poor silver-haired man.

I asked him, "Where is Carol?"

He replied, "She did not come home last night." He mumbled, "This always happens when a foreign man appears in this town. Two months ago, it was that damn man from Cayman. Now, it's an Englishman. What on earth is happening to me!" he screamed, holding his head with both hands in a distressed manner.

He then continued walking towards the town with his face to the ground. I stood watching him until he was out of sight. I felt his pain. I then proceeded toward his house. When I got there, I shouted "Carol" twice but got no reply. For some reason, I thought Carol went home to prepare her daughter for school, but I found out later that she went straight to work at KFC. On reflection, I did believe she acted irresponsibly, but at the time, we were both ruled by lustful passion. The Englishman and the Jamaican—how hot, the *ice melts!* Around 9:20 A.M., I returned to my parents' mansion. I sat down for a while, thinking what to do. I decided to do some washing because all my designer clothes were dirty. I could not believe the amount of washing I had done that day. I placed the washed clothes on the line at approximately 11:30 A.M. I then went to KFC because that was my girlfriend's place of work. She was there. I asked if she was okay.

She replied, "Yes, but I am leaving early today."

I waited for her. We then proceed back to my parents' palace at approximately 12:00 P.M. When I got there, I said to Carol, "I did some washing today," but it was not on the line. All my clothes were gone, including my underwear, and if you think that was funny, even the clothes pegs were gone!

I then turned around and said to Carol, "What do you think happened?" She laughed until she almost pissed herself.

She said, "I did not know that they did this kind of thing in this area. This is due to the fact that were mansions all around.

I went to my parents' business premises and told my mom what had happened. I told her that I was going to the police, but she advised me not to go. She said anyone who was seen with my clothes could be arrested, and if charged by the police, they might come to harm me and could burn the house down. This is what they are like in this country, so I left it. My mom and I continued speaking. During the course of our conversation, she made me extremely upset by saying, "If you were not chasing a red woman's crutch, this would not have happened."

I went to Carol's house, upset as I was, and I told her of the argument between Mother and myself. She took it all as a big joke.

She replied, "The next time you do any washing, if you have any clothes left, stay by the window with a gun pointing towards the clothes' line until the clothes are dry."

I did not find it funny. All I had left of my clothes were two pairs of jeans. Luckily, I was due to return to England. Involving myself with Mrs. Woodburn had started to be disastrous. I had no clothes to wear. *Looking back, it was purely self-destruction. Never take another man's wife (or another woman's husband)— but I did. The sins that brought me to my knees.*

I went to the unravelled mystery woman's house. She wanted sex, but the thought of him touching her was inside my head. *I was so saturated by these thoughts* that they caused me to have a refusal of an erection. No matter what she did, the erection failed.

She asked me what was the problem, and I said, "Nothing. I am okay, but I am just not in the mood." In spite of my horrific revelation, I still thought she was beautiful.

She then said to me, "I want to talk to you."

I asked her, "what about?"

She brought me a slice of chocolate cake that she baked for me. "I baked this for you," she uttered and gave me a cold drink.

I never gave it a second thought. I grabbed the cake and downed the drink in one in the sweltering heat. She looked deep into my eyes. She spoke *in patois,'*(Jamaican accent) saying, "Me love yuh, (*I love you*) yuh know, but mi married."

"I know you are married. Think about it. Last week, at the ackee factory, a young lady called you Mrs. Woodburn. I was also told that you are married to Mr. Woodburn, the manager of Super plus. I saw him, but I thought he was your grandfather." I described him to her in details. At this point, she burst into tears.

She said, "I am married, but I am separated. Although we share the same home, we have separate lives."

I said to her, "Don't worry, I will get you out of this, if it is the last thing I do" *What on earth possessed me to say that?* I asked myself. Upon reflection, what a fool I had been. *Could it be that she had fed me something to tie me to her?* There is an ancient African tradition, a potion that some women could use (supposedly) to make a man fall in love with them. Does it work? That, I will never know!

In my final week, I couldn't wait to get on that *iron bird* to return to civilisation—home—England. Shock, shock! horror, horror!

My girlfriend approached me. To my surprise, she asked me if I still love her. Did the potion work? Indeed, it did. I responded "Yes," but I was so scared. Whatever I was fed, it was very powerful. Don't forget Nadine tried, but I refused to drink, so I was certain it was a similar potion.

After saying yes to the woman who I fell in love with (*unnaturally*), she requested that I meet her husband. She claimed that it was his request. I was blown away. It was as if I stood in front of a cannon at point blank!

At this point, I started stuttering in my speech. She asked me to give her a day when I was able to meet him. I then plucked up the courage and said, "Tomorrow." Did I sleep that night?

The next day, I went for the meeting and met Mr Woodburn, the same silver-haired man, just like Mr. Bojangle! But guess what, it was the same man I saw in the supermarket, the same Mr. Woodburn!

My mother was right! In fact, mothers are always right (*That was the general assumption*). Listen to them; *they are full of wisdom.*

As I stood in front of him, he stared at me as if his world was about to collapse. My world sure did!

He uttered, "So you are the English man who managed to steal my wife."

I said, "Pardon me."

He said, "You come from England in your big jumbo jet with the pound in your hands, and you frightened my wife because she thinks you are rich. You know what it is like when a foreigner comes out to Jamaica."

I said, "I don't know."

He said, "Let me tell you, we work for dollars, and you work for pounds. One pound is equal to 110 dollars. When you change 100 pounds, you are a rich man in our eyes. Our women fall for this all the time."

"What is your intention, my son?" he asked.

At this point, my shirt was saturated with sweat, as if I was standing in a sauna. I was sweating like a PIG! But I had no fear.

He said, "I was told you are going back to England at the end of the week."

I said, "Yes."

He said, "So tell me, what are you going to do about my wife?" He asked in a soft voice, "Are you going to marry her or what?"

I said as my voice trembled with fear, "Don't you think this conversation is a bit heavy?"

He laughed. "So what did you expect me to say? Do you think you could just come to Jamaica, sex my wife, go back to England, and laugh at me?"

I could not believe my ears.

He said, "Man to man, my wife is in love with you. I think you should make up your mind. Are you going to marry my wife?'

No need to ask; the sweat continued even more profusely. I felt like a rat cornered, and any direction I took, I knew I would be killed. Indeed, that was a fact.

I said, "*Ye, ye, ye, yes,* I will marry your wife." He looked me in the eyes, and I saw death. Little did I know he was looking at my death!

He shook my hand with a grip as tight as a vice and said, "Good luck, my son. I am old, but the thoughts of you will keep me alive."

Believe it or not, those words still haunts me even to this day!

On reflection, my dear friends, Mr. Woodburn was telling me something, but I was too blind to see! There is no way a man would give his wife to another man without a fight if she was a good woman. As it stood, Mr Woodburn knew what he was doing. The woman was no damn good. She used men to better her life without working—a common gold digger. If it was me in his shoes, there would be bloodshed. I was warned by the locals that Carol was a prostitute for foreign men, hoping to get a break from Jamaica. I did not listen to these truthful people because at the time, prostitution did not seem to be of her character. But how wrong I was. On reflection, fifteen years later, I thought I should have listened, but at least it is all behind me now, fizzled away in a huge explosion, just like when the sunlight hits a vampire full blast!

At present, any man who has the audacity like I had in 1993 (did what I had done then) deserves to die; a man's wife is like a precious stone that he should cherish and not pass on to another man.

I have mentioned this to several friends, and they asked me if I was a lunatic because of that experience. They said they *would have been gone for dust.*

But don't forget, *I knew I was fed something* because I would have been gone, but I stayed. It was still a mystery to me.

I flew back to England, and just like with Nadine as mentioned previously, I was having telephone sex. I eventually sent money to Mrs. Woodburn to pay for her divorce. After six months, I sent for her to visit me in England. I was living in the same studio apartment when I was with Nadine. Although I was running a small business, I left Carol in England whilst I returned to Jamaica on an emergency trip. Here I met someone whom I fell in love with naturally. She had her own business and was doing quite well.

A beautiful woman, I may add. We had good times together, and the sex was electrifying. We made love on the beach, on the boat, and in the Triple Arrow Hotel, which was owned by my friends.

I returned back to England with my head spinning. I kept my relationship with Barbara very quiet, but I was confused. Thinking back, I did love Barbara, but why I did not end up with her? That was a mystery to me. Barbara wrote to me frequently at the business address; it was all good. However, I often send my current girlfriend to the business premises to check on things. To my surprise, she discovered that Barbara was writing me love letters. She collected all the letters and read them, which was a criminal offence and an invasion of privacy in the United Kingdom. This happened over the course of six months. I received a phone call at home from Barbara. She seemed very disturbed. She said that she had received a letter from my girlfriend written in red ink, threatening to have her killed. I confronted Carol the next day. She was very upset, and we had an argument. She presented me with the letters that was sent by Barbara, which she had intercepted. I must admit the letters were sexually explicit. Some of them had her lipstick impression on them.

A week later, Carol had asked me to have sex with her. I remember it quite clearly. It was a Thursday night in November. I had never experienced sex like this with her before. In fact, now that I am not with her, the memory makes me cold.

I went to work Friday morning after she made me a packed lunch. As I drove to work, I began thinking. It was quite unusual—hardcore sex and packed lunch. I began adding up again, and still, 2 + 2 equals 6! *Why was she so nice to me? I was truly puzzled.*

Her behaviour was quite peculiar. To my utmost shock, when I arrived home that Friday evening, the apartment was turned upside down as if a tornado had passed through it, *and* she was not at home! I picked up the phone, and I rang everyone who we both knew. No one had seen or heard from her. I was at a dead end. Then it hit me. I thought she might have returned to

Jamaica. But it was just a thought. It turned out that my thoughts were right because looking around the apartment, there were no sign of any summer clothing; only the winter clothing were left behind. I knew she had to be gone somewhere hot, but it wasn't Spain.

At this point, I rang Mr. Woodburn in Jamaica, the ex-husband. *Remember him?* He answered the phone. I asked him if he knew anything because Carol had disappeared.

"Disappeared?" he said. "She has not. She's on a flight coming back to me." That was what he said on that day he handed her to me. How foolish indeed. How foolish of me. I should have known.

I was astounded, but at least I stopped worrying.

I said, "Thank you," then hanged up the phone.

I cleaned up the apartment, made myself something to eat, had a drink, and put my feet up, watching the television. Jamaica was six hours behind the United Kingdoms, so when it was 8:00 P.M. in the United Kingdom, it was 2:00 P.M. in Jamaica. I worked out the time difference. I also worked out the landing time and taxi journey time to Mandeville. I then set the alarm to wake me up at an appropriate time—when I knew she would be with her ex-husband. I had to find out why she did this.

The clock alarmed at 8:00 P.M., which was 2:00 P.M. on Saturday for her. I rang Mr. Woodburn's house once, and believe me, Carol answered the phone as if she was waiting for my call.

I said, "Hello." She was speechless. I repeated hello again and said, "Speak to me." She began to weep hysterically.

I said in a soothing voice, "What is the matter, Carol?"

"I can't believe what I have done. I have lost my opportunity to be in England when I booked the flight one-way. I thought I could go back to my husband. When I looked out of the window of the plane, I started crying because I did not know what I was doing."

"You didn't know?" I asked.

She said, "No, I didn't. I wanted the plane to turn around and take me back to Gatwick Airport. I sat on the plane thinking about you, regretting what I have done. It's your fault."

She said, "It was the pictures and love letters that were sent by Barbara that drove me to do this."

I said, "You must be a fool." Indeed she was.'

She said, "You have two women in Jamaica now. Which one do you love?" Still crying, she said, "You have to choose one of us. Barbara or me?"

Earlier, I mentioned *she was a fool indeed*, but I am the real fool here!

I said to her, "Don't worry, darling. Just take a week or two holiday." Then I made the biggest mistake that I kept on making—giving her second chances. Keeping her in my life was not only a mistake but also a disaster.(*I guess I will never learn.*)

I do believe upon reflection, that I had murdered myself in cold blood! Two weeks later, I booked a flight for her return, costing me £900 because it was high season and it had to be a return ticket in order for her to gain entry. "What a waste, what a waste, what a waste," I now sing! If I had booked a one-way ticket, she would not have been able to enter the United Kingdom. *So you see, I was a fool. Never let your heart rule your head.* Can you imagine taking another man's wife and allowing her to go back to him on a holiday? Was I a fool, or was I?

She arrived at Gatwick Airport, and I met her there. The immigration stamped six months in her passport—the usual procedure. However, to her utmost shock, they had changed the ticket departure date that I had listed from six months to three weeks. At that time, immigration had just began to clamp down on Jamaicans due to alleged contraband activities here in mainland Britain. She was devastated to see what they had done. When she walked through to the meeting point, and I saw her, she looked as if her mother had died. I did not realize the significance of being in Britain to her. I gave her a hug, and she felt extremely heavy, as if she was going to faint on me. She explained what had happened at the immigration.

"Three weeks," she said, "I can't believe it."

I said to her, "Don't worry. When we get home, I will make a few calls to see what I can sort out. I have heard of cases where people are turned back within hours of arrival, so count yourself lucky you are is still in England." Carol had fulfilled her childhood dream—destination England. Wasn't she lucky!

When I got home that day, I rang British Airways and explained to them that I booked a six months return ticket for my girlfriend, and the immigration had changed it at the airport. I insisted that the ticket be changed back to its original status.

"Okay, Mr. Francis, that is done for you."

I then said, "Thank you," and hanged up the phone.

I told Carol and she was ecstatic. She asked, "How did you do that?" as if I had performed a miracle. Yes, indeed, it was a miracle, considering the circumstances. Two months later, I married her in order for her to obtain British citizenship. Her troubles were over, and mine had just began. She had returned to Jamaica one year after this incident as Mrs. Francis, and my life had been in turmoil since. *The day in March when I said, "I do," to Carol was despicable. I did not know I was on the road to hell. Trust me.* I was told by Carol that my sister Jane told her she was too good for me. I do believe she was mistaken. Thank God, I was happily divorced after getting out of this emotional prison. *Read on...it gets better.*

Her trip to Jamaica was paid for by myself, of course (muggings). I told her to stay for six months, and I would join her at a later date. Indeed, I joined her one month later. She had a lot of family in Jamaica, but I could not understand why she chose to stay with her ex-husband now that she was my wife. Indeed, I was a fool to allow this to happen.

She came to the airport to meet me, but what I found quite strange was that during the short time I stayed at my parents' mansion, she stayed with her ex-husband. A week after I arrived, she took me to an STD clinic as if I had a sexually transmitted disease. On reflection, a woman of her sexual thirst genetically passed on by her father platehead who is known to fuck anything that smells like a fish. I dare say it was a string from the old bow. Bad genes ran in the family. It was plain obvious to me that she had a disease that she did not want me to catch. It was said by a local who was a friend of Carol and I, that if I had a pound for every man she slept with whilst on holiday, I would have been a rich man! But I was a naïve fool who was blind to the facts. Before she went on holiday, believe it or not, one day I got home from work, she had love bites on her neck and in her vaginal region. I questioned her about these marks because at the time we were not having any intimate contact with each other. Obviously, she did not do this herself. I dare say I never thought I would see the day that when I went to work, my wife has not been screwed by another man, or as Carol claimed it, a ghost that screwed her when we both lived at 13 Laurel Grove. What a day that must have been for her. How bizarre.

She said then, "I was held down by a ghost, and he actually had sex with me." And you know what I did? I actually believed her! How naïve I was, indeed. It is only now, thinking back, that the penny had just dropped. I totally understand. The doctor explained to me that my wife had an infection that I might catch. I was shocked and disgusted by this. He prescribed a course of medication for me. I took them without asking my wife any questions about her sexual activities. Could it be that she had caught a disease? That I would never know because I never questioned the facts. I must have been a lunatic. I then started to question myself, *What have I done to myself?* Well, it was too late to find things out because no matter what the situation, I was married, and I had to live with it. I decided to execute an investigation by asking family members about Carol.

I was informed by a blood relative of Carol that indeed, she was a whore, and she disgraced the family by sleeping with older men from the age of fourteen. However, due to the fact that there was no law in Jamaica against it, the men got away with it. I was also informed by the same person that she was the product of an unfaithful father. She was the daughter of a mentally ill woman by the name of Nancy who was a cleaner at her father's bar/pub (Easton Nembhard strikes again!).

"Her father was married to my mother," the woman said. I also learnt through research that Carol's dad would sex anything with a hole in it that smelled like a fish. People called him Solomon, but in my eyes, he was not the wisest man! Others called him platehead due to the fact that he had a metal plate in his head as a result of an accident.

When Nancy gave birth to Carol, she left the newborn child cold and unloved on the bed and vanished. Due to her mental health, I doubt if she knew she had given birth. Perhaps, this could have contributed to her disappearing act. The child (Carol) was cared for by a non-family member, an old woman called Curdell who lived in the village.

"And that is the woman you marry?" She said, "I am glad she got someone younger than Woodburn. Good luck, you will need it."

I could not believe what I had picked up on my shoe, but I fell in love with it. Could you imagine the life such a person had to offer in adulthood? I could see clearly why she did what she did—survival, of course. That was all she knew. What she did to me was unnecessary—*bit the hand that fed her*—but I am still alive, considering three failed suicide attempts due to my imprisonment and the distressing lifestyle I had experienced and endured with her.

Childhood reflection can be dangerous in adulthood because it determines the type of adult you become. For someone who had no form of love from the onset, this must be damaging, in my opinion. So here I was with an unsuitable person for me, but due to the fact that I was married and no one got married to divorce, I took it in my stride to give it my best shot. We both returned to England and set up home in my studio apartment.

She got a job in the local Sudbury's supermarket and in spite of the hustle and bustle of life, I still tried to keep things together. The business I had at the time was not doing too badly because I was able to pay the mortgage for the property. You might wonder, "What property?"

Well, in 1992, my parents had taken early retirement, although they had not yet reached retirement age. They went back to Jamaica to live there. They used to own a pub in the East End of London called The Rising Sun. My father had borrowed a substantial amount of money against the family home. That money was used to build their mansion and opened a family business. Before my father left for Jamaica, he took me to the Halifax Building Society to introduce me to the manager and put me in charge of the repayment of this massive loan. In fact, the repayment was £1000 per month. I paid it comfortably for two years due to the fact that I turned the family home into rented accommodation letting the rooms privately. This was illegal, but it was the only way I could afford the monthly payments. When my dad left England, I discussed what I have done with the bank manager in order to pay the mortgage.

He said, "I will turn a blind eye to the fact that you have let the property. All I need is the regular monthly payments."

That was the agreement I had with the Halifax in 1992, off the record. I also had a verbal agreement with my father that upon the sale of the house, he would get a £10,000 lump sum payment. Although he had borrowed against the property to finance the new business in Jamaica and build the mansion, his percentage was already taken by himself. Due to my trustworthiness, I had no documentation drawn up by a solicitor. My wife, Carol, at the time, had mentioned on a few occasions that she did not think this was right, as if she knew what was brewing, and *I was sure it was not beer!* I now realized that I was a naïve person because I did not foresee this event; neither would I expect this to happen to me.

In 1997, Carol gave birth to a beautiful little girl. I named her Rochelle Ann Francis because I wanted us to have the same initial—RAF. Six months later, we were offered a two-bedroom house with rear and front gardens in a lovely cul-de-sac. It was newly built by Wimpey and owned by London and Quadrant Housing Association.

Our lifestyle improved because I was working as an engineer, earning a substantial salary. The mortgage for my dad's property had been decreased from £1,000 to £700 per month. I had no financial problems. I furnished our new home with top quality furniture, the best carpet, and made the small room into a nursery. In the normal sense, this was meant to bring happiness, but to be totally honest with you, it was the beginning of the end, and I was still hanging in there.

My daughter grew close to me. She refused to sleep at nights if she was not in my arms. This was a lot of work. At one point, I even had to take her to work with me. This continued for three years.

My daughter became obsessed with her daddy. Every feeding time or nappy change, it was always me. I could not understand why a baby could show so much affection—could it be that she sensed the love I was giving, perhaps?

It was said by my wife that I was not the child's father. This had somewhat distorted me, on top of the other problems I was facing in the marriage. My wife became abusive towards me, and I could not understand why.

I decided to take a trip to Jamaica. Taking my wife and the baby, we went as a family. I had made arrangements from England to stay in a guesthouse, but upon arrival, my wife decided to go to her ex-husband's home where she stayed with our baby. This, I could not understand. I stayed at a friend's home that night. The next day, we met at the marketplace and went to the guesthouse. We had a wonderful three weeks, and then we return to England.

Upon our arrival at the airport, we took a taxi. As soon as we got home, she said to me, "Don't make the mistake of thinking we are friends."

That night, she slept in the nursery, and our daughter slept with me. There was a double bed in the nursery, just in case we had visitors to stop over. Since that night, I had never woken up next to my wife! The nursery became her bedroom!

In the early part of 2000, my mother became very ill (She was actually ill before, but I was unaware of this). It was brought to my attention when she came over to England for chemotherapy; she had breast cancer. The chemotherapy had done a lot of damage to her, in my opinion; she had excessive hair loss. At the same time, I was fighting against my dad because he came to reclaim the property that I had been paying the mortgage for since 1992, and to which he had never contributed a penny.

My mother stayed in England for one year and my father also came back. At the start of the family feud, I instructed my tenants not to pay me any rent as I am the only landlord they knew. Other family members had tried to obtain rent from them.

In 2001, it all came to a crunch when I had to tell my tenants to vacate the property with all the rent money they had accumulated from their Housing Benefit. That was two years worth of rent, at a payment of £1300 per month. It was a sad occasion, but the tenants were very happy because they lived rent-free for two years. This I had to do due to my pride. I did not want my parents to say I was collecting rent and not paying the mortgage.

I had also informed the bank manager of the situation. At the time, he shook my hand and said to me, "You are the best customer I have ever had. I don't blame you for giving up because I knew all along that this would happen. You did not get any legal documents for the property to say you were paying your father's debt, and now, he is simply giving you a kick in the balls." He shook my hand and said, "Good luck, my son, and take care." (I learnt the hard way; I had trusted my own father.) *My dear friends, if it was not written and signed, don't go near it; walk away from it. I made a mistake.*

Although my mother was in a decaying state when the house was repossessed, she was still strong enough to get hold of the rest of the money after the bank sold the house and took their share. My mother had given what was left over to my sister Judy by to pay for her funeral expenses when she departed from earth. She knew she was going. Six months later, after returning to Jamaica, she went to meet God. I did not go to her funeral because, believe it or not, my wife's mother died one day after my mother. Incredible coincidence! It was almost as if they had planned it.

I sent my wife to Jamaica to represent me at my mother's funeral and to enable her to attend her own mother's funeral. My daughter and I spent two unforgettable weeks together. We were both very happy.

My main reason for stopping the payment of mortgage for my parents' house was due to the fact that my parents' house was meant to be mine automatically, as I was directly responsible for paying the mortgage. It was agreed that my dad gets £10,000. However, he came back and demanded £20,000 when it was arranged for me to get the money. He requested that I take the back the seat and give him the house, with all the furniture and the tenants. I objected strongly to this, so he instructed his solicitor to write to me in order to remove my landlord status from the property. The agreement we had was verbal—huge mistake! My father became avaricious, causing him to lose everything including a tight-knit relationship with me.

My mother was buried, but her funeral expenses were paid for from another source of income and not from the money that was left from the repossessed house after it was sold by the bank. The money from the house was given to Sister Judy by Mother dear, as, in the event of her death, it would be used for her burial. Sister Judy used the money to do other personal things. However, Father dear had no idea that the money was spent. He dragged Judy through the court system but failed to retrieve a penny. How unfortunate for him. Before dear Mother died, she had also joined in the fight against me to reclaim the property known as 4 Hawstead Road. At that time, all my family could see was money. During that period, I was running the family house that I verbally bought from my dad as a business. The rental income was paying the mortgage comfortably. Due to my lavish lifestyle, the family looked at the house like it was making me rich. They did not look at the fact that I was a hardworking engineer also. I was begrudged of my lifestyle, not knowing how I financed it. Mother dear was fighting a losing battle because any money that came into her possession would have been taken away by father with his avariciousness to support his mistress. At the time, Father dear was desperate for money because the building of the house for his mistress was taking too long. Nevertheless, it was now completed. On reflection, I could barely see the point of the trouble because she was now living with him in the mansion built with the money extracted from the house known as 4 Hawstead Road that I paid the remortgage for a long six years. Unbelievable!

The family wanted to build a tomb for Mother. They asked me to make a contribution, which I did with an aggrieved heart. Well, unto this day, I had not given my father much thought.

Two weeks later, my wife returned from Jamaica after attending the funeral. The twelfth disciple of Satan had emerged. She started to behave in a strange manner. I did not know if it was due to the close relationship between my daughter and I, but something was not right. At times, she would lock me out of the house for no apparent reason. When she decided to let me back into the house, she would follow me and spit wherever I walked.

I had not, in any way, provoked her, so I saw no motive for this irrational behaviour. I occasionally retaliated, and she would then call the police. This carried on for two years. The officers always asked me to leave the home, although they had no evidence and there was no bruising on her. It was alleged that I was a wife beater.

This, I could not understand. I was simply not that kind of person. I had a phone call on my mobile in August 2001 from an officer called DC Gad. I was at work at the time when he requested that I visited Ladywell Police Station.

He did not explain what this was about, but I felt I obligated to go. I left work at 1:00 P.M. and drove all the way from Sittingbourne, Kent, to Ladywell to see the officer. I was asked my name and address. Upon giving this information, I was arrested and thrown in a van. All I could hear was the sound of the sirens. The van was driving at high speed, overtaking everything in sight! It was very uncomfortable for me because I was handcuffed, with my hands at my back. I ended up at Bromley Magistrate's Court, but still, I had no idea why I was brought there. A judge emerged from the chamber. She asked, "Who is this man?" The officers stated my name and address. The judge replied, "He is not scheduled to be in court."

She said, "Remove him from my court immediately."

I had no understanding of the law nor the way it worked. The officers looked at each other in shock. I knew they had made a mistake. They did not set me free at the court. I overheard them asking each other, "What shall we do with him?"

I was brought back to Ladywell where I was thrown into a cell. I really had no idea what was going on. I was allowed a phone call. I rang my sister's husband, John, who informed me that Carol had made an allegation against me, and she was on her way to the station to make a statement so that I could be released. I was bemused, absolutely astounded, and with no knowledge of what was happening. The officers asked me if I wanted to make a deal. "What deal?" I asked. They asked me to accept a caution and walk free. I did not know what a caution was, but I accepted it in order to get out of there. *It was the beginning of my hell!*

The officers said, "We will set you free, but we cannot let you out by the front door." They asked me to leave by the side door that led to the exit of a factory. This, to me, seemed suspicious. On reflection, I should have got myself a solicitor because to date, the caution was still against my name. The officers claimed that I kicked my own front door, causing £10 worth of damage, conned by the police because I did not know the law. I did not question the facts, nor did I question my wife when I got home.

Two months later, I discovered that my wife had been building a dossier in order to have me removed from the marital home as she had other plans. I discovered this one day when she was out. I had a look at some papers she kept in the bottom of the wardrobe. She was simply following instructions given by a solicitor. I still did not question her about it as I could not see the relevance.

December 2001. Carol told me that she could get anything for free from Sudbury's. I asked her, "How is this possible?" She told me she had a friend who worked on the till. She then explained to me how it was done. You simply go in the store and pick up ten items that were inexpensive. Then you pick up items of any value. The inexpensive items would be scanned to make a beep sound. Then you move your expensive item across which would be free. No one would ever suspect this action because other surrounding cashiers would hear the beep sound of the scanner. I decided to give it a try. My first hit was a DVD player with £250 value. Only a can of beans for thirty pence was scanned. It worked like magic. Then there was a kettle for £50 and lots of items and clothing that she had put into the trolley. I estimated about £350 that night that included the ten cans of beans that was scanned. The trick was that, each time a can was scanned, an expensive item was moved across by the scammer. I could not believe how easy it was. I then used Carol's credit card to pay just for show because when I got my receipt, the part I signed using her signature was also given back to me. Believe it or not, not even the beans were paid for that night! I went home with a huge smile on my face, riddled with disbelief. It was so easy. All you have to do was to have a friend on the till who was *willing to take the risk!*

My second hit was all the items I needed for a huge Christmas party: two large bottles of Mòet et Chandon Champagne, four large bottles of Baileys Irish Cream, six bottles of white wine, three bottles of Vodka, bottles of Brandy and Christmas presents for everyone I know at the time, four children's coats, shoes, sweets, books, and clothing for myself. The trolley was so packed, I could hardly push it to the car, not forgetting the tins of beans, my inexpensive items for scanning! I estimated that night. Beyond no doubt, my takings were between £250 and £300, and the total cost to me was £10. This time, I actually paid cash! I was still in disbelief. I wished I knew this earlier because I had actually shopped in Sudbury's for a very long time, spending approximately £50 per week before I discovered the pot of gold at the end of the rainbow, and yet, it was someone else's idea, not mine. I would add that she was an absolute genius. I wondered what the staff thought when they saw the husband of a co-worker shopping at such a high level. At today's rate, in 2007, I would simply say, "Rubbing shoulders with the Beckhams." *If only they knew,* especially since times were so damn hard. I still continued going. I even went back with a friend who knew the cashier quite well, so she had to do the both of us. At this point, for the first time, I felt a bit scared, but I still managed to pull if off. That night, I got a Philip VCR, more clothes, and more drinks. In fact, I went to the head of the Electrical Department and asked for the latest Philip VCR. I told Carol what I had done, and I had never seen her in such a state of panic. I assumed she was also scared. However, I did the usual. Yes, I got away again, but I did not feel contented until I got home.

    The next day, I saw another guy who was doing the same scam. He pulled it off, too. We spoke about setting up a business called "Sudbury's Scammers," but it did not work because of greed and jealousy. It was not for me anyway. I disliked what I was turning into. I classed myself as a respectable and decent member of society. On reflection, two previous summers ago, my wife and I went to several parks in London, and I did believe that this was where this culture developed. I was not very happy with myself because I did believe that I caught a disease that only I could cure.

During visits to the park, Carol would always put her mark on a certain plant or flower that we must have. Peckham Park was her main target. Believe it or not, it was causing me great embarrassment to say this, but we used to go thieving flowers and plants from the park so that our garden was the best on the street where we lived. I wondered what people thought when they suddenly saw exotic plants sprouting up in our garden the following day! I must be crazy because I was the one doing the digging. The burning bush was my favourite. It grew like a head of afro hair. After a week, it turned red, hence the name, burning bush. It was very easy to pull from the soil unlike some of the others. On reflection, I was not proud that I had done this, and to think I had a three-year-old child with me at every strike in the park.

Looking back, it made me feel somewhat tearful to remember what I was doing in the presence of my child, although she was totally unaware of the situation. Perhaps, it was a curse that led to the Sudbury's strikes. I do hope that the Greater Power above would forgive me for such drastic actions committed out of sheer greed. Although it was not my idea, I was just as guilty. I could not say where this bad habit came from, but I was totally riddled with relief that I was no longer in that circle. I thought it was all a blessing, but in fact, it was a curse. I was heavily influenced by my former wife. Never let anyone lead you astray; have courage. Being influenced could be very dangerous to one's health and well-being. Let's go back to the Sudbury's saga! I knew I was doing wrong, but I did it anyway as a result of the duress my wife had me under. However, I did not enter Sudbury's again until a Wednesday, on April 6, 2005, three years after my divorce. When my "new girlfriend" had a craving for coconut bites, it almost seemed like *she was desperate* for them. She asked me to buy some for her, so I drove to Tesco in Elmer's End. I was unsuccessful in my quest. On the way back, I stopped at every grocery shop en-route, and still, I was unable to find coconut bites. It was also something that I like eating, too. I then remembered when I was a *straight* (honest) Sudbury's shopper, I used to buy this regularly there. Where did I end up? Yes, you guessed right! In Sudbury's. There was one packet left on the shelf that I picked up and paid for. I was so frightened that I had flashback. That tense feeling arose inside me. It was almost as if I was a murderer knowing one day, I would be caught. As I stood in the queue, the feeling of guilt was enough to kill me. *I felt like I had died a thousand deaths and still could die some more! The experience was unbelievable, and yet, I had no problem in any other branch of Sudbury's or other supermarkets. "Thou shall not steal"* because one day, you might feel like this, and trust me, it was not a pleasant feeling—when you reach the cashier to pay for something legal and you start sweating like a pig. How could I free myself from this? I asked, "How can I free myself from this?" By telling you my readers, now I know I am free.

December 2001 was the year when I became a person outside of my character. Yes, I was a proper thief influenced by a *Jamaican woman* whom I was unfortunately married to. I had the biggest Christmas party on the block. There were food and drinks galore. The guests had food and drinks to take home after the party. In fact, what they took away could be used for another party, and still, there was enough left in the house to have another two parties if we wanted to. I still could not believe what we had. This was way above my means and everyone on the block together; it was crazy.

The family members were overwhelmed with their gifts, and the children were overjoyed. I wondered what they really thought at that time. Okay! I had a well-paid job, but reflecting back, could I have the liberty to call that the *good old days* because for the past two Christmas no one got sweet *f.a.?* Think about it. Such was life. There was not any *f—ing* money around, and yet, someone else was doing my *f—ing* job! At the moment, I did not know anyone on the till. I did not think I would do that again.

My wife made a huge mistake by calling the police once too many. If I sneezed too loudly, the police would be on our doorstep in minutes, but this time, my cup runneth over. On a Sunday morning, we left home and went shopping. We also went to Yes Car Credit in Sidcup.

In January 2002, my wife and I went to visit her sister who was visiting her daughter in London. Carol overstayed her visit. I was very hungry and irritable, but she was very comfortable, feeding her face and making jokes whilst I sat downstairs on my own. Six in the evening was fast approaching, and I had not yet cooked my dinner. All I wanted to do was to go home. I had plans to have a barbecue that day.

I went to the toilet. While on my way back to the seating area after using the toilet, I saw Leigh, Carol's sister, coming towards me down the stairs.

She asked me, "What's up with the long face?"

I replied, "I have been trying for months to get Carol to visit you at your home (in Chatham). As you know, it is not far from my work place (At the time, I was working in Sittingbourne, Kent.). Carol always refused." I found it strange that she never wanted to go out of her way to visit, but that particular Sunday, I bent over backwards just to accommodate her so she could see her sister. I did not wish to be blamed for her not seeing her family. It was said that I was possessive, but that was an obvious lie.

We left her niece's house at approximately 6:45 P.M., and boy wasn't I starving! *A horse and its rider on the menu would be fine, thank you!* On the way to the car, I was carrying our daughter.

Carol said to me, "You *fucking cunt,* why did you say that to my sister? Now, she's not going to leave me anything in her will."

We got to the car still arguing. She was still calling me all the names under the sun. I drove off in an erratic manner. I turned the corner on a deep slope on the hilly road. I threw the vehicle round the bend, and I felt it tip slightly. The speed bumps on the road were as if they were not there. Nevertheless, we got home safely. As I parked the car, Carol said, "Get ready, Rochelle. We have to get in the house quickly."

At this point, I knew that I would be locked out again as she had always done throughout the marriage! I pulled into the parking bay and got out of the car before the engine stopped turning, although the keys were in my hand. I went into the house, leaving the front door open, went upstairs, and lay on the bed. I was so stressed, I wish I were dead. I was truly "at the end of my tether." *I must remind you, my dear friends, that I brought this all upon myself. I took another man's wife! The flashback was coming again. Do you remember the silver-haired old man who shook my hand and said "Good luck, my son?"* I could see *him staring at me now. Bizarre, isn't it? I remember him having a bell which he would ring when he was in need of attention from Carol. One night, during sex in Carol's bedroom, I heard that bell ringing constantly. I knew Mr. Woodburn needed his wife to do something important, or perhaps he could hear the noise of the bed? But the sex was so intense, the bell just continues ringing. Looking back, I was so pleased with the end result. I didn't have to ring a bell for attention. Come to think of it, would it be answered if I had a bell to ring? The tears of the old man appeared like raindrops in my mind from time to time. Now, it was my turn to feel the pain. The sins that brought me to my knees.*

I got up and went downstairs; it was time for action. Little did I know that this woman came to England and studied the system to her benefit! *The law was an ass.* I looked at her with my arms folded.

She said, "Aren't you going to cook, you arsehole?"

I said, "I would appreciate it if you speak to me with some respect."

She said, "Aren't you going to get the shappin from the car?"

At this point, she was giggling hysterically in a provoking manner. *I did believe that at this point, the Pope would have said, "Fuck you."* I held her by the lapels of her jacket and pulled her towards me as close as possible. I could feel her *exhaling* breath on my face, the tip of our noses almost touching. Then I said what the Pope *would not have said, "Fuck you."* I let go and went upstairs to cool down. I stood by the window with my arms folded, looking out. I called my friend, Sabrina, a woman whom I have always been sexually active with throughout the marriage. *As you know, my dear friends, the marriage was a sham.* Whilst speaking to Sabrina on my mobile (cell) phone, I heard screaming coming from downstairs. Murder! Police! Police! There was crashing of glasses.

I said to Sabrina, "Just listen to this." I held the phone by the entrance of the stairwell so she could hear. I then continued with our conversation, walking back to the window facing the street. I stood there for at least fifteen minutes, then I said to Sabrina, "A Police car has pulled up into the close." This part is very difficult for me to write, but I must bite my tongue and carry on as the teardrops from my eyes trickled down on the paper. As I estimated, they stopped at 4 Thomas Dean Road as usual. The doorbell rang. She answered it, and this was what I heard: "Officer, he beat me up again. He kicked me in the belly and punched me in the face."

"Is there any bruising?" they asked.

I must tell you, my *dear friends*, my wife at the time was three-quarter caste. She had very little black blood; she was 75 percent white. On the subject of bruising, she once told me that she was raped by a ghost. I did see bruising at the time; however, they were love bites and scratches on her back that she could not have possibly done herself. It was rather obvious, looking from the outside, that one of her male companions was involved in this *gothic* attack. On reflection, whilst I was having sex with Mrs. Woodburn in Jamaica, it certainly did not cross my naïve mind that she would do the same to me after I marry her. Whether or not the ghost story was true, we would never know. This happened whilst I was at work, but between you and I, it was neither the milkman nor the window cleaner! Nevertheless, I was sure as hell that it wasn't me who caused the gothic bruising!

One of the officer said, "Calm down. Who called us?"

She replied, "It was me."

I started walking down the stairs towards the two officers who were standing in the hallway. My God, they were huge, over six feet tall and built like tanks, but more gentle than you could find it was almost beyond belief. We went into the lounge, and they stood there, speechless for a few seconds. One of them asked me what kind of work I did for a living. I told him I was an engineer.

He replied, "My God, we are in the wrong game." He said to his colleague, "This pad is a bit posh, isn't it?"

One of them took Carol to the kitchen, and the other went upstairs with me.

He said, "I want to hear your side of the story," and I told him.

He said, "Down at the station, we have a file on you which is getting bigger by the minute. Have you got anywhere you could stay tonight?"

"Oh yes," I replied as always!

They consulted each other for a short while and then accompanied me to my car, which was in the parking bay.

One of them said to me, "Can't you see what she is doing? She is taking you for a mug (fool). "Listen, mate, just leave her; find someone else." That was the advice I was given, then they both said, "Good luck," and went to their patrol car.

As I drove down the road behind their car, they stopped to let me pass. They followed me towards Penge, to the *love nest* where I rested that night.

Throughout the marriage, I dare say, the best sex I ever had were on the nights when the police asked me if I had somewhere to stay! It was good for me, but if only I knew her motives! One day, I might have to give up the affair I was having with Angelina Jolie because during sex with the woman that I stole from her husband and marry, the only way one could maintain an orgasm was to think of sweet Angelina; it worked every time. In those days, the picture on the Tomb Raider DVD was the best. It really could make you gush. Unfortunately, when it was all over and the eyes were open once more, the eyes registered on Carol: how disappointing. I once overheard a telephone conversation between Carol and her friend. She was informing her that the easiest way to obtain citizenship in England was to find a man who was a British passport holder. "Marry him, and all your troubles will be over. You will be home and dry," she said. I had no suspicions that this was her plot to gain British Citizenship (by marrying me), and indeed, it worked for her. I had been told many stories of fellow countrymen and women who were used to get a foothold in this paradise we live in, not only Caribbean people I may add. However, I do believe that this is a worldwide problem. Is it true, is England really heaven on earth? Perhaps to some! Depending on your birthplace. But the question is, where is hell? The word was out that Jamaican women are the true pirates of the Caribbean. I really could not answer that. Perhaps you could. I was told a story recently of a Jamaican woman feeding her man crushed glass in his food for months; it had almost killed him. Other stories that I was told made me feel very lucky to have escaped. On reflection, during the turbulence of the marriage in 2002, Carol had returned from Jamaica. For someone who disliked cooking, she actually cooked me my favourite meal—curry goat and rice that was served to me only whilst she and the children ate a totally different meal. I offered Rochelle a spoonful of my food, and Carol shouted almost as if she was afraid, "Don't' eat that, Rochelle. Eat your own food.". I did not consume a bite because I was one step ahead. *What was in the food?* I asked myself. That, I would never know. Perhaps, I would have been dead by now! Who knows?

I don't understand what possessed me to marry Carol. From the day I met her in Jamaica, she was cooking for me. The question is: Was the food spiked? What was in it? I would never know! Jamaica is filled with beautiful women. Why did I take Carol away from her husband? Why did I marry her? Why? Why? I hate myself for it. She obtained her British Citizenship for free. What hurt me most of all was that a very close friend of Carol had enlightened me that she often bragged that the day she got married was the best day of her life, not because she was *in love,* but because "the door to achieving 'British Citizenship' has thrown itself open to me," she said. "Now, I am home and dry," she continued to brag. "Britain is in the palm of my hands."

How bizarre, I thought, knowing that at the time I married her, a young lady from Jamaica offered me £5000 to marry her in order to obtain British Citizenship. On reflection, I should have grabbed that £5000. It cost me £500 to marry Carol including the hiring of the wedding dress and food cost of £400 for the guests was money thrown away, but perhaps not, because my guests did enjoy the *Chinese meal!*

My dear friends, I could have gained £5000 by marrying the young lady who made me that substantial offer. What a fool I was. When I was released from prison, I received the divorce papers that I gladly welcomed. "Thank you so much, Carol, you are the best!" I was thankful that the thorn in my side had removed itself, or was it by the hands of the Almighty? The bill from her solicitor, believe it or not, *my dear friends,* was running in the region of £10,000. For what, might I ask? How could a wedding that cost £500 result in a £10,000 bill to dissolve it? How could this be?

Throughout the turbulent, loveless, and deceitful marriage, she gained what she wanted—her *British passport*! In all honesty, what did she really get? Through my eyes—nothing! The question I always asked myself was, "Why does people from poor countries flock England?" Is it because England is known as heaven, or is it a sanctuary? If England is heaven, Tony Blair must be God! *Ooops!* Sorry, I meant Gordon Brown! Think about it.

But now, it was transparent, although it was 200 years or more too late! I might add, on top of all this, my undying love for my daughter, Rochelle, grew and grew.

The next day after the night of the police visit, I went home from work, and put my keys into the door, thinking it was locked or changed (although I was paying the rent). The door opened, and I went in. I said, "Hello." She reacted as if nothing had happened the day before, and I had no feelings of guilt of my sexual infidelity whatsoever.

Two weeks went by. She approached me almost every night after work and awoken me from my deep slumber, asking me, "Are you tired tonight?" *Don't forget, my dear friends, that we had never woken up in the same bed!* We lived in two separate rooms in the house, and she would remove our daughter who always slept cuddled up tightly in my arms from the bed. After sex was over, she would bring the child back to my bed. She would do it occasionally, on her nights off (her working hours was 7:00 P.M. to 1:00 A.M. in the morning). I always got home by 6:30 P.M. to let her go. Then I left London at 6:30 A.M. each morning to drive to work in Sittingbourne. Come to think of it, I must have had some remarkable stamina! To think that I was up at 5:00 A.M., out the door by 6:30, then driving back home, arriving by 6:30 P.M., looking after the baby, get some sleep, get up again when she came in at 1:00 A.M. to service her, go back to bed, wake up again, and *not forgetting my other women who need servicing, too!* Then she had the audacity to make allegations of sexual harassment and rape. Ludicrous—that was what I would say.

Those two weeks in January 2002 were the best two weeks that I wished I were married for *love*. Then I arrived home late on the last week. I started having the feeling of not wanting to go home after work. I brought myself a Dictaphone, which I used to record all events in our home. She found out I was doing this. I did this to use as evidence against her, but she always said to me, "Don't hurt me. Please don't hurt me. I didn't do anything wrong.'" Then she would scream at the top of her voice, almost as if she was using my Dictaphone at her disposal to frame me. She always ruined my recordings with her ridiculous outbursts, and then she would laugh at me.

However, at this point, it was all over. On this particular Sunday, I got fed up with her calling the police. She came home from work. The dinner was not ready, so she was acting horribly towards me. I always made sure that dinner was ready on a Sunday before she came home from work, almost as if I was afraid of her. She asked me, "Why the dinner was not ready?" I told her I was not in the mood to cook, and she told me to fuck myself.

I asked her, "What do you mean by that?"

She replied, "Suck your mother." *(This is an insult.)*

I was very upset. I went outside and sat in the car for approximately twenty minutes. I decided to go back inside the house, but when I got to the door, it refused to open. I had the child with me. She then started to shout through the letterbox in a scandalous manner, "You fucking batty man (gay man)!" She repeated this several times, screaming as usual. I loathed this type of behaviour, as I am quiet by nature. All I wanted was a quiet life and a loving family. I wanted to gain entry to the house so I could put the baby to bed. Each time I tried, all I got was verbal abuse through the letterbox. I was so fed up, I kicked the door a few times. She opened the door because the baby was crying.

She said, "Give me my baby, you fucking batty bwoy."

I went inside the house, but at this point the neighbours gathered together for the free (but indeed embarrassing for me) entertainment, with the great performance of my wife. Within no time of putting the baby to bed, Carol looked at me with a grin and said, "I am going to destroy you, you cunt, and I am going to use the law to do it." *She then started to giggle in a gothic manner with that very eerie sound, like witches cackling, leaving a chill down your spine.* Then she went downstairs. After about ten minutes, I also went downstairs where I saw her drinking undiluted Jamaican white rum.

She then repeated, "I will destroy you using the law." It was quite apparent now that this was not an empty threat. I did not know her motives for this. Apparently, this was not the first time that Carol had fabricated a plan to destroy me. At the age of two, Carol made an allegation that Rochelle was sexually abused. However, she was inspected in my presence, and the result was negative. It just dawned on me in 2008 that I was the suspected abuser. Carol's attempt to destroy me had failed, leaving her room for a second attempt, which, as you would see, also failed. I went upstairs and sat on the bed, looking at Rochelle sleeping peacefully. In fact, I thought to myself, *How wonderful it would be if this family was happy. If I was happy* To my utmost shock, the doorbell rang, and it was—who was it? You tell me! Yes! You are right; it was the police. I rushed downstairs and said to Carol, "The police is at the door."

She said, "Yes, I know that."

I then opened the door and there was the usual statement, "We were called to this address." They both came into the house and stood in the hallway.

I said to Carol, "I am going to tell them everything about SavaCentre, I swear on my life." I took both officers into the lounge. I opened the drinks cabinet and said, "All those drinks in there are stolen: the DVD, video, saucepans, kettle, cutleries, and plates. Carol stole them from SavaCentre, so the person you should arrest is her." The police had no interest whatsoever in the articles that were stolen. *What a Sunday that was!*

At the time, there was not an actual marriage out of love; it was to secure a British passport *(a marriage of convenience)*. We both knew this, but I, like a fool, was breathing heart shapes from the water bubbles. What an asshole I was indeed! The mistake she made was she had been planning for years to get residency of the rented house. She tried every trick in the book to get it so her sibling in Jamaica would *have a home to come to once she had successfully executed her plan.* May I pause and say, "God bless Michael Howard in 2005 for his stance on immigration, especially on Jamaicans." Now, I would continue. She was building a dossier on me, something that may stand up in court as evidence, allegations upon allegations. Now, I was not bragging, so please do not get me wrong. I have always been a playboy; one of the allegations against me was rape. However, I did not know this until 2003 when I was imprisoned for allegations made by my then wife against me. How could someone like me be accused of such an act when pussy was easy to get? Women had a habit of falling over me. As I say, I was not bragging. The day I got married, I rang a female friend who was dear to me in many ways and told her that I got married. She started crying on the phone as if someone close to her had died. I went over to comfort her, and the only comfort she would accept was, well, I am certain you could imagine what I had to do, the day following my marriage to Carol, or should I say Mrs. Woodburn? A man had to do what a man had to do! They see me, but they do not know me.

So you see, it was extremely difficult for me to accept any form of sexual allegations. It was not in my character, and it was simply not my style. I did not need to travel down that defamatory road.

On reflection, I remember the day in January 2002, as I might have said before, after the wild Christmas party at the end of 2001. Obviously, you could see by now that the marriage between my wife and I was really an act of convenience for her. She promised me, and I believed that it was a sincere promise, although I took the words of the promise very lightly. This was after the visit to her sister who was visiting London in 2002, as I had previously mentioned. She used her Jamaican bad habits on the way back from her sister's home, and as I might have mentioned previously, I was driving erratically. When I reached home, it was just a matter of who got into the house first. At the time, I knew if she got into the house before me she would lock me out, bolt the door, and then do what she did best—shout a barrage of abuses through the letterbox. It was the typical Jamaican expletives: batty man, batty sucker, bombo-claat, etc.—all the Jamaican abuse you could think of. I must stress that at this point, it was extremely refreshing. Not hearing those Jamaican slanders in July 2005 was almost like drinking clean pure water! At last, I have to show you my dear friends, that the air was clean. So there was a God after all. Did you get my drift? *I knew you would! Let's continue* to the day in question. You might be wondering if I did get in the house first. Indeed, I did! Believe it or not, twenty minutes passed, and all three of us were in the house: me, my wife, and my lovely daughter who was aged four. I loved her then and I still love her to bits now.

My wife uttered in a Jamaican tone of voice, "Yu nah go get de shappin out a de car?"

I looked at her, and then she started with an annoying giggle. She repeated this giggle several times. That annoyed me, I dared say, but still, I just kept calm. She wanted me to go outside so she could do her performance. However, it so happened that I suddenly realized that I did not have my mobile phone with me. I then went to the car. I retrieved the bags of shopping and my phone, of course! I returned to the front door, expecting what I always had from her. Obviously, indeed! The front door was locked and abuse, in abundance, came howling through the letterbox in the usual Jamaican style. To refresh you with a few: cock sucker, pussy licker, batty man, etc., the usual expletives. To add to it all, my dirty clothes from the wash basket—including underwear—came flying out of the upstairs window, followed by important documents like bank statements, etc. Was this normal behaviour? I wondered. I had not experienced this before I asked myself.

Then I remembered the woman who had retrieved her from the hospital bed after her mother pushed her out and left her at the age of zero. My ex-wife's sister had led me to believe that the woman who was known as Curdell used to do the same thing that my wife was doing to me to her husband. So at this point, I dare say, my friends, it was simply an act of childhood reflection, and for that reason and that reason only, my daughter, who was now 7 years old, was what some people would call spoilt! However, I do hope that her adulthood would be filled with love and happiness because that was all her childhood would reflect.

Going back to the heart of the story, when my belongings went hurling from the upstairs window like debris falling from space into the atmosphere, I could no longer sustain my calm. I kicked the front door a few times, in fact, that I hurt my toe. But

I do thank God that the door did not give because at that point, anything could have happened. I picked up my belongings in front of the neighbours who were gathering into a crowd for the X-rated entertainment as they always did. This was a typical display of her power in which her dominance was shown, portraying herself as a victim of domestic violence. It was a fact that in some parts of the world, including the United Kingdom, and might I add that this type of behaviour seem prevalent in deprived neighbourhood because their morals are lower. I retrieved my belongings, loaded them into the car, and drove off, looking at my four-year-old staring at her daddy's car as I disappeared around the bend.

Could it be that my wife treated me this way because she knew it was a marriage of convenience? Or was it because she detected I had been unfaithful? Throughout the turbulent marriage, revenge, as always, played a part. Whatever she did to me, I always get even and *vice versa*. On reflection, the question I would ask myself in July 2005 was what was the meaning of this now that I am extremely happy? I might look back and ask myself, why? It was like being free from cancer cells!

As I drove around that Sunday night, early in January 2002, I was totally distorted with the events in my life. I went to see a girlfriend whose advice to me was to go home and talk. So I returned home at approximately 11:00 P.M. of the same night. I got home, inserted the key into the lock, and to my utmost surprise, the door opened. I went upstairs, feeling sick with emotions, not knowing what to do or say. I went back downstairs; I was gasping for a cup of tea. My wife came into the kitchen and made a Gothic giggle. At this point, I flipped. I turned around trembling in anger. I pulled her by the lapels of her dressing gown and whispered in an angry tone, *"Don't fuck with me."* Her nose was literally touching mine. I then let her go, went upstairs, and phoned Sabrina, the same lady friend who encouraged me to talk.

I remember having a conversation with Sabrina about the situation that kept recurring when I heard screaming and smashing of glasses coming from downstairs.

I said to Sabrina, "Just listen to this," almost like déja vu. I then said to her, "Do you see what I have to put up with?"

At this point, Carol was on the landline phone, calling the police. The screaming, shouting, and smashing of glasses were to alert the neighbours, to make them think that I was attacking her when in fact, I was nowhere near her. The police came, and as usual, after trying to ascertain what the problems were, asked me if I had somewhere to stay. As usual, I said "Yes."

I then said to the police, "If anyone is to be arrested, it should be her." I told them about the scam at Sudbury's as I had mentioned previously. At this point, my wife ran upstairs, packed a bag, and disappeared through the front door. They asked, "What has happened? Where did she go?"

I said, "I have no idea." The police then left, as I might have mentioned previously. The next, day she came back and got dressed for work as if nothing had happened.

I then told her that I rang Sudbury's and informed the Head of Security what we had done. Also, as I had said previously, I could not stand the emotional state she was in. I then went to Sudbury's to see the Head of Security personally. That was my reason for going there. I had made up a story that someone was trying to get her into trouble. I informed the security of a phone call with a threatening nature that came through to the house to get my wife sacked. My dear friends, at this point, you might call me whatever you wish, but I felt sorry for the bitch. On reflection, I should have made her fry. Her job with them was again secured. Believe it or not, the Head of Security told me to go home, ask her to come and see him, and he would sort out the matter. They had actually believed my sob story about her innocence. However, the evidence was in our house. Most of the stash that was taken was still in the house.

Amazingly, when I got home from work the next day, the stash had disappeared! I asked her, "What's happened to all the goods?"

She then said, "Don't worry, they are safe."

"What do you mean safe?" I asked. At that point, I was gasping for a glass of *free* champagne.'

She said, "I got rid of the stuff because something similar happened to a colleague of mine. Her property was searched, and goods were found that came from the workplace that could not be accounted for. Some items still had the security alarm still attached. That caused her to lose her job, so I have to be one step ahead of them.'

One month went by, and we both agreed amongst ourselves that the dust was settled and our relationship was back on track. In fact, she had led me to believe this. One week after intense sex and playing catch-up, I received a letter, believe it or not, that was hand delivered by a process server. To my utmost surprise, it was a summons for me to attend court in March 2002 for eviction from the marital home. "How crafty," I may say, "old chap." Carol struck again, punching below the belt once more!

Apparently, this had been the reason for her calling the police even if I sneezed too loud. She had been building up a domestic crime file of ill-treatment, and indeed, she had succeeded. I was ordered by the Family Court to leave the marital home on Good Friday. On that day in March, I believed it was a Wednesday, I saw Carol at the bus stop on her way from court whilst I was driving. I offered her a lift, but she declined, saying it was not necessary because her solicitor may be coming her way *(I think she was really trying to tell me something else.)* I was given two weeks to vacate the property. That evening, I was cooking a meal. She came home much later than I did. She came into the kitchen, and she then hugged me in exactly the same way Judas did to Jesus when he pointed him out to the killers who crucified him, and just like Jesus, I rose again! To my utmost horror, she uttered these words, "I have got what I wanted at last, and I am still not happy." She had the audacity to try to seduce me. I could not believe my fucking ears! At this point in 2005, I was still blown away by that moment. I was also still riddled in disbelief. Is there a name for someone like this? Is there? I really don't know.

Good Friday came quicker than I estimated. It was almost as if two weeks had passed within two days. So, did I get myself a placard? "Homeless and hungry." Well, that was how I felt at that time. However, my pride would not let me sink to such a low level. The day before Good Friday, we were both discussing what to do and how to spend the holiday. I had almost forgotten that it was the day for me to vacate the home. I suggested we go to Hastings or Margate. She then turned to me and said, "This won't be possible, although I would love to. My solicitor stated that you have to vacate by mid-day. So if we went out, we would not have gotten back in time."

So there you have it. My deadline had arrived. I packed my bags and said good-bye to all my furniture, to all the comforts I had built up over the years. She agreed verbally that I could see our daughter whenever I wanted to. This carried on for several months until one day, I rang the marital home and was told that Rochelle was having a bath. I really wanted to speak to her because that little voice *healed many wounds—excuse my tears. I could hear a voice. It sounded like a male* voice amongst the splashing of the water. Apparently, it seemed that another man was bathing my pride and joy. Everything in my view became RED. It was very difficult for me to absorb this. I almost had a brain haemorrhage, and you know what! Even the reflection made me mad as I was writing this story.

Another month passed. Injunctions after injunctions were upon me not to go within 100 yards of the marital home. So when I want to see Rochelle, I had to go to Sudbury's car park where her mother delivered her every Saturday. On Sundays, I go to Sudbury's car park to meet her mother in order to return her. It began to feel as *if she was borrowed property that I was returning.* One Saturday, I went to collect her from the usual place. Sabrina was with me. She was a friend that went way back. We used to be lovers, too, before I met Rochelle's mother. She knew Rochelle since birth, but she had not seen her for a while.

When she saw Rochelle, she said, "Hello, Rochelle, do you remember me?"

She replied, "No."

Sabrina said, "Who's that man driving the car?"

Rochelle replied, "Raymond."

Sabrina said, "Is that who you know him as?"

Rochelle replied, "Yes."

Sabrina said, "Is he not daddy?"

She replied, "No, my daddy is Michael."

At this point, I stopped the car because my vision had changed to *RED* again. I went totally mental.

I uttered to Rochelle in a soft mental tone, "Who is Michael?"

She said, "My daddy."

I said, "Rochelle, you listen to me, and listen carefully. You have only one daddy, and that is me. Do not let anyone tell you anything different."

She replied, "Yes, daddy."

At this point, Sabrina started chuckling.

I said, "Sabrina, don't laugh. It is not funny." I then said to Rochelle, "Who told you that Michael is your daddy?"

She replied, "Mommy."

Thinking of my present situation, I was with a woman who had a six-year-old child. On several occasions, she called me daddy. Was this what Rochelle went through at that time? I would like to believe that more than anything else. I just thought I would explain to give a better understanding of the situation.

Back to where we left off! I literally told Sabrina to shut up because I was fuming, not that I meant any harm, but I was in a state of shock, being extremely embarrassed by Rochelle's denial of my fatherhood status.

Sabrina said, "What kind of madness is this? He is your daddy, Rochelle. Can't you see? You look just like him.'

On reflection, when Rochelle was conceived, Carol had a male friend who was always at the house. He was an employee of BT at the time. This young man would connect Carol's telephone calls to anywhere in the world using a special pin number. I understood that these calls were free! Carol had mentioned that this young man was the actual father of Rochelle. She also claimed that Michael was Rochelle's father, but for some strange reason, D.N.A. result claimed that I was her dad, which I happened to believe due to the fact that she had an enormous amount of my characteristics, including the chromosome defect! The neighbour had confirmed that each morning, as I leave for work, another man would enter the house and stay almost half the day. Apparently, it was the same man who was issuing the free phone calls. This was revealed to me after the divorce. During the marriage, I was too naïve. I actually thought that Carol was getting the telephone calls for free, but I should have known that she was simply paying the price in the same manner that she used to get herself into England. *She blows a mean trumpet! I did believe her best attribute was blowing, not the trumpet I may add! Think about it.*

I rang Sudbury's Super Store where Rochelle's mother worked. I was put on hold for approximately ten minutes. Then I heard her voice saying "Hello."

I said, "Listen, you *fucking slut*. Don't fuck with the head of my child. Don't confuse her more than she is already confused." She hanged up the phone on me. My blood was at boiling point. I was on my way to Sabrina's house, which was in Crystal Palace. I then turned the car around rapidly. Believe it or not, I ended up in Sudbury's Super Store all the way back in Sydenham. I felt a huge amount of pressure building up in my head, almost as if my skull was going to explode. I went on the shop floor, looking for her. She was nowhere in sight. I questioned a few of her co-workers who usually worked with her. They said she was not feeling well and went home.

I replied, "Gone home sick? I just spoke to her on the phone less than five minutes ago."

Her colleague, Maggie, replied, "She left in a hurry, saying she was ill." I breathed in heavily, and then I walked off, holding Rochelle's hand. I left the store and went back to the car.

Sabrina said, "Are you okay?"

I had no memory of giving her an answer. *My dear friends, try to analyse the situation.* Two days later, I learnt that if I had gone to the marital home, I would have been arrested and sent to prison for breech of injunction, and that would be playing in Carol and her cronies' hands. Carol had anticipated my movement, but how wrong she was. The trap that was set by Carol and the police had failed. The police were simply waiting for nothing, though the marital home was literally two minutes away by car from the store. Apparently, the threat that was given in January 2002 was destined to take effect, but as per usual, they could never outsmart me. Just think, looking at all the avenues, this was a set-up. She tried to have me arrested. *Could you not see that it was simply a set up that did not work?!* But why use the child this way? I went to the Sudbury's Super Store to question the facts of why my child was led to believe that I was not her father. Little did I know I was walking into a trap. I was the rat, she was the cheese, and the CPS (Crown Prosecuting Service) and the police were the trap. I did believe this was professionally planned, looking back.

But at the time, I had no idea. Sabrina encouraged me to forget my past, even to forget my child and start a new life. However, due to my strong love for my daughter, my only child, it was impossible for me to abandon her or to forget about her existence. How could I forsake her? When I was told by Carol that I was not Rochelle's father, it had not crossed my mind until now, as I was reflecting on the incident that there was a man who worked for BT who often visited the home. He always gave her free telephone calls to anywhere in the world she wished. Free telephone calls, however, came with a price attached because there was no such thing as freeness. I knew this man also had sex with her during the marriage, not that it bothered me. But until the facts of the D.N.A. result had been revealed, I did suspect that he could have been Rochelle's father. Although D.N.A. proved that I am her dad, I still had my doubts.

During the breakdown of the turbulent marriage with Carol, it was suggested by one of my dearest auntie (Velma's mom) that I should disappear.

She made me an offer for me to go over to Canada to live with her and her husband. After deep thoughts, I could not make a decision. The thought of leaving Rochelle was my greatest deterrent. I just could not bring myself to leave her, my little pet. This thought had haunted me for months because it was an offer that could only be refused by a fool. Would this be the end of my problems, or would it be the beginning? That was the question I asked myself for several times.

On reflection, when I met Mrs. Woodburn, she also had a four-year-old child. The question was "How could she leave that child and come to England to me?" Here I was in 2005, telling you exactly what had happened due to my love for my daughter. I was still in England but suffering at the hands of the mother no more; she was out of my life forever and ever. I was still here, giving my love to Rochelle because I do believe that every living creature, whether it was a man or an animal, needed some form of stability from both parents. How dared Carol confuse the child?

The day Rochelle was born, my sister, Jane, and I had helped to deliver her from the miserable cocoon she had to endure for nine months before seeing her daddy's face. During the birth, the baby kept moving. A clamp was placed on her head to keep it in place, which resulted in a cut. Immediately after she took her first breath of air, the nurse handed her to me. She cried a little. I comforted her, then she stopped. She was a whopping 10lb 8oz at birth weight. I looked at her little face. I felt proud of my little girl as I stared down at her. She wriggled her fingers and toes in different directions, and I gave her, her first cuddle. She was given antibiotics and kept in hospital for two weeks; this was the longest two weeks of my life! I had loved her ever since, so to be told that she was not my child was a sudden blow to my whole system. I do believe that Carol was extremely confused because she had told me that it felt so right, that she wished Rochelle was her first and only child, and forgetting the fact that she had an older child by the name of Erica in Jamaica.

It appeared that at the age of four, Rochelle had shown symptoms of minor learning difficulty. A test was carried out that included a blood test from both parents to determine which side the defect was from. To my utmost shock, when the result was presented at Guy's Hospital, an appointment was made for both parents to attend. Rochelle's big sister, who at the time lives in Jamaica, was also present at the reading of the result; she was here on vacation. The doctor asked if any of us had any family member with learning difficulty. Carol did not hesitate to shout, "It is the father, doctor, it is the father."

I did have two family members with difficulties: one was wheelchair bound. I did not know the medical nature of his disability. I also had a cousin with a speech problem and intense learning difficulty. Carol did not hesitate to put this forward to the doctor as if it was some kind of a blame issue. I did believe, from a personal point of view, that a woman of this nature should not be let loose with any information pertaining to the family.

Carol and I lived together as a man and wife for seven years. Due to the build up of her British citizenship, she always stressed that she did not need British papers. However, beneath all that talk and (This is exactly what she wanted.) under lock and key in the bedroom that she resided in, were papers—application forms seeking British residency. Carol happened to know everything about me and my family, including the *alleged* rape charge against my dad, the embezzlement charge that my dad committed against a brewery in 1992, and another *alleged* rape charge that had taken place in Jamaica in the early 70s. She had mentioned several times that the victim was a close friend of hers.

She always mentioned this to me in a mocking manner. During arguments, she would shout, "Your daddy is a rapist," in order to provoke me to react to her comments. She used everything in her power to get a reaction from me, but the most hurtful ones were when she shouts batty man, batty sucker, or batty licker through the letterbox when I was outside and she locked the door so I could not get in. *Sorry, my dear friends, I got a bit carried away, but the truth causes great pain. I just wanted to show you what I had to endure.*

The doctor at Guy's Hospital said, "Mr. Francis, we do have the result, and this is how it reads, 'Carol Francis, normal. Raymond and Rochelle appear to have abnormality of the same type.

Carol and her daughter looked at each other, and they both looked at me with a grin on their faces. Before anything else was said about the abnormality, the doctor asked if any immediate relative from Rochelle's generation had learning difficulty. I did believe that the doctor was asking me that particular question. However, Carol, being the character that she was, did not hesitate to answer yet again!

"Yes, doctor," she uttered in a giggling manner. "His brother's son, Mark. He is eleven years old and cannot read. His other brother also has a daughter who has *dyslexia." (difficulty in reading or learning to read, accompanied by difficulty in writing and spelling correctly).* I did believe, from a personal point of view, that a woman of this character was a danger to anyone she had information on. She would put herself out to seek information about any individual, especially myself and my family, but nothing about her and her family should be disclosed; hers must always remain a secret. Little did she know that a close member of her family had been feeding me with information since her birth about her, from the day her mentally ill mother pushed her out from her cocoon and left her in the hospital bed *loveless*. It all stemmed from there, believe it or not!

The doctor said, "Mr. Francis, you have a chromosome disorder, and your daughter has exactly the same, almost like a mirror image. Rochelle has nothing in her genetic make-up from the mother." My mind was at total rest because no one on earth could tell me that I was not Rochelle's father. So that settled that, my chromosome disorder had no impact whatsoever on my life. New technology dictated that a disorder such as this could cause learning difficulty and confusion. Well, all I could say was from my experiences, I am afraid I would have to say it was not applicable. I had no learning difficulty, nor did I suffer from any brain disorder that slowed me down in any way.

I went through school achieving O level in maths, English, biology, and social studies. I also achieved through college engineering qualifications, parts 1, 11, and 111 of the City and Guilds Certificates. These qualifications might not look impressionable today, but when I got them, they were great achievements. I had always worked as an engineer. My last job after I was released from prison was a precision engineer for VW (VOLKSWAGEN). *From August 2005* to date, I am working as an engineer for Paramount Products. I am capable of reading engineer drawings of any type and produce components to British Standard Specifications. I also work unsupervised, executing my own inspection. So where does my chromosome disorder fit in? I was in the music industry for a while; I had my own recording label. I played the keyboard, but due to marital commitments, it phased out, partly because of the long distance travelling to work and a lack of time also. The doctor explained to me that number four and fourteen chromosomes were switched. Therefore, if you were reading a book and you reach page three, the next page appeared to be page fourteen, instead of 4. Then, further on in the book, you were reading page thirteen and the next appeared to be page four instead of fourteen. I then explained to the doctor the non-effect this disorder had on me. He then explained that it could be a generation skip. "Luckily, for you, Mr Francis, these chromosomes within your genetic make up is switched off. Therefore, you will not experience any form of learning difficulty. But in your daughter, they may have been switched on." My daughter was attending a mainstream school, which, on several occasions, I visited. I observed her thoroughly, and what I noticed was a lack of concentration. I, too, had this problem at a young age, but by the age of eleven, I remembered so clearly. I was given a composition to write at school, saying what I would be like in ten years' time. I wrote an impressive composition saying that I would be in England as an engineer. My teacher at the time gave me full marks.

My daughter was removed from the mainstream school and placed in a special needs school. I couldn't believe how well my little girl was doing. She read everything, and she asked questions which enhanced her learning. At age seven, she was doing much better than I did at the same age. Up to age thirteen, I was never settled or focused on my education; I was always out playing truant.

I was one of the few children at school who owned a bicycle. The other children would flock me to get a ride. I always charged them fifty cents a ride. Oftentimes, at the end of school days, I would go home with between thirty and forty dollars in my pocket; I was quite happy with this arrangement. Several months ago, I visited a close friend with my daughter. I happened to leave her upstairs and went to the shop to buy a drink. When I returned, my friend told me that she couldn't believe how bright my little girl was and it was almost as if she was me. Apparently, I was told by many people that my little girl appeared to be me. Somehow, I didn't understand this. Currently, my little girl tended to do things that I used to do as a child; it was quite uncanny to watch her. She had oftentimes said to me *"I want to be just like you, Daddy."* Judging by the life I had lived and the *womaniser that I was,* I do not wish for her to be like me. However, genetically, it appeared to be unstoppable. I know she was my child, and I love her with every breath I take. I also hope that the chromosome disorder the doctor had pulled out of his hat does not have any impact on my little angel's wellbeing.

It was December 2002. The threats of January 2002 had raised its ugly head again! On December 23, 2002, I was arrested for kidnapping Rochelle and harassing her mother—another setup involving the police, myself, and HM Prison Belmarsh. Do not be too shocked by what you are about to read. It happened, and I was telling it like it was. It was December 22, 2002. It was a Sunday. I remember it vividly, almost as if it was happening now. I went to visit a friend by the name of Linda to whom I hade been acquainted with through a health club. I had my daughter with me. Linda and I chatted about everything and nothing over a glass of wine. After a few hours of talking, I suddenly realised the time was going faster than I imagined.

I then said, "I have to leave now because I have to take Rochelle home." I was quite surprised that my phone did not ring. Rochelle's mother had a habit of phoning me every Sunday without fail. However, she did not phone me that day—at least I thought so. I left Linda's place and went to see my sister Judy. I chatted with her for at least ten to fifteen minutes. I then said to her, "I can't stay long because I have to take Rochelle home." Whilst speaking to Judy, her phone rang. She said, "Hello." All I heard was, "Yes, okay, talk to you later."

Judy said to me, "What's going on between you and Carol?"

I asked her, "What do you mean?"

She revealed to me that her phone conversation was with Carol. "She asked if you were with me."

I then asked Judy, "Why did you not let me speak to her?"

She said, "Carol did not want to speak to you. She just wanted to know where you were."

I said, "If she phones you, and I am here, obviously, I have the baby, then that is what she is phoning about." I reached into my pocket for my mobile (cell) phone to call Carol, and I discovered that the phone had a blank screen. It had not been working. (*Maybe this was the reason why she had called my sister*). Nonetheless, I began to panic because I know she must be upset by now.

I said to Judy, "I have to go now."

She said, "Phone me later to let me know how you got on." (She also reminded me of the injunctions against me.)

I told her not to worry because I would be fine. I just wanted to get the child home.

Perhaps I was not as clever as I claimed to be because if I was, I would have taken my dear child to the nearest police station with a tag attached. But how could I do this to my baby? The thought was there, but my heart would not let me do it. Still, I wished I had done so.

I drove to Sydenham Sava Centre car park, the meeting point to drop Rochelle off. I rang Carol from the phone box.

I told her, "I am in the car park, please come and get Rochelle."

She said, "No, I am not coming."

I did not understand what was going on. I drove to lower Sydenham train station where I could almost see the back of the marital home. I rang Carol again from the call box at the station.

I said, "Listen, you *fucking bitch,* I am at the train station. If you look out the window, you can see me. Come and get the child because I have to go to work tomorrow."

On reflection, I coul see now what she was trying to do. She was trying to lure me to the front door, as this would be a breach of the injunction she took out against me. As I said previously, *she was the cheese, I was the rat, and the police was the trap.* Looking back, what her intentions were at the time was now crystal clear.

Introduction to Statements

My dear friends, I present to you all the statements that were used in court during the period of my trial. They were stored at Ashley Smith & Co Solicitors for a period of six years. I obtained copies purely for this book. These were known to be facts, not that they were true facts. However, please read them carefully because Carol's statements did not appear to be true to the judgement. At this point, you might find yourself being the judge, jury, and executioner. Your understanding of these statements should be clear. Thus, before you condemn me to prison or set me free, study the case carefully. Silence in court. You may be seated.

The *twelve disciples of Israel* found me not guilty on all counts. What do you think? Was I guilty of kidnapping and harassment or was it just a plot for D. C. Duffus to get his pants down yet again?

During my time in prison, I had received a crime file stating I had several criminal activities against my name such as rape, sexual assault, and grievous bodily harm, all against Carol Francis who was now my ex-wife, thank God! If I was guilty of any of the above, I would gladly served the time with no stress. In fact, the only crime that I was guilty of committing was taking Mrs. Woodburn from her husband in 1993.

My dear friends, I must say that Carol was beyond professional. She happened to fool the doctor, the police, and the housing officer. However, she was unable to fool the twelve members of the jury that set me free. When she pretended to collapse in the courtroom, motionless, as if she was dead, I thought I was dead! But at that point, she simply shot herself in the foot. Apparently, she left the courtroom with a limp. Who was laughing now?!

He who laughs last, laughs best. That was me!

CROWN PROSECUTION SERVICE

V

RAYMOND FRANCIS

UNUSED MATERIAL DISCLOSED

THESE ARE THE ORIGINAL STATEMENTS

OF:

RAYMOND FRANCIS

01-MAY-2003 17:32 FROM EWING & CO TO 02084639191 P.03/47
No

INDICTMENT

IN THE CROWN COURT AT WOOLWICH
THE QUEEN v. RAYMOND FRANCIS
RAYMOND FRANCIS is charged as follows:
Count 1

STATEMENT OF OFFENCE

PU'ITING A PERSON IN FEAR OF VIOLENCE BY HARASSMENT, contrary to Section 4(1) of the Protection from Harassment Act 1997.

PARTICULARS OF OFFENCE

RAYMOND FRANCIS, on days between the 28th day of November 2002 and the 24th day of December 2002, caused Carol Francis to fear that violence would be used against her by his course of conduct, which he knew or ought to have known would cause fear of violence to the said Carol Francis on each occasion.

Officer of the Court

URN: OIPL 03984/02

The following information is a record of my interview at the police station accompanied by my solicitor.

Form MG 15

RECORD OF INTERVIEW

Record of interview at police station accompanied by solicitor

Person interviewed: FRANCIS Raymond   Police Exhibit No. HAD/2
Place of interview: Lewisham Police Station   Number of pages: 5
Signature of interviewing office producing exhibit
Date of interview: 23.12.02
Time commenced: 3:27 P.M.   Time concluded: 3:50 P.M.
Duration of interview 23 mins.   Tape reference Nos (') T2931636A
Interviewing Officer(s): D. C. Duffus
Other persons present: Mr. Rayment, Solicitor

Tape counter Times (')	Person Speaking	Text
		Introductions: Persons present introduced themselves.
1:00	D. C. Duffus	Caution given and explained. D. C. Duffus explains to Raymond the reason for his Arrest for Harassment on his estranged wife, Carol Francis. On 29th November 2002 at Bromley County Court, you were served with an order for breach of an injunction. I later gave you a harassment warning, telling you not to make contact with Carol." Raymond pointed out that he had to contact Carol to get his child.

"Were you or were you not given that warning?" |
| | Raymond FRANCIS | "I was told some rubbish. If I don't contact the woman, how am I going to get my child?" |

	D. C. Duffus	"What was your arrangement with regards to your access to Rochelle (your daughter)?"	
4:03	Raymond FRANCIS	"That I should pick Rochelle up from the Sava Centre car park. Sometimes, I wait there, and the mother didn't turn up and gives me the run around.'	
		Raymond stated the arrangements were made through his wife's solicitor who he had also spoken to.13:30	
13:30	Raymond FRANCIS	Raymond stated that he had pleaded with Carol for them to talk and be civilized to each other.	
		Raymond explained that on speaking with Rochelle, she told him that her daddy was called "Michael." Raymond explained this is Carol's new boyfriend. "On hearing this, I was fuming and phoned Carol up. I asked her why Rochelle was telling people that Michael is her daddy."	
18:41	D. C. Duffus	"What happened this Saturday? Did you threaten her?"	
	Raymond FRANCIS	"I told you, of course, I didn't threaten her."	
16:43	DC Duffus	"Did you say to her, 'See you, see you, I can smell death'?"	
		"You explained to her that you were making some big tool at work so you could kill her with it. You then followed her on foot to her care, say a woman in the care, and said 'You've brought a witness with you. Is that your witness?	

		"Later on, you telephoned the house. The woman's two-year-old son picked up the phone, and you hurled abuse down the telephone." Raymond stated that he said, "Get Carol on the phone. Will you now?" to whoever picked the phone up
		"Did you hurl abuse down the phone?"
	Raymond FRANCIS	"No, I did not. I did not put no abuse down the phone."
18:20	D. C. Duffus	"On Saturday, 14 December, Carol says you telephoned her at work and accused her of having another man and he was living in the house." "Is this true? Did you phone her up and accuse her of having another man and that he was living in the house?"
18:55	Raymond FRANCIS	"I said, 'Don't put another man in my baby's face because I would never do that with another woman."
18:57	D. C. Duffus	"Did you tell her that you were going to kill them and chop them up?"
		"You then accused him of driving the car."
		"Did you mention about him driving the car?"
19:15	Raymond FRANCIS	"I don't remember. It's not my car. It had nothing to do with me."
19:22	D. C. Duffus	"You then said that what has happened to her car previously is nothing compared to what will happen next time."
	D. C. Duffus	"Did you say these things?"
	Raymond FRANCIS	"No, I did not."

19:40	D. C. Duffus		"She says you were ranting at her, and she hung up on you.
			"Is that right? Did she hang up on you when you telephone her?"
	Raymond FRANCIS		"She hung up on me."
19:54	D. C. Duffus		"What did you do then after she hung up on you? Did you go to Sava Centre and have a row with a member of the staff in there?"
	Raymond FRANCIS		"I did not have a row. I went in Sava Centre, asked for Carol, and this woman told me that Carol wasn't there. I said she was lying because I had just spoken to her on the phone. She called me Michael. I shouted and told her never to call me that name again."
20:32	D. C. Duffus		The woman in the store called the police who attended Carol's address to wait for you but you didn't go there
			"Carol says that you have threatened her with violence since November on numerous occasions.
			"Carol has stated that she is going away on holiday to Jamaica, to which you have said that if she goes, your cousin will kill her."
			"She says the calls in November stated that you want her back and want to start afresh." Raymond agreed and stated that a child needed both parents and most of all, her dad. "I asked her to be friends to start with."
			"Carol refused, and you have been threatening to harm her. She is terrified of what you will do to her."

11:44	Raymond FRANCIS		Have you threatened her?" "No, I did not."
24:03	D. C. Duffus		D. C. Duffus recapped that Raymond, since November, had made contact with his for wife several times. "You deny you have threatened her. You admit that you have been to her work, and you spoke to her manager. Raymond stated that he phoned Carol several times about Rochelle and had been to Rochelle's school. "Why did you telephone her at work in December when you already had Rochelle?"
25:19	Raymond FRANCIS		"I telephoned her to say to her, 'Look, I don't want Rochelle confused.' Rochelle has told me that some bloke is her dad."
25:17	D. C. Duffus		"You admit making the phone calls, going to her work, and you deny all the abuse and the threats."
26:37	Raymond FRANCIS		Raymond stated that his daughter meant everything to him. D. C. Duffus also pointed out that Carol had stated "You love your daughter and at no stage did she ever think you would harm Rochelle."
26:38	D. C. Duffus		Form 987 served
26:38	D. C. Duffus		INTERVIEW CONCLUDED AT 3.50 P.M.

FORM OF NOTICE OF APPLICATION FOR BAIL
IN THE CROWN COURT

Application for Bail

Take notice that an application for bail will be made to the Crown Court at Woolwich on Friday, 28 February 2003, at 10:00 A.M. on behalf of

Full name:　FRANCIS　　　Forenames:　RAYMOND

Crown Court reference number: 220030044

Place of detention:　HM Prison Belmarsh
　　　　　　　　　　Prison Number: HP6441

Particulars of proceedings:	Defendant awaiting trial at the Crown during whichApplicant was at Court committed to custody. Indictment alleging one offence of putting Carol Francis (his wife) in fear of violence by harassment contrary to Section 4(1) of the Protection from Harassment Act 1997. At the Plea and Directions Hearing on 20 February 2003, the Defendant pleaded not guilty. Matter in Warned List for 24 March 2003.
Details of any relevant previous applications for bail:	8 January 2003 at Woolwich Crown Court whilst matter pending in the Magistrates Court. Bail refused on grounds that it was feared that defendant would commit further offences and a risk of further threats to the complainant.
Grounds of application for bail:	The Defendant has no previous convictions, one caution for criminal damage to his wife's property. The allegation amounts to verbal threats only arising out of an argument regarding

child custody and contact. It was not followed up by the complainant using the injunction between 14 December and 22 December or calling the police on 22 December since she waited until 23 December.

The complainant who has lived at the former matrimonial home, 4 Thomas Dean Road, Sydenham, London, SE26, has now left that address and is presently in the West Indies.
The child of the parties, Rochelle, born 16 December 1997 who has learning difficulties and has previously relied upon the support and assistance of her father, has been left by the complainant mother with strangers whilst she has travelled alone to the West Indies.

The Defendant has the support of his sister, Judy Maxwell, of Hollywood House, Denver Street, London. She lives there with her two children and can provide accommodation to the defendant and, if necessary, to his daughter.
Alternatively, the defendant's brother, Rupert Francis, of Lanyard House, Pepys Estate, London, SE8, can provide him with accommodation.

The Defendant, until his remand in custody, was employed by Precision Engineering Medway and believes that he can return to work for them.

The Defendant has now been in custody since his arrest on 23 December 2002 and his subsequent first appearance at Greenwich Magistrates Court on 24 December 2002.
The Defendant would suggest that suitable conditions of bail would be residence, non contact with the complainant, save through solicitors for the purpose of arranging

access to his daughter, and that he should not go within 500 meters of the complainant's address at 4 Thomas Dean Road, Sydenham, London, SE26, or any other alternative address which she should be living at. That he should sign on at the local Police Station.

Notes: The appropriate office of the Crown Court should be consulted about the time and place of the hearing before this Notice is sent to the Prosecutor. A copy of this Notice should be sent to the Crown Court.

Form 5029

STATEMENT TO ASSIST MY TRIAL

RAYMOND ANTHONY FRANCIS, PREVIOUSLY RESIDENT AT 9 LANYARD HOUSE, GROVE STREET, DEPTFORD, SE8, CURRENTLY IN CUSTODY AT HMP BELMARSH

WILL STATE AS FOLLOWS:

I am now forty-two years old, having been born on the October 26, 1960 in Kingston, Jamaica.

Prior to my remand into custody in relation to the present allegation, I have been living at 9 Lanyard House which is my brother's address. I have been living with him since Good Friday, 2002, which was when I separate from my wife, Carol Francis, who is, of course, the complainant.

I came to England when I was between twelve and fourteen years of age. My parents had come over here to find work, and I stayed with an aunt in Kingston until they sent for me.

I attended the Catford Boys School until the age of 17 years when I left to pursue an apprenticeship with Swift Precision Engineering. I worked at Swift whilst paying my way through college, attended the South East London College, and studied for a City & Guilds Certificate in electrical and mechanical engineering. I stayed with Swift for nine years before leaving to work for Elmec Engineering in East London. I worked at Elmec for four years before going to Precision Engineering, which was where I was employed at the time of my arrest. I have worked at Precision Engineering for three and a half years without any problems, would consider myself to be a highly regarded member of the staff, and I believe that my employment would still be available for me if and when I am able to secure my release from custody.

I would like to say that I have a British passport and notwithstanding what my wife has said about me within her statement. I do not consider that I have or have ever had any mental health problems.

An application for bail was made on my behalf at Woolwich Crown Court and on January 8, 2003. I was refused bail upon the basis that the judge stated that if released, I would commit further offences and would interfere with the complainant.

On the January 28, my case was committed for trial to the crown court at Woolwich, and I was committed for trial in custody.

On February 20, I appeared for a plea and direction hearing. I entered a plea of not guilty, and on the February 29, a further application for bail was made and adjourned until March 3, on which occasion bail was refused again upon the basis that I would commit further offences and interfere with witnesses.

It is right to say that on April 30, my case was transferred from my previous solicitors, namely Ewing & Co, to my current solicitors who now act for me.

I understand that following the listing of my case for trial on May 7, my case was stood out and is not to be listed at any time on or after May 14, 2003.

It is therefore right to say that I remain in custody and appreciate that, given that my trial will take place in the very near future and given the number of applications for bail already made on my behalf, I will now remain in custody until my trial.

FACTS OF CASE

The history of this matter is as follows:

It was on March 23, 1996 that I married my wife, Carol Francis, whom, as I have said, is the complainant in this case. I had met Carol in 1995 whilst I was on holiday in Jamaica at the time, and in fact, she served me a meal when I was a customer in a restaurant. At that time, she was, in fact, already married, and I actually met her husband whilst in Jamaica. Subsequently, Carol and myself had an affair. Her husband knew of the affair and asked to meet me. We met, shook hands, and he said to me, "Good luck to you." Initially, I came back to England alone, although I sent money to Jamaica so that they could get divorced, and Carol could then come over to this country.

Carol came over to England, and as I have said, we were married on March 23, 1996.

Our daughter, Rochelle, was born on December 16, 1997. Obviously, since I had been in custody, Carol had looked after Rochelle, although I was aware that in February of this year and whilst in custody concerning this matter, Carol went to Jamaica and left Rochelle with people unknown to me. I do not believe that she is a particularly good mother.

There were problems in our marriage from the very beginning, and I suspected early on that the marriage was not right. I began to realize that she had married me simply because she wanted to come to England, and I suppose the greatest problem was one of culture. Although I was born in Jamaica, I considered that I am more British than Jamaican whereas because Carol had lived longer in Jamaica, I believe that she considered herself primarily to be Jamaican. Indeed, when she returned to Jamaica, from time to time, she would, in fact, stay at her former husband's address.

She began to lock me out of the house and intimidate me. We were living together at 4 Thomas Dean Road, Sydenham, SE26, which was a housing association property in both our names.

In January 2002, she locked me out of the address and said words to me to the effect of "When I finish with you, you will wish you were dead." She went on to say that she would destroy me and would use the law to do so.

We eventually separated on Good Friday, 2002, and as previously stated, since that time, I was living with my brother until my arrest on December 23. I moved out of the property as Carol had previously gone to Bromley County Court, stating that she could not live with me, and I was ordered to leave the address by the court. She alleged that I had assaulted her, and because I was not represented at the injunction, the court decided that I should not be allowed to return to the house. In relation, to access arrangements for Rochelle, it was agreed that I would collect her and drop her back at the Sava Centre car park in Sydenham. I was allowed to speak to Carol only in relation to our child.

I would confirm that I had never been violent toward her. Although we had had a lot of arguments, there had never been any violence whatsoever.

On September 9, 2002, she managed to persuade the police to arrest me. She told the police that I had been violent toward her and had threatened her. This simply was not true. In relation to the facts, I had gone to Sava Centre in Sydenham to collect Rochelle and had parked at the usual spot. I had gone to the toilet, and when I had returned, I noticed that my car was scratched. I suspected that it was either Carol or her friend, and when Carol arrived, I said words to her to the effect of "Your friends done a good job." Carol flew off the handle, came to have a look at the damage, but did not say a great deal. This incident was on, I believe, a Wednesday.

On the following Saturday, Carol's car was scratched, and she blamed me, although I had no involvement in her car being scratched whatsoever. We both went to the police, and the police stated that as we were both making cross allegations, there was nothing that could be done. I decided to pay £300 and had my car repaired. When I picked up my car on Friday, I thereafter went to pick up Rochelle, saw Carol, and said to her, "It looks good, doesn't it?" She just looked at me as if she wanted to do something. I then went into the house, took possession of an ice pick from one of the kitchen drawers, and handed it to her, stating, "Go on, put the scratches back on if that will make you happy, if that's what you want to do." At that point, she ran into the house and started to abuse me. She called me batty man and batty sucker, which were West Indian terms and was the lowest form of Jamaican insult.

I kicked the door a few times, and I then left. I made a telephone call to her and remember saying to her words to the effect of, "Don't ever abuse me like that again."

She then said, "The police are on your case." I got in touch with the police. They said that I was not wanted, although three days later, the police telephoned and asked me to go and see them. I was, in fact, arrested and went to court at Bromley, although the case was later discharged.

I could confirm that I had never made threats to Carol in the Sava Centre car park or elsewhere, and certainly, I would never make threats in front of our child.

On December 14, 2002, which if I remember correctly was a Saturday, I had collected Rochelle from the Sava Centre, i.e., the usual spot, and we had gone to see a friend, namely, Sabrina. She was talking to Rochelle and said to her, joking, "I bet you don't even know who I am, do you?" She went on to say, "and I bet you don't know who he is either," laughing and pointing at me. She went on to say, "That's your daddy."

Although, Rochelle then said, "That's not my daddy. My daddy's called Michael."

I had previously called Carol the day before at her house and had heard a bloke's voice in the background. When Rochelle made this comment, it caused me to stop the car, and I asked her what she meant. She said that her mummy, i.e., Carol, had said that Michael was her new daddy.

Not surprisingly, this greatly upset me. I telephoned Carol whilst she was at work at SavaCentre. She worked there as a Sales Assistant. I asked her why she had told the child that I was not her dad. I remembered that Rochelle was put on the telephone, and I asked her why she had said that Michael was her daddy. She said, "Mummy said Michael is my daddy." At that point, Carol started shouting and swearing, saying that she had not said it. I then made my way to SavaCentre where I saw Maggie whom I note had now made a statement against me. Maggie worked with Carol, and she said to me, "Listen, Michael," and then went, "whoops."

I said to Maggie, "What did you say?" and she said "Nothing." I said to her words to the effect of "Look, don't ever call me Michael." However, I did not say anything that, in my view, would have caused her any fear at all. I did not have, and have never had, any complaint against Maggie. I then went to my brother's. I do not accept that Maggie could possibly have been so frightened that she had to telephone the police.

I should say, at this stage, that the address at 4 Thomas Dean Road could be seen from SavaCentre, and it was, in fact, a stone's throw from one to the other.

I remember that at SavaCentre, there was lady aged about thirty-eight years, wearing glasses, who stood nearby and who could be a witness, although I accept that the possibility of tracing this witness was remote, unless the CCTV evidence of that date could be seized.

In relation to the arrangement between Carol and myself for collecting and dropping off Rochelle, the arrangement was that I would pick her up on Friday, at 3:00 P.M., and drop her back at about 10:00 P.M. of the same day. That was after Carol had finished work.

On Saturdays, I would pick her up after work at a time between 2:00 P.M. and 2:30 P.M. and drop her back on Sunday evening at a time between 7 P.M. and 9 P.M.

I had been shown the witness statements, and I would be making comments in relation to those statements in due course.

I noted that within the statement, Carol stated that I would have her killed when she went on holiday to Jamaica by my cousin. That was complete rubbish because I would not even know where to find my rude boy cousin, and furthermore, I did not know that she was going to Jamaica.

It was right to say that on one occasion, I suggested that we get back together, as when Rochelle had been born, we had both agreed to stick by the child and do everything that we could so Rochelle could have a good life. I also, at one point, accepted that I asked Carol to give Rochelle to me as I earned a lot more money than she did and could look after her a great deal better.

On Saturday, December 21, 2002, it was right to say that I went to SavaCentre in order to collect Rochelle. However, I completely deny that, at any time, I tried to make Carol think that I was going to crash into her car. I went there as normally as I could and asked Carol to get in the car because I wanted to ask her if I could have Rochelle over Christmas. We had previously discussed this on the telephone. At no time did I say anything to the effect of "See you, see you, I can smell your death." That was just a ridiculous comment and allegation to make against me. Nor did I refer to any tool that I was making at work to kill her with. That was complete nonsense, and there was no way that I would have said that, especially in front of Rochelle. She did have a friend with her, and I noted that, that friend did not appear to have made a statement. I did go to the car and said words to the effect of "You have got a witness." I said this because I knew that she was plotting things against me.

She did not get in the car, but she did say to me that she could not talk at the time about Christmas arrangements. I remember saying that I wanted clothes for Rochelle, and she told me that I would have to come around and that she would leave the clothes in a bag by the front door.

I did call Carol later that day to talk to her and finalise the arrangements to keep Rochelle over Christmas. Christine answered the phone and then put Carol on. I asked her if I could keep Rochelle, and she said that I could, but she refused to give me any more clothes for the child. The intention, had I not been arrested, would have been that I would have kept Rochelle until returning to work in January, following the Christmas and New Year holiday break.

On Sunday, December 22, I had Rochelle and took her to visit a friend. I remember saying to my friend that at 7:30 P.M., on the dot, the phone would ring. I know that Carol would telephone at that time. However, the phone did not ring, and I remember leaving my friends and going to my sister's address at 14 Hollywood House. My sister told me that she had been trying to call me on my mobile but could not get through. I then realized that my phone was not working and there appeared to be a problem with the SIM card. When I eventually switched my phone on, I saw that I had missed six calls. I was quite sure that Carol would have telephoned me and told me to drop Rochelle off at the car park.

At about 8:30 P.M., my sister's phone rang, and she answered it. My sister told me that Carol had said to her on the telephone that she should not tell me that Carol was on the phone, although I could not understand why she would have made such a comment. However, following the conversation, I then telephoned Carol. She asked me, on this occasion, not to drop Rochelle off at the car park but to take her to an area close to where Carol lived. I refused to do this as I was not allowed to go there given the injunction, and I thought she was going to try to get me trapped. At no point did I ever say anything about wanting to rip her face off, and I never called her a coward. I did not say that I was going to get her, but I did say to her, "Pick up point, fifteen minutes." At that point, I hung up and obviously, by making that comment, I meant that we would meet at the usual destination, i.e., the SavaCentre car park. I then took Rochelle to the car park, telephoned Carol, and said that I was at the car park and that she should come and get Rochelle.

She said to me, "I am not coming out," and she then hung up. I telephoned her again and asked her what was going on. She told me to leave Rochelle to a friend of hers whom I know was called Kenneth and who lived in Upper Sydenham. At no time did I say that I was going to get Carol, although I do accept that I kept calling her and asking her to pick up Rochelle from the car park as would be the normal arrangements. She kept saying to me that she would not do that and that I should bring Rochelle to the close. As I have said, I did not want to take Rochelle to the close because of the injunction.

Having suggested that I take Rochelle to a friend of hers living in Upper Sydenham, which I would not do as she should come and collect Rochelle, I told her that I would drive to Lower Sydenham, which was near to Carol's house, and that she should come and collect Rochelle from that location. She told me that she still would not come and told me to bring Rochelle to her front door. She hung up. I then drove to the entrance to the close, telephoned Carol, and said, "I'm outside, come and get her."

She said, "Bring her to the front door," although she knew full well that I could not go to the door. At that point, I simply refused, said that I had to go to work in the morning, and was not messing around any longer. I decided there and then that I would not go to work the following day. That was the end of our conversation that evening

The following day, which was Monday, I telephoned my work and said that I could not come in as my wife had refused to collect Rochelle. Obviously, I had kept Rochelle with me. At no point did I ever threaten to kill Carol.

I would confirm that the only times I have ever communicated with Carol was when I had to get access to my child, for that was my only interest. All I could say was that if Carol was terrified of me, then why would she continue meeting me to give me Rochelle?

Another incident, which I believed proved that she was not terrified of me, took place on December 15, 2002. I had been away to Paris with a girlfriend, and when I returned, I went to pick up Rochelle. Carol then started asking me how old the woman was.

She asked if I had slept with her, and I said that I had. She then said, "Was she better than me?"

I said words to the effect of "She's okay, but maybe not better."

She then said, laughing, "Can she handle you?" If she was terrified of me, I do not believe that she would have spoken to me in this way.

I had never threatened her with violence or put her in fear of me. All that I was interested in was seeing my child, and I believe that she was going to stitch me up. I could not help but recall her words sometime last year when she said to me, "When I'm finished with you, you will wish you were dead." She told me, at that time, that she was going to try to ruin me, and it now looks like her threats to ruin me are in motion.

In relation to my arrest on December 23, I had, as stated, telephoned my work place, explaining that I could not come in because I was with Rochelle. The supervisor, Carl, said that I should not worry and that I should take the day off. He said to me that he would see me back at work in January.

I then said to Rochelle that after I had washed some clothes, I would bath her and before I bathed her, I remember putting some money in my wallet, which would remind me to pay my credit card.

At about 12:30 P.M., my telephone rang. It was my brother. He said that he had someone who wanted to speak with me. I asked who it was, but my brother did not reply. He put the person on, and this person turned out to be D. C. Duffus from Lewisham police station. He asked me if I had Rochelle, and I said that I did. He then said that he wanted to see me, and I remember saying to him, "Why? It is Christmas, and I want to be left alone." I then accepted that. I put the phone down, and a short while later, at around 1:00 P.M., my brother's girlfriend opened the front door. Before we knew it, a number of police officers entered the premises. I was handcuffed in front of my daughter, and that was the last time I had seen her.

I was taken to Lewisham police station where I was interviewed. During the course of the interview, I answered all questions put to me, and at the conclusion, I was then charged and detained in custody, pending my production before Greenwich Magistrates' Court.

As I had said, I had been shown the witness statements with regard to my case, and I had made comments in relation to those documents elsewhere.

In relation to any possible reasons why Carol would make up allegations against me, it was right to say that she came from a poor family and always made it quite clear that during our marriage, she wanted a house for herself. Indeed, after one of the previous County Court hearings on February 2002, she said words to me to the effect of "I've got the house, and I am not happy."

I thought that she also wanted revenge for the fact that her car was scratched, and I believe initially that she had no idea how matters would escalate once she had made the allegation against me.

I could confirm that her cousin, George, visited me approximately once a month. During one of his visits toward the end of February or early March 2003, he said to me that Carol had telephoned him upon her return from Jamaica, asking where I was. She went on to enquire as to whether I was out of prison. When she was told that I was still in prison, George stated that she appeared to be in shock and said that she thought I would receive twenty-eight days. As I had said, George visited me about once a month and had told me on more than once occasion that Carol simply could not understand why I have not been released on bail.

I did not know whether Carol would attend court in order to give evidence against me, although I would not be at all surprise if she decided that she could not go through with repeating false allegations under oath.

In summary, it was my intention to contest the allegation prepared against me, and at this stage, I had no further information to provide.

Statement to Assist Complaint Part Two:

Witness Statement
(CJ Act 1967, s.9 MC Act 1980, ss.5A (3) (a) and 5B; MC Rules 1981, r.70)

Statement of Raymond Francis

Age if under 18 'Over 18' (if over 18 insert over 18) Occupation: Engineer

This statement (consisting of **two** pages each signed by me) is true to the best of my knowledge and belief and I make it knowing that, if it is tendered in evidence, I shall be liable to prosecution if I have wilfully stated anything which I know to be false or do not believe to be true.

Signature   Dated

Tick if witness evidence is visually recorded (supply witness details on rear)

On Wednesday, September 3, 2003, at 1800 hours, I attended Norbury Police Station together with my solicitor, Joe N'Danga-Karoma, to meet with Detective Inspector McQueen and Detective Constable Dace from the Directorate of Professional Standard to discuss complaints. I wish to be fully investigated against D. C. Duffus. Further to my statement, dated September 1, 2003, which I made to my solicitors and of which I had provided a copy to D. C. Dace, I wish to clarify the following aspects of my complaints:

1) On November 29, 2002, I was in attendance at Bromley Family Court relating to a civil matter between myself and my now ex-wife. D. C. Duffus was present at these proceedings for reasons I did not understand, as these were civil matters, not criminal. At the time, I had no idea he was a police officer. I was not shown any form of identification, and he was not wearing uniform. D. C. Duffus intimidated me immediately after the civil proceedings by approaching me outside of the Courtroom, saying, "If you so much as breath heavy on Carol, I'm going to come down on you like a ton of bricks." I felt a little confused as I had never seen the man before. I laughed and just walked off.

2) As a matter, of course, I had custody of my daughter, Rochelle, at weekends. There was an injunction in existence against me which prevented me from going to my (now ex-wife's) home address. With this in mind, on Saturdays, Carol dropped Rochelle off in SavaCentre car park in Sydenham, and I took her from there. On Sunday evenings, I, in turn,

dropped Rochelle off in the same car park, and Carol collected her from there. On the December 22, 2002, my mobile phone wasn't working (Carol phoned me religiously at 7:30 P.M. every Sunday.). I was at my sister's home. Judy said to me, "What's going on? That was Carol on the phone. She told me not to tell you." I found this quite strange, as I was awaiting her call to drop off Rochelle.

I used a second mobile phone and said, "Drop off point, fifteen minutes," and hung up. Carol did not arrive. A couple more phone calls took place, and Carol still refused to collect Rochelle. In the end, I went to the end of her road and called her, yet she refused. Rochelle stayed with me that night. On December 23, 2002, I received a telephone call on my brother's landline. It was 12:00 P.M.

3) The male on the phone said, "Are you Raymond?" He said it was D. C. Duffus. I hung up. Some time between 12:30 and 13:00 P.M., D. C. Duffus come to the apartment and arrested me for harassment in front of my child. I was then handcuffed very tightly. D. C. Duffus laughed when I said they were too tight; I wish to complain about this. It was at this time that I recognized him from court on November. I felt that the arrest was unlawful, and because D. C. Duffus failed to investigate the matter properly everything that happened to me. I was remanded in Belmarsh for six and a half months. My health deteriorated, I lost my job, and I was blacklisted for not paying my credit card bills.

4) I believed that D. C. Duffus coached my ex-wife. This was on information from my barrister and solicitors. I also believed that D. C. Duffus delayed my trial in order to do this.

5) During my time on remand, I longed to see my daughter. As a direct result of advice from D. C. Duffus, my wife would not allow it.

I wish for D. C. Duffus to be fully investigated in relation to unprofessionalism and malicious manner in which he displayed throughout my case.

Statement during turbulence

STATEMENT OF THE RESPONDENT
RAYMOND ANTHONY FRANCIS
March 14, 2002

I, Raymond Francis, of 4 Thomas Dean Road, SE26, 5BY, was the respondent making a statement against the allegations alleged against me.

I had been married to the applicant since March 23, 1996, and we had one child from the relationship. My wife had one child living in Jamaica with her ex-husband.

I met my wife whilst on holiday in Jamaica. At the time, she was married. The ex-husband requested to meet me, so I accepted the invitation. He then asked, "Are you going to marry my wife?" He shooked my hand and wished me good luck without hesitation. Until this day, a man passing over his wife to another haunts me.

They got divorced, and I married her after several trips to Jamaica. Whilst she lived in England with me, she worked very hard for her living. I thought we could make it because we are both "hardworking people." We previously lived in a bed-sit, and after the birth of our baby, we obtained a two-bedroom house at the current address.

After we moved into the property, I began to see changes in my wife's behaviour towards me.

1. She would lock me out of the property.
2. She would throw my belongings from the top bedroom window unto the garden.
3. My wife shouted verbal abuses through the letterbox, which caused me great embarrassment, as neighbours would gather round to laugh. This pattern continued on a six-month basis since I began to log these events. It happened, to the best of my recollection, on January 2000.
4. On June 2000, my wife locked me out, and I had no access to the property. That night, I slept in the car, in the car park of my work place in Sittingbourne, Kent. When this

happened, it brought great distress to me, not to mention the stress involved, at the same time, with being the rent payer. I never stopped loving my wife because I think something was not right with her way of thinking. Thus, I continued to live with the situation up to January 7, 2002, the latest occurrence.

5. I visited my wife's sister with my wife for a five-minute "hop" on January 6, 2002. My wife had overstayed the time given by myself. This caused me great distress because I had not eaten all day, and it was 7:00 P.M. I said to my wife, "let's go now." Her sister asked me what the problem was, and I told her Carol did not want to visit her on previous requests, so why couldn't she leave now? We left, and upon arriving at the car, I was verbally attacked by Carol. An argument started.

6. My wife started to swear, and as a result, I started to drive erratically.

7. At home on January 6, my wife tried to get me to go to the car to retrieve the shopping. At this time, I knew that she wanted to lock me out, and shouted abusive words through the letterbox. I felt extremely intimidated by her because she was laughing at me, stating that I never dared to go outside.

8. My wife intimidated me so much, I could not hold back from arguing.

9. My wife called the police. I started talking to them and told them, at this point, if I lose my baby or my home, it didn't matter because I had had enough. I started relaying to them the events which led up to the confrontation.

10. My wife walked past both the officers and myself with a bag. I revealed to the offices what caused my wife to disappear out of the front door. What was said would remain, I repeat, anonymous! At this point, I still loved my wife and had not wish to use anything against her. I should never had mentioned it to the officers. My wife did not return home that night.

11. "Sex monster" as it was alleged. I had not forced sexual activities upon my wife. I had not had sex with my wife or

any other woman for the past four months to date. Several times my wife was in the bath or lying in the bed, I had not made any attempts to engage in any sexual activities. The sex allegations were not true! If this were so, the police would know about it by now.
12. "Stress." I agree that my wife was stressed, but I was not the cause. The reports from the doctor may have indicated stress and other factors of illness, but none of them were caused by myself, the respondent. I do believe the stress was work-related, with her colleagues saying things, which would also remain anonymous for private reasons.
13. "Guilty." The only thing I would plead guilty to, at this point, and any point was the fact that I loved my wife more than life itself. If it was my fate to be executed or beheaded because I truly loved my wife, so be it. It was my wish to be with my wife until the dust of our bones blew in winds, scattered upon the surface of the Caribbean sea. Then she would know that true love prevails.
14. "Finances." I work fifty-one hours per week and travel 100 miles to work per day. My petrol costs £80.00 per week. I also paid the weekly rent of £76.00 and bought the food, just to make my wife comfortable. Six months ago, I bought my wife a car at a cost totalling £8,000.00. At this point, I was trying to return it to the finance company, but the company would not accept, so I was stuck with it. It was very expensive to maintain such a vehicle, but I only did it to give her comfort and protection against the weather.

The "monster" that I was alleged to be would not go through such vigorous measurements to stabilize his family. I loved my family and I wished to remain so as a family, seeing my daughter every night after work. As a result of these expenditures, I found it hard to afford a solicitor to represent me, as the quote I got was £760.00 plus the VAT. I would prefer to give that sum to my wife to sun her body.

THESE ARE THE ORIGINAL STATEMENTS

OF:-

CAROL FRANCIS

Here, I was embraced by the jaws of death. I must say thanks to Mrs. Woodburn. Or should I say, Carol Nembhard!

It had been a pleasure, I must say, to have received the divorce papers. I dare say that it was the happiest day of my life, as I might have said previously. At this point, I must take the pleasure of apologising to Mr. Woodburn for taking away his wife in 1993. I do wish he would find it easy to forgive the Englishman who stole his diamond, but indeed, his diamond was something I stepped in whilst walking in the bushes. *Sorry, old chap, the things people do to get British status was incredible!*

My dear friends, after reading Carol's statements several times, it occurred to me that this statement was not of someone with a sound mind. This character appeared to be somewhat confused. Please read carefully and see if your thoughts equated to mine.

Due to Carol's allegations and to prove to you, human beings/my readers, one night, I went home late. My present wife was asleep. I laid on top of her as an experiment to see if she would notice my body weight. It was alleged by Carol that I had sex with her for several nights without her knowing whilst she was asleep until the next day when she discovered a flow of discharge. *I dared say she either had a "wet dream or the ghost from Laurel Grove had found his way to Thomas Dean Road"* where we both reside at the time of the attack! The same ghost that had sex with her at Laurel Grove, and left her dribbling from the fountain of lust and visibly bruised in her sexual regions to be seen by myself, i.e., on her neck and pubic area, the ghost was always coming back for more. That was what I call a sex-mad ghost. The semen found by her forensic friends on her body was not of my D.N.A. Obviously, if it was, Duffus and his cronies would have been all over me like flies on shit! Come to think of it, at that time of my life, Carol was hooked on American crime dramas. *Was it possible*, I asked myself, that *these programs had really damaged Carol beyond reasonable repair?* That was the question. Let's get back to the experiment. As the weight of my body pressed down, Zora responded immediately in her French accent, "What are you doing?" I began to laugh as I told her the facts of the matter. She replied, "Your ex-wife was an idiot. Good night.'

My dear friends, at the end of this book, I would place an e-mail address for your response. Please let me know if it was at all possible, in any way, for sexual intercourse to happen during sleep without knowledge of the sleeper. I was told by a very close female friend of mine that having sex whilst asleep was on the top of her fantasy list. I was sure, by hearing that, I was going crazy.

In my opinion, when a person is sleeping, many functions were closed down, but that was my opinion. What was yours?

<INSERT ARTWORK HERE>

| Family Court—Statement to obtain marital home |

IN THE BROMLEY COUNTY COURT   CASE NO:
                                   BROOFL0014
IN THE MATTER OF THE FAMILY LAW ACT 1996
BETWEEN:
                          CAROL FRANCIS Applicant
                                  -and-
                          RAYMOND FRANCIS
                                Respondent

STATEMENT OF APPLICANT

I, Carol Francis, of 4 Thomas Dean Road, Sydenham, London, SE26 5BY
MAKE THIS STATEMENT:

1. I am the applicant herein and I make this statement in support of my application for a non-molestation and occupation order against the respondent.

2. I am making my application on a "Without Notice" basis, as I truly fear that should the Respondent believe I am taking action against him, that he will subject me to further incidents of violence, and he would evade service of any court documents.
3. I married the respondent on the March 23, 1996, (C. Francis) and we have one child from that relationship namely: Rochelle Francis D0B: 16.12.97. I do have another daughter from a previous relationship. The child from that relationship, namely Erica Woodburn, DOB: 28.10.86, currently lives with her father in Jamaica.
4. The property at 4 Thomas Dean Road aforesaid is rented in joint names from the London Borough of Lewisham. Prior to moving to this accommodation, I lived with the respondent in a property that was in his sole name, which always made me feel that he had more rights over me and that he was able to throw me out whenever he wanted to. With the joint tenancy, I feel more secure.
5. Throughout the marriage, there has been violence. I have been badly beaten by the respondent in the past, but now, the respondent is mentally causing me severe damage. The respondent will sit in front of me. He will come up and put his face right in front of my face and tell me that he loved me. The respondent will then keep me up all night long, telling me that he cannot live without me. The respondent comes up, pokes me in the face, and says, "I cannot breathe if I think I am going to lose you." The respondent will keep on at me over and over again to the early hours of the morning, until I eventually said that I will not divorce him or take any action against him. Then and only then will he let me go to bed and sleep. I often lay in bed feeling terrified because I am not sure what is going to happen.
6. There have been many incidents of violence throughout the marriage, far too many to mention, but I will briefly give details of some events that have taken place.
7. On one occasion, the respondent threw me to the floor. He had beaten me so badly that I had to hide the bruises on my face and could not go out for some time. When I did venture

out, I had to wear very thick make-up to hide the marks inflicted by the respondent.
8. On another occasion, the respondent banged my head against the wall, punched me in the ribs, and kicked me in my private parts. At the beginning of all these assaults, I was too scared to seek help from the police.
9. During the pregnancy with my daughter, Rochelle, the respondent was only verbally abusive and did not harm me, but as soon as my daughter was born, the violence continued.
10. More recently, the respondent has grabbed me around the neck. He has swung me up against the wall and then thrown me to the floor. On one occasion, the respondent kicked me so much that I ended up falling to the ground. Then, he just kicked me non-stop until he had ran out of energy and could not kick me anymore.
11. Additionally, the respondent did start to pack my clothes in a bag. I ran down stairs and all I know is that I was hit across the back with some force. The next thing I remember is that I was back in my bed. I do not know how I got there and can only assume that during my loss of consciousness, the respondent had carried me back upstairs and put me in the bed.
12. The most recent incidents have caused me concern. The respondent seems to think that he has a right to have sex with me, and although I have told him that I do not want anything to do with him, he ignores my pleas. The respondent is now forcing me to have sex against my will.

The respondent swears at me and is extremely abusive. Then he will ask me to try to reconcile our differences. He changes his mind like the weather. The respondent has also said that he will kill himself if he cannot have me, and I truly believe that he is so unstable that he would not only take his own life but may consider doing me some serious harm.

13. Over the Christmas period, the respondent forced me to have sex on three separate occasions. On one occasion, it was 2:00 A.M. in the morning, and I was in my daughter's room. The respondent came in, pulled me to another room, and then forced me to have sex with him. It is not worth me trying to put up a fight because I know I will just be strangled, beaten,

or kicked. It either means that I am forced to have sex or may get beaten. On one of these occasions, I believe it was December 21, I called the police who attended and calmed the respondent down. One of my neighbours had also telephoned the police, having heard my cries.

14. More recently, again over the Christmas holidays, I came in from working nights at 3:00 in the morning. I woke up at 6:00 A.M. with a heavy feeling only to find the respondent laying on top of me, eventually forcing me to have sex with him. Despite my pleas, the respondent will not stop.

15. On Monday, January 3, 2000, the respondent came into my room. He said to me, "Come and pay your debt." I took my daughter to bed, and the respondent told me to hurry up because he was waiting to have sex with me. Again, the respondent forced me against my will.

16. I contacted the police because I could not bear this, but the Woman Police Constable told me that unless I am saying the word "No," they cannot charge the respondent with rape and cannot take any action against him. They have also told me that as I have no proof that I had been beaten, they cannot assist me in anyway.

17. The respondent is now threatening me on a daily basis, saying that he is going to have sex with me, and making comments like "Will it be before or after work?" I am living on a knife's edge, not knowing when the respondent is going to force me to have sex with him, also knowing that if I try to prevent this from happening, I will receive further beating.

18. The respondent does have other places that he can live. There are family and friends with whom he could stay. On January 4, 2000, he tells me that I can have a divorce if I wanted and told me he had lots of places to stay. I, on the other hand, need to be able to stay in the home to give my two-year-old daughter some continuity of security. I have a childminder nearby who will care for the while I am at work, but I cannot afford to pack my bags and move. The respondent works for an engineering company, and I believe he earns £300 per week. I believe he could afford to rent alternative accommodation.

19. My two-year-old daughter is now reacting very badly. She has become withdrawn and quiet and clings to me all the time. She has seen some of the beatings and can obviously sense the tense atmosphere between myself and the respondent. I am very nervous, keep crying, and am worried that every time the respondent comes in, I am going to be forced to have sex or beating.
20. I am truly terrified of the respondent and believe that unless he is restrained by this Honourable Court, such assaults will continue, and my injuries will escalate. I therefore humbly request that this Honourable Court do grant me the following relief:
I attended my doctor's surgery at the beginning of February because I was distressed. My doctor then took it upon herself to write a letter to my instruction solicitors. There is now produced and shown to me, marked "CF2," a fax from my doctor, Anita Alexander. Indeed, my doctor had to sign me off work because I was in not fit state to work and after speaking to her and telling her what I have endured over the last couple of years. My doctor told me I was in a very vulnerable situation and needed to be living faithfully in my home with my daughter, without any problems from the respondent. My doctor is fully aware that I have no family or friends to support me in this country. I am on my own and have no one to turn to for help.

Over the past couple of days, the respondent has gone from being aggressive, abusive, and threatening towards me to being very depressed and apologetic. He follows my every move. If I go to work in the evening, he will ring up to make sure I am there. If I am at home, he will ring to check up on me. When he comes in from work, he sits in front of me and makes me promise to him that I am not going to move. The respondent also comes right up to my face and tells me that if he cannot breathe without me, there is no point in living.
1. An Order under Section 42 of the Family Law Act 1996 that the respondent is forbidden to use or threaten to use violence

against me and must not instruct or encourage, in any way, any other person to do so.
2. The respondent is forbidden from intimidating, harassing, or pestering me and may not encourage in, any way, any other person to do so.
3. An Order under Section 36 of the Family Law Act 1996 that the Respondent should leave 4 Thomas Dean Road, Sydenham, London, SE26, 5BY, forthwith. Having left, the respondent should not return, enter, attempt to enter, or go within 100 metre radius of 4 Thomas Dean Road, Sydenham, London, SE26, 5BY.
4. That a Power of Arrest be attached to this Order.

Carol Francis' statement before the trial to gain maximum imprisonment for Raymond Francis.

Witness Statement
(CJ Act 1967, s.9 MC Act 1980, ss.5A (3) 9a) and 5B; MC rules 1981, r.70)

Statement of Mrs. Carol Francis

Age if under 18 'over 18' (if over 18 insert over 18) Occupation: sales assistant

This statement (consisting of five pages, each signed by me) is true to the best of my knowledge and belief, and I make it knowing that, if it is tendered in evidence, I shall be liable to prosecution if I have wilfully stated anything which I know to be false or do not believe to be true.

Dated   23 December 2002
Signature   C. Francis

I live at an address known to the Police, and I live there with my five-year-old daughter, Rochelle. I have lived there for the past four and a half years. I am married to Raymond Francis, although I am proceeding with a divorce, which has been to court, and I am awaiting a completion date.

My married life with Raymond began in 1996, and throughout our relationship, he has been violent towards me.

This has gone on for some years, although I have had him arrested for this but not prosecuted for any offence on me. I began divorce proceedings in January this year, and since then, he has constantly harassed me by telephoning me and threatening me. He has access to our daughter every Saturday until Sunday at 7:00 P.M. I drop Rochelle off in the car park at Sava Centre in Sydenham, and I collect her from there. This is an arrangement we have had for the past 12 months. Unfortunately, Raymond has made direct threats towards me on occasions at Sava Centre, and he has recently continued in this vane by threatening to kill me. The threats have increased and the severity of the language and threats are increasing.

On November 29, 2002, I attended Bromley County Court to obtain full injunction order against Raymond. This is not the first injunction I have obtained, but it is the third one. Raymond has no respect for the injunctions or the court, and he was warned at the last occasion that he would be sent to prison should he breach this injunction. I am also aware that D. C. Duffus, at the court, warned him that he should not contact me, and he would be committing an offence under the Harassment Act. I am also aware that D. C. Duffus warned him back in July this year for the same offence of harassment.

Sainsbury's Sava Centre in Sydenham employs me, and he has attended my workplace. On Saturday, December 14, 2002, he telephoned me on my work telephone. I spoke to him, but he did not threaten me. He accused me of having another man and that he was living in my house. He told me that he was going to kill him and chop him up. He then said that my car was being driven by this other man, and he told me that what happened to my car the first two times is nothing compared to what will happen to it next time. I am seeing another man, but our relationship is in early stages. The last thing I want is him being involved in these incidents. He really is a quiet man. Raymond was ranting at me on the telephone, and I hung up on him. I realized that he would attend the shop, and I asked if I could go home. The manager, who is aware of the situation, sent me home, and about ten minutes after I returned home, Maggie Harris, who is my team leader at work, telephoned and told me that Raymond had attended the store. He was now on his way to my house. Maggie also told me that she was so frightened; she telephoned the police to have them attend my address. Raymond never attended at my house, but the police did.

Prior to this day, and since November 20, 2002, Raymond has bombarded me with telephone calls and threatened me with violence. He is aware that I am going to Jamaica on holiday in the early part of the year, and he has threatened me that he will have his cousin in Jamaica kill me. I am now extremely reluctant to go on this holiday as I am terrified of what could happen to me should I go. I believe that Raymond is saying these things to stop me from going on holiday, but I have a nagging doubt that he is capable of having someone harm me whilst I am away. I have received a large number of telephone calls on my home telephone number since November 29, 2002, and these calls have started from him saying he wants be back and he wants us to start again. I have refused this, and he had gone on to threatening me that he will harm me. It has got to the stage that I have contacted D. C. Duffus directly and asked for him to intervene and stop Raymond from harassing me. I am terrified of what he will do to me. I now live with my lights on in the house, and sleeping is very difficult. I really fear that Raymond is on the brink of carrying out his threats, and I am more terrified of him now than I have ever been. I believe that Raymond has a mental problem, and he has no respect for anyone except himself and Rochelle. He has never threatened to harm our daughter. I had arranged to see D. C. Duffus today at Ladywell to make this statement.

On Saturday, December 21, I dropped Rochelle off at the SavaCentre, Sydenham, at about 3:30 P.M., and I took Christine Knight, a friend of mine, with me. As I entered the car park, I could not see his car. All of a sudden, Christine said, "There he is, coming towards us." He appeared as if he was about to ram me, but he stopped and pulled into one of the bays. I then left my car, took Rochelle's bags from my boot, and placed them into the back of his car. He asked me to get in to his car as I put Rochelle into the car, but I said "No." He said, "See you, see you, I can smell your death." He then went on to explain that he was making a big tool at work to kill me with. He works in an engineering plant in Kent. I walked back to my car. He followed me on foot, and he said, "You have brought a witness with you. Is that your witness?" I got back into my car and drove home. The telephone rang, and I left it. However, Christine's two-year-old son picked it up. Christine took it from him. It was Raymond. He was swearing at the little boy and Christine, and she hung the telephone up.

On Sunday, December 22, I ended up my shift at work at 8:00 P.M., and I went home to telephone him to let him know that I had finished my shift. This was the usual arrangement. I will telephone him to let him know, and he would then attend the SavaCentre Car Park. Yesterday, he did not answer his telephone. I left a message that I was at home, and I asked him to drop Rochelle off at the entrance to my close rather than the SavaCentre. This was because of what happened on Saturday, and I cannot face going into the SavaCentre Car Park at that time alone. The car park would have been dark, and no one would have been about. I really feared that he might attempt to harm me.

Then, at about 9:00 P.M., Raymond telephoned me, said, "Pick up point, fifteen minutes," and then hang up. I sat there at home and did not move as I was terrified. He telephoned back, about 9:30 P.M. and said, "Are you coming to collect Rochelle?" I told him that I was not and could he drop her at the close. He said, "Come and get her, you coward, and I will rip half of your face off." He then kept on saying, "I'm going to get you." He must have said that at least ten times. It was the way he was saying it which concerned me most.

I hung up. He telephoned me back, called me names, and then said, "I will kill you, if it is the last thing that I do before I die." I hung up again. He telephoned me about five or six times more during the night, was repeating his threats to me as I have previously said. He did not drop Rochelle, and he still has her. I do not believe that he will harm Rochelle, as it seems to me that I am his target. I even offered for him to drop off Rochelle at a friend's house, but he refused. I have not seen Rochelle since Saturday, although I feel that she is not at risk with him.

I can only describe the last three weeks as the worst time of my life. Raymond really has made an effort to put me in fear, and

I feel that he is capable of attacking me and causing me great harm. I am living a life of fear, and I cannot take anymore. He has threatened to damage my car again and had told me that I have been hiding it, which I have as a result of the amount of damage it has received recently.

I am more than willing to attend court, as I feel that he will not stop and he will harm me.

THESE ARE THE ORIGINAL STATEMENTS

OF:-

D. C. DUFFUS

> **Witness Statement**
> (CJ Act 1967, s.9 MC Act 19780, ss.5A (3) 9a) and 5B; MC rules 1981, r.70)
>
> Statement of H Duffus
>
> Age if under 18 'over 18' (if over 18 insert over 18') Occupation: Detective Constable
>
> This statement (consisting of two pages, each signed by me) is true to the best of my knowledge and belief, and I make it knowing that, if it is tendered in evidence, I shall be liable to prosecution, if I have wilfully stated anything which I know to be false or do not believe to be true.
>
> Signature   Dated

On Monday, December 23, 2002, I was on duty at Lewisham Police Station. I spoke to a woman I know to be Carol FRANCIS. I obtained a full statement from her. As a result of that statement, I attended a shop in Malpas Road and spoke to a man I now know to be Mike FRANCIS, and I asked where his brother, Raymond, was with his daughter. He telephoned a number and gave the telephone to me. I said, "Is that you, Raymond?"

He said, "Get off my case and fuck off. Leave me alone." He then hung up the telephone. I asked the brother where he was, and we made our way to 9 Lanyard House, SE8. I asked for assistance from uniformed officers. I arrived at the scene with D. C. EDDINGTON and attempted to gain entry to the premises. However, there was no occupier. I then telephoned the brother, and he told me that he had spoken to Raymond and he was in the apartment. After some time, Miss FRANCIS (Mike's wife) arrived. We gained access with keys, and we entered the apartment. Raymond FRANCIS was bathing his five-year-old in the bathroom, and I asked him to come out and speak with me. After about three to four minutes, he came out, and I said, "I am arresting you for harassment of Carol FRANCIS and for the threats you have made to her." He was cautioned at 1:20 P.M. There was no reply. He was handcuffed rear stack (handcuffs 362425) to custody at Lewisham Police station, arriving at 1:35 P.M. Facts to PS 76PL after delivering Rochelle to her mother at Lewisham. On

Monday, December 23, 2002, at 4:20 P.M, I was on duty in plain clothes at Lewisham Police Station, in the custody suite. I was present when Raymond FRANCIS was charged with the offence of harassment. The charge was read over, and he was further cautioned, to which he made no reply.

Witness Statement
(CJ Act 1967, s.9 MC Act 19780, ss.5A (3) 9a) and 5B; MC rules 1981, r.70)

Statement of H. Duffus

Age if under 18 'over 18' (if over 18 insert over 18) Occupation: Detective Constable

This statement (consisting of one page, each signed by me) is true to the best of my knowledge and belief and I make it knowing that, if it is tendered in evidence, I shall be liable to prosecution if I have wilfully stated anything which I know to be false or do not believe to be true.

Dated   23 December 2002
Signature: H Duffus D C

On Monday, December 23, 2002, between 3:27 PM and 3:50 P.M., I interviewed Raymond Francis in the presence of his solicitor, Mr. J. Rayment. The interview was conducted on tape. I sealed that tape with T2931636A, and I produced that tape as exhibit HAD/1. I was present when he was charged and cautioned at 4:20 P.M., but he made no reply.

I then completed a SDN of that interview, which I produce as exhibit HAD/2.
Signature   Signature witnessed by

Statement of Judy before the Trial

I, Mrs. Judy Maxwell, of Hollywood House, Denver Street, London,
WILL STATE AS FOLLOWS:
I am now aged thirty-four, having been born on November 20, 1968.

I currently reside at the above address, and I am employed as a PA at Lewisham College.

I do not have any previous convictions or cautions, and indeed, I have never been arrested.

I have been requested by my brother, Raymond Francis, and the solicitors currently acting for him if I would be prepared to attend court and give evidence at any time on or after June 23, 2003 concerning the matter for which he is to stand trial.

I understand that Raymond is charged with an offence of harassment toward Carol Francis, his estranged wife, and that the offences said have taken place between November 28, 2002 and December 24, 2002. I confirmed that I would be so prepared, and on the June 5, 2003, I provided the following information.

I should say at the outset that I first met the complainant, Carol Francis, before she was married to my brother, Raymond. I was aware that they married in March 1996.

I would describe Carol as a nice person, and we got on perfectly well until the incidents in question which I would deal with and which took place on December 3, 2002.

Both Carol and myself had children, and we therefore had something in common. I had two children.

I was able to confirm that, although I was aware of the difficulties between Raymond and Carol, I did not know that they were going to get divorced until near Christmas of 2002.

The first difficulty that I really knew of any major significance between them was after he had been arrested.

I am aware that on December 22, 2002, Raymond came to see me together with his daughter, Rochelle Francis. Prior to Raymond visiting me, I had left a message on his mobile phone for him to call me. When I asked Raymond if he had got my message, he explained that he was experiencing problems with his phone and did not seem to be getting his messages. A short while after this conversation, his messages started to come through. At around 7:00 P.M., I received a telephone call from Carol who asked if Raymond was there. I said that he was, and she then explained that she had phoned his mobile, and he had not responded. I explained to Carol that I had also left a message on Raymond's phone, but he was experiencing problems with it and had only received messages a short while ago. Carol asked me not to tell Raymond that she had called, so I did not as I did not want to get involved in differences between them.

At around 9:00 P.M. that evening, I received a call from Carol who told me that Raymond and herself had been arguing and that she did not want to go and meet Raymond in the SavaCentre car park. I told Carol that it was too late for Raymond to have Rochelle out, and that they should not be arguing in front of her. I told Carol that I would telephone Raymond and tell him to bring Rochelle back to my Brother Mike's house where Raymond was living, and he should bring her back in the morning. Carol agreed. I therefore telephoned Raymond, and he took Rochelle home.

Following my brother's arrest by police on December 23, 2002, my other brother telephoned me to say that Raymond had been arrested. I then telephoned Carol to ask her what it was all about, and she told me that they had been involved in an argument. I could confirm that I had not spoken to Carol since.

I was, as stated, willing and able to attend Woolwich Crown Court in order to give evidence on behalf of my brother if so required.

Statement of Mrs. Judy Maxwell during the trial:

September 10, 2003

I was waiting outside the courtroom during July/August (trial actually took place on July 2.) as I had not given my evidence yet. Everyone started coming out of the court. My sister, Jane, came down from the public gallery and said that there was going to be a retrial, and that the jury had to be changed as D. C. Duffus's statement had been misleading to the jury.

As we had not booked an appointment for Raymond that week, my sister decided that we had better make a booking. Jane took out her mobile phone and called the booking service. Someone picked the phone up, but when Jane said, "I would like to make a booking for Raymond Francis," she was told that the booking line was closed and that she should call back later.

When D. C. Duffus heard that Jane was making a call to book a visit for Raymond, he immediately called Carol, saying, "Hello, Carol, it's me. Looks like there is going to be a retrial. You need to remember (memorise) dates and times. It's important that you get hold of Maggie. You need to remember dates and times." He then asked, "What are you doing now?" She must have replied that she was going out as he said, "I will come round and see you later."

- Unprofessional to discuss the case in front of Raymond's family members.
- They were too friendly. (D. C. Duffus's body language.) "Hello, Carol, it's me."
- Going to her house to discuss the case (Why not at the police station?).

Statement of Raymond Francis's complaint after the trial regarding: D. C. Duffus

In The Matter Of Mr. Raymond Francis's
Complaint/Claim against Metropolitan Police Service (MPS)

STATEMENT OF MR. RAYMOND FRANCIS

1. My name is Raymond Francis. I am making this statement in support of my complaint against D.C. Duffus of the Metropolitan Police Service, Lewisham Borough Division.
2. My complaint is about the unprofessional and malicious manner in which DC Duffus conducted himself, leading to and during my trial at the Woolwich Crown Court. On November 29, 2002, I attended the Bromley Family Court in the matter of my ex-wife's application for an injunction against me. Although to the best of my knowledge and belief, this matter had nothing to do with the police, D. C. Duffus was present in court.
3. After the hearing, I took my jacket and hat and left the courtroom. D.C. Duffus followed me and said to me that, "If you breathe heavy on Carol, I would come on you like a ton of bricks." I just laughed and left the court building.
4. On December 23, 2002, between 12:30 P.M. and 13:00 P.M., D.C. Duffus and some other police officers came to my brother's house where I was staying and arrested me. I was bathing my daughter at the time of my arrest.
5. Prior to arresting me, on December 23, 2002, I received a telephone call from D.C. Duffus. This was at about noon. He asked for my name, and I asked who he was. He told me his name, and I then said to him, "Get off my case, you couch potato."
6. When D.C. Duffus arrested me, he said to me, "All I wanted to do was to talk, but because you are too cheeky, you are going to prison." He said this to me at the police station.

7. I had been in custody since I was arrested on December 23, 2002 until when I was acquitted and discharged on July 7, 2003. During this period, I lost my liberty and my job, my health deteriorated, and I suffered severe psychological conditions including depression and stress. On three occasions, I tried to take my life, and I was placed on "suicide watch" for a month.
8. I believe that this happened to me because of the unprofessional and malicious manner in which D.C. Duffus had conducted himself. I believe that D.C. Duffus did not investigate the allegations against me properly. His intention all along was to have me sent to prison maliciously. His intentions became very clear from the way he conducted himself during the trial.

Signed: *R. A. Francis*   Raymond Francis
Date: 1/9/03

IPCC REPORT next page

My dear friends, please study the IPCC Report thorougly. You would find, in this chapter, enough evidence to tell you that D. C. Duff was up to no good. However, the witnesses that saw him suddenly appears to have been put into silence, in my opinion. Although he was seen with Mrs. Francis engaging in an inappropriate behaviour in the court building, i.e., having a kiss and a cuddle, the evidence seemed to have disappeared!

The law protected itself from the public eye. How did D. C. Duffus get away with it? Frankly, I was stunned. What do you think?

IPCC Report of their investigation of my complaint

Mr. R. Francis

IPCC
independent
police complaints
commission

90 High Holborn
London WC1V 6BH
Tel 020 7166 3000
Fax 020 7404 0430
E-mail: enquiries@ipcc.gsi.gov.uk
Web: www.ipcc.gov.uk

IPCC Contact Toby Pragasam
Casework Manager
Your Reference
Our Reference IPCC/PCA/4336

Date   15 July 2005

Dear Mr. Francis,

I am writing about the complaint you made against the police on 23 December 2002.

Your complaint has been investigated by the Metropolitan Police Service. The investigation was then reviewed by a chief officer and has now been submitted to the Independent Police Complaints Commission, which replaced the Police complaints Authority on 1 April 2004. The role of the IPCC, which is totally independent of the police service, is to satisfy itself that the complaint has been properly investigated, and to decide if there is sufficient evidence to justify misconduct proceedings against any officer.

As explained in the enclosed notes, the IPCC is required to review the investigation under the rules that applied to the Police Complaints Authority, as your complaint was recorded prior to 1 April 2004.

The investigation into your complaint:

You made a statement, dated 1 September 2003, and subsequently made a follow up statement in order to clarify your complaints. You have complained that:

i. D. C. Duffus attended the Bromley Family Court for an unknown reason and used intimidatory language against you.
ii. D. C. Duffus used excessive force when handcuffing you and then laughed when you asked him to loosen them.
iii. D. C. Duffus wrongfully arrested you on 23 December 2002.
iv. D. C. Duffus abused his authority by advising Ms. Francis not to let your daughter see you in prison.
v. D. C. Duffus deliberately misled Woolwich Crown Court, giving him time to "coach" Ms. Francis in giving evidence
vi. D. C. Duffus conducted an unprofessional and malicious investigation against you.

D. C. Duffus has been interviewed under caution in response to your complaint.

The relevant police records have been obtained, including a copy of the original complaint form.

i. **D. C. Duffus attended the Bromley Family Court for an unknown reason and used intimidatory language against you**

The solicitor who represented Ms Francis in the family court states that she requested D. C. Duffus to attend the hearing. As they left the court, the solicitor says that D. C. Duffus approached you and gave you a formal harassment warning. She says that she clearly heard the officer give you this official warning, and maintains that he did not make any threats towards you.

D. C. Duffus has been interviewed under caution in response to your complaint. He states that he attended the court after being requested to do so by Ms. Francis' solicitor, in case he was needed to give evidence. At the end of the hearing, D. C. Duffus says that he went over and gave you a final harassment warning.

He denies saying any of the words that you attribute to him. In response, he says that you told him to "Fuck off."

Ms. Francis corroborates that above accounts. She recalls D. C. Duffus following you out of the courtroom. When D. C. Duffus returned, Ms. Francis states that he told her and her solicitor that he had given you a final warning.

There is no independent evidence to support your account of events.

ii. <u>D. C. Duffus used excessive force when handcuffing you and then laughed when you asked him to loosen them.</u>

D. C. Duffus cannot recall whether it was he who handcuffed you when the police came to your address on 23 December 2002. From his incident report book, he is able to state that you were handcuffed to the rear and then taken to custody by uniformed officers. He maintains that the arrest was carried out in a professional manner and denies that he refused to loosen the handcuffs or laughed when you asked him to. He suggests that you were handcuffed because the violent nature of the allegation against you suggested that you could be a threat to the officers' safety.

A police constable who assisted in your arrest 23 December 2002 has provided a witness statement. He says that you initially locked yourself in and would not answer or open the door. The officer cannot recall who handcuffed you nor does he remember you complaining about them being too tight at the time. He maintains that it was not D. C. Duffus who handcuffed you and also suggest that this officer did not accompany you back to custody.

A doctor examined you on 23 December 2002 at Lewisham Police Station where you complained of police brutality. The doctor states that you had handcuff bruises over your right wrist, but that the skin was not broken and there was no swelling. He suggested that you would have been fully recovered after a few hours.

There is a degree of uncertainty as to which officer it was who actually handcuffed you. Furthermore, D. C. Duffus has provided adequate reasoning for the use of handcuffs. There is no independent evidence to support either your account or that of the officers whilst the doctor's evidence does not suggest that there were any significant wrist injuries.

iii. D. C. Duffus wrongfully arrested you on 23 December 2002.

On 23 December 2002, Ms. Francis attended Ladywell Police Station and provided a full statement detailing the ways in which you had harassed her. It is not necessary for a warning to be issued prior to arrest under the harassment Act. However, D. C. Duffus states that he did give you a warning at Bromley Family Court on 29 November 2002. This has been corroborated by two other witnesses.

Section 24 of the Police and criminal Evidence Act 2984 gives a police officer the power of arrest for an arrestable offence. You had previously breached four court orders against you.

D. C. Duffus therefore states that he considered there to be sufficient evidence to arrest and interview you. Furthermore, he says that he believed that without police intervention, you would have killed your wife.

Your detention was also authorized by the custody sergeant at Lewisham Police Station. The evidence suggests that D. C. Duffus was within his powers to arrest you under the Harassment Act on 23 December 2002.

iv. D. C. Duffus abused his authority by advising Ms. Francis not to let your daughter see you in prison.

In relationship to your daughter visiting you in prison, Ms. Francis says that she sought advice from her solicitor and mentioned it to D. C. Duffus. She denies that the officer influenced her decision in any way.

Ms. Francis's solicitor also recalls giving Ms. Francis advice in relation to this issue.

D. C. Duffus recalls Ms. Francis mentioning this issue to him, but says that he believed that she had already made up her mind. He admits saying to Ms. Francis that visiting prison would not be a pleasant experience for Rochelle, as she would probably be searched.

There is insufficient evidence to suggest that D. C. Duffus abused his authority in relation to this aspect of your complaint.

v. <u>D. C. Duffus deliberately mislead Woolwich Crown Court, giving him time to "coach" Ms. Francis in giving evidence.</u>

Ms. Ghantiloupe has also provided a statement under caution. She suggests that D. C. Duffus intentionally caused a retrial in order to give him time to "coach" Ms Francis in giving evidence. At the retrial, Ms. Ghantiloupe says that Ms. Francis was much more confident and was able to remember specific times and dates in relation to the evidence.

Ms. Francis has denied that D. C. Duffus gave her any help whatsoever in terms of the evidence that she gave in court.

D. C. Duffus maintains that although he was aware that an agreement had been breached between the prosecution and defence counsels, he was not willing to answer any questions dishonestly in court. He also denies "coaching" Ms. Francis in giving evidence or even seeing her at any time between the two trials. The officer admits calling Ms. Francis when he left the courtroom, but says that he just wanted to explain to her why there had to be a retrial and to inform her that they should attempt to get another witness to testify.

The prosecution and defence counsels have both stated that they had come to an agreement before the trial that there would be no mention of your conduct during your criminal interview. The prosecution counsel has stated that D. C. Duffus simply answered the questions asked of him in an honest way and suggests that the office inadvertently mentioned the interview, contrary to his instructions. The defence counsel is critical of D. C. Duffus and suggests that one of his answers led to the retrial.

They typed transcription from Woolwich Crown Court that outlines the judge's address to the jury. The judge stated that there had been a misunderstanding but that "this is not a criticism of anybody…. it is just what happened in this case." This transcript also shows that D. C. Duffus apologised to the judge and stated that there was no intent on his part to mislead the court.

There is insufficient evidence to suggest that D. C. Duffus deliberately caused a retrial or that he coached Ms. Francis in giving evidence.

vi. <u>D. C. Duffus conducted an unprofessional and malicious investigation against you.</u>

You have suggested that D. C. Duffus had an inappropriately friendly relationship with Ms. Francis and that this biased the officer's investigation.

Both D. C. Duffus and Ms. Francis have firmly denied these allegations.

The defence counsel has suggested that two witnesses saw D. C. Duffus and Ms. Francis engaging in inappropriate behaviour in the court building. However, she refused to provide contact details of these witnesses, but stated that one of them was a member of the court staff.

Enquiries were made with solicitors, firms, and court staff who were present during your trial. No one recalled seeing any inappropriate contact between Ms. Francis and D. C. Duffus.

The prosecution counsel has stated that D. C. Duffus is a "naturally enthusiastic officer" and that he "was very pleased with the way he had investigated [this] particular case."

There is a lack of independent evidence to suggest that D. C. Duffus conducted an unprofessional or malicious investigation.

We note from the file that the investigation was submitted to the Crown Prosecution Service, which independently reviewed the evidence and decided that there was no realistic prospect of conviction of any officer involved.

The Commission's Provisional Decision
On the evidence available, the IPCC is not satisfied that there is a realistic prospect that a tribunal would find that the conduct of the office felt below the required standard. We are therefore minded to conclude that misconduct of proceedings cannot be justified.

Your Right to Comment

As explained above, your complaint was investigated by the police, and the summary in this letter is based on the police investigation that I have reviewed. Before the IPCC makes a final decision, we wish to give you the opportunity to comment and to send any further information or evidence you may have. If I do not hear from you within that time, the IPCC will make a final decision.

I enclose a reply form which sets out the choices open to you. Please use this form if you wish to comment. You can also telephone the number at the top of this letter if you want more information.

Yours sincerely,

Toby Pragasam
Casework Manager
For the Commission

EXPLANATORY NOTES

The accompanying letter informs you of the provisional decision on the investigation into your complaint against the police. A copy of the letter has been sent to your solicitor, if you have one. Although the investigation was undertaken by the police, the final decision on your complaint must be taken not by the police but by the Independent Police Commission. We, not the police, are responsible for writing to you to summarize the findings and conclusions of the investigation and reporting to you on the disciplinary action, if any, which it is proposed should be taken against the officer(s) you complained about. You have an opportunity, and the enclosed letter tells you how to go about doing this and the time limit for doing so.

The Independent Police Commission replaced the PCA on 1 April 2004 and is totally independent of the police service. As the enclosed note explains, the legal powers IPCC has with regards to your case are found in the Police Act 1996. Its Commissioners come from different backgrounds but none have been employed by the police either as a police officer or in a civilian capacity.

Our purpose is to see that a complaint made about the conduct of a serving police officer is dealt with fairly, thoroughly, and objectively. When reviewing investigations, the IPCC must have regard to the evidence gathered, to law, and to the provisions of the Police Code of Conduct. If it considers that more information is reasonably required before it is able to finalize its decision, then it has the power to seek this from the police.

Allegation of Criminal Conduct by a Police Officer

In some cases (such as where the complaint is of an assault or theft), the Crown Prosecution Service (CPS) will have considered whether the evidence gathered during the investigation of that complaint justifies the officer facing criminal proceedings. If this applied in the case of your complaint, you may already have been told of the CPS's decision. Any disciplinary outcome resulting from a complaint is only considered after the question of criminal prosecution has been decided, and any trial has taken place.

The Investigation Review

When reviewing an investigation and the recommendations made to it by the police, the Commission is not bound to adopt the conclusions of the investigation officer nor does it have to agree to those recommendations. If the police force has not already proposed this, and there is evidence to support what you allege, the IPCC has the legal power to recommend to the force that an officer's conduct should be referred to a disciplinary hearing (called a misconduct tribunal). It can direct this to happen if the police force refuses to accept a recommendation.

Standard of Proof

However, before the IPCC can recommend or direct formal misconduct proceedings, we must be satisfied that there is a realistic prospect of showing that the officer's behaviour has fallen below the standards set out in the Police Code of Conduct. This has to be proved on a balance of probabilities, which means that the tribunal must decide that it is more likely than not that an allegation is true. The degree of proof required increases with the gravity of what is alleged. A serious allegation, for example, of an unprovoked assault causing injury, will need to be proved to a high degree of probability.

Other Disciplinary Action

Many complaints, even if supported by the evidence to the required standard of proof, do not justify, in the public interest, an officer facing a formal hearing, and in these cases, the IPCC can propose that an officer be given a formal written warning or "Advice" (a police term equivalent to an oral warning) by a senior office. A formal written warning will be recorded for twelve months on the officer's personnel record. Even if the evidence does not reach the required standard, we may propose that an officer should receive guidance or further training to prevent a recurrence of the incident or behaviour giving rise to your complaint.

This is the end of the authentic statements submitted by author.

This is my dear daughter, Rochelle, aged four years old. This photo was my inspiration for living, my hope for the future, when I was in HM Prison Belmarsh. Each night, I would always look at it before going to sleep

RAYMOND FRANCIS
PRISON NO: HP 6441
4 Jan 03
<u>Letter to Rochelle during Incarceration:</u>

My Dear Rochelle,
    I wish you were older because I know you would understand. I am still in prison. In fact, Christmas and New Year, prison has been my home. It is not a very nice place, but what can I say? Anyway, my sweet, I am thinking about you, as always. I miss you so much. I feel a pain in my heart. Today is Saturday. Every Saturday, I normally pick you up and take you swimming or shopping, then take you to the fun park, and then take you to uncle Mike where I give you a bath and feed you, then put you to bed and read you a story. When you fall asleep, I used to enjoy watching you sleep, thinking to myself, my pretty little baby. Rochelle, you are only five years old. Did you know you are my best friend? Believe it or not, you are. For the past two weeks in prison, the love I have for you kept me alive. Rochelle, I don't know what I am going to do, how am I going to face life without you? That's why I said I wish you were older. Up to the day of my arrest, I try to be the best dad to you. At this point, I feel as if I've let you down. Your Christmas present is still in the car. I feel so bad. It's not my fault, you will see one day.
    Rochelle, my dear, I know that one day you will go looking for daddy, and when that day comes, I will be waiting for you because I've always loved you, and I always will. Rochelle, even if you find a gravestone with my name on it, I want you to know that your daddy loved you. I will always keep you in my thoughts and in my heart until the day I die. Rochelle, my dear daughter, one day we will meet again, and the choice will be yours. As I said, you are too young to understand at age five. I wish you all the best in school and whatever you do in life until we meet again. Rochelle, my dear daughter, I will always love you.
    My love is yours; the love of God is ours

Love you always,
Dad, xxx

This artefact was made by myself as an expression of my love for my daughter, whom I love deeply, in case I did not leave prison alive.

All praises be to Allah for bringing me forth to see the dawning of a new day.

Chapter Three
Trial and Imprisonment
Francis
V.
Francis

December 23, 2002. Mission accomplished for Carol! She finally cracked it to have me arrested. Her revenge on me had now started to flourish. I was arrested at 1:00 P.M., December 23, 2002, by a man calling himself D. C. Duffus. He was approximately twenty stones in weight, more like a refrigerator with a head. Duffus thought he was playing a role in Tom Cruise's movie, "Minority Report," where potential criminals were arrested before the crime had happened. That was exactly what he did; it was almost like a joke! I asked myself, "Under what 'act' was I arrested?" D. C. Duffus claimed that I was a danger to the public. I gathered he arrested me under the "mental health act" due to the fact that I must had been mental to find myself with such a floozy. Another question I asked myself was, being arrested under the mental health act I presume, "Why did I have no form of medication to protect me from myself and the public?" Therefore, this arrest was purely malicious. He arrested me whilst I was bathing my child. I was handcuffed and dragged away, leaving my four-year-old daughter covered in soap. I really wondered what was going through my little girl's mind when she saw eight policemen and the so-called detective dragging her daddy down the stairs with his hands cuffed behind his back. I was taken to Ladywell Police Station where I was fingerprinted, photographed, and a D.N.A sample was taken. For the first time in my life, I could not believe what was happening to me. I was also interviewed by a duty solicitor from the firm Ewing. I did believe that the so-called solicitor was working with Duffus because he did me no favours. This must had been a traumatic experience for little Rochelle in the same week when she suffered the trauma of finding herself wandering alone on the platform of West Wickham train station, not knowing where to turn. She was discovered by the platform assistant whilst her mother was at home, entertaining her male friend. My dear friends, could you imagine a four-year-old child getting on a train from lower Sydenham to West Wickham in search of her daddy whilst still in her nappies? She had recently revealed to me at the age of ten that she left home that day because she wanted to be with me. The impact of hearing these words did not fail to bring tears to my eyes. It was days after she was found in West Wickham. Her birthday was due. I did what every loving father would do for an adorable daughter. I went to her school and asked the teacher's permission to have a party for her fourth birthday. The teachers were delighted that I took such an interest in my daughter, knowing my predicament, and gave me permission without hesitation. They also said that they wish that some of the other parents would do the same for their children. Yet, it was alleged by Carol in court during the trial that I had gone to Rochelle's school and disrupt the classroom, and the teachers were very upset by this. If that was the case, how could I have entered the school in the first place? There was the security. The security at the school was very stringent. There was an entry door system and also a CCTV at each entrance and exit. How could I possibly get in the school to have a party without the teacher's permission? I found the allegation by Carol incredibly malicious. My solicitor contacted Adamsrill School and found that Carol was lying as usual. The reason for Carol to lie like this on oath, I would never know, but I guess God knows.

I was taken to Ladywell Police Station in the back of a van. When I got to the station, for some odd reason, the handcuff were removed in the courtyard before I entered the building. This was done to disguise the fact that I was handcuffed, so the superiors had no knowledge that I was handcuffed. Apparently, this is done to most black males when they are arrested. I complained on several occasions during the journey that the cuffs were very tight; both of my wrists were badly bruised and swollen. I was interviewed by D. C. Duffus in the presence of a solicitor from the firm Ewing. During the interview, I was very exasperated because of what had happened to me. I could not imagine that such a crazy thing could happen to someone of my nature. After the interview, I was examined by a doctor who claimed to have found no substantial injuries. Obviously, it was a police doctor. I was then thrown into a cell where I stayed for the night. Indeed, it was a night to remember! During that night, I was severely stressed beyond my limit. I heard different types of abuse through the flap of the cell door. Some of these abuses were racial, and some were calling me the wrong name; I guess to annoy me or to provoke a reaction. I rang the bell, and it was answered one hour later. They were not interested in the cause as to why I was ringing. The flap of the cell door slammed open, and a voice shouted, "What do you want? It had better be good," then slammed shut the door again.

I then decided that I came to the end of the road. I took from my pocket a charge sheet which stated "kidnapping and harassment." I tore the paper into hundreds of tiny pieces, and I then use the little pieces of paper to write on the floor as in white pebbles from a birds eye view.

I wrote, *Goodbye, Rochelle. I will always love you. Dad.* At this point, there was no doubt in my mind that I was going to kill myself. I took the laces from my trainers, tied them round my neck, and started to pull. Yes, I was beyond being traumatised; I became a deranged man!'

I almost succeeded because I remember feeling very dizzy as I fell to the uncomfortable piece of plastic that was meant to be the bed. The cell door opened and a voice shouted, "What the fuck do you think you are doing? You stupid bastard!"

From that point onwards, I was on suicide watch. They removed the laces from my shoes and all the items that could be use for self-harm. The next day, I was whizzed to Greenwich Court where I asked to see a solicitor, which I did, one from the same firm, Ewing, who had spoken to me previously. On reflection, I was charged with kidnapping and harassment. Between the station and the first court appearance for pleas and direction, one of the charges had disappeared. I had now only to answer to the harassment charge. I guessed D. C. Duffus was in a state of panic, but that I would never know. It came out in court on the night before my arrest.

Carol's car was badly damaged, believe it or not, my dear friends, right outside her front door. It was alleged that the vandal was myself. In fact, D. C. Duffus had investigated this thoroughly using the forensics team that was at this disposal, purely to impress, of course! There was no D.N.A. or footprints found that belonged to Raymond Francis. The allegations had exhausted themselves because it was alleged also, that there was no question about the vandal. "Raymond Francis had plastic bags on his feet, and he was wearing a mask," said D. C. Duffus and his forensic team. My dear friends, I wonder if D. C. Duffus meant to say "Sudbury's bags!" It was due to the fact that his girlfriend, Carol, at the time, worked for Sudbury's—pathetic fools.

I do not think he had any payment in kindness that night from Carol. What a joke! My dear friends, it was quite simple. I had nothing to do with the vandalisation of Carol's car, but it was alleged that I was the vandal. Who knows? Could it not have been Duffus himself just to score points? Think about it.

Carol called the police to collect Rochelle the night before my arrest. D. C. Duffus was not on duty at that time. Carol was told by an officer that the police was not a taxi service. The next day, I was arrested for the above allegations. Why didn't the police arrest me on the December 22, 2002 when Carol called them? If I had committed a crime, indeed, I would expect to be arrested. D. C. Duffus was not available on that day, a Sunday. Question: Could any other officer make an arrest on the Sunday?

It was clear to me, and the blind man, that D. C. Duffus was acting on personal grounds.

The solicitor asked if I had anyone who would stand bail for me. I gave my brother's details, the same brother who had given me shelter at the time. The solicitor contacted my brother and asked for surety. Indeed, he agreed. However, I was not granted bail because D. C. Duffus thought I was far too dangerous to be let loose on the streets of London. On reflection, Under what context? I asked. Damn liberty! I was not granted bail, and to my utmost shock, I was taken to Belmarsh, AA category, maximum-security prison. For what, may I ask? I do believe D. C. Duffus had manipulated the law to suit himself for sexual gain—that was what it was all about. He was getting sexual gratification from a vulnerable Jamaican woman who, unfortunately, for me, was my wife at the time. I guess he just had to do what he had to do to prolong his pleasure. I arrived at Belmarsh. I was taken to the hospital unit of the prison where I was placed in a dormitory that housed six prisoners. Dangerous prisoners were kept in cells by themselves, but stressed, suicidal, or ones with any other mental illnesses were placed in a six-prisoner cell where there was constant closed circuit television (CCTV) in operation, even when you go the toilet. How about that for a luxury hotel? After one month of being in this hospital unit, I started meeting some very interesting people. One night, while I watched the news about a hardcore paedophile, he was then in the exercise yard, rubbing shoulders with me the next day.

One interesting person that I must mention with high respect was Sir Ronnie Biggs, the great train robber. I found him to be a very interesting person. However, I disagreed with the way in which he was treated during my stay. They had taken his dignity away from him, and I truly believe it was wrong. We were all in the hospital wing because, obviously, some of us were sick and some had other problems. Feeding a man through a tube in his side in front of all the other inmates was something I found very distasteful. I was sure other inmates take this as cheap entertainment, but again, British justice had raised its head. On reflection of the British justice, a very close acquaintance of mine got arrested. He was thrown in prison for rape. On visiting him, I learnt that it was he and three women, an experience that I myself would have liked. Unfortunately, the women, together, made up a story and accused him of rape. In the News Today, on June 2007, it was said that since 2001, 1300 cases of rape was let off with a caution. Rape to me was quite a serious act that should be dealt with severely by the law. The question was, What did I do in 2002 to end up in Belmarsh maximum-security prison as an A category prisoner? That was the question.

My dear friends, could you imagine one man raping three women at the same time? My acquaintance gave me vivid details of the incident with the three women. Although he was explaining to me what had happened in a prison as environment, my imagination wandered, putting me in his shoes at the time. I really couldn't see how a man could be put in prison for having sex with three women with the use of condoms and performing orally. It was virtually impossible. All that I could say was that his legal team were total shit. They were working with the police to get a conviction. I did believe at this point, if I might take the liberty of saying, that my colleague was entitled to a retrial. However, I don't think he would ever get that because of the British injustice. I do not think I would ever have three women in a bed, but then, I guess that was every man's fantasy. My acquaintance had that opportunity, and he is still, at present, in prison in the Isle of Wight, serving ten years, believe it or not, because of British injustice! The objective of the police was to fill the prisons with as much blacks as possible because to them, blacks were simply monkeys that belonged in cages. On saying that, statistics showed that three-quarters of young black men were on the D.N.A. crime file register. This is outrageous!

I observed Ronnie Biggs being fed on several occasions with whatever they were pouring in the tubes that led from his side to his stomach. The contents oftentimes overspill and made a terrible mess; the so-called care assistant who executed his feeding showed no interest in him as a person. I do believe they had no idea what they were doing. I may add that these assistants appeared to have no training.

I asked them, "Why don't you clean him up?"

They replied, "This is a prison, in case you don't know."

Sir Ronnie Biggs was almost helpless. He had no use of his mouth to speak; he communicated by using an alphabet pad. He pointed at letters to make up words to say what he wanted. If you were quick, you could catch on to what he was trying to say. This was a very difficult and lengthy process for an able-bodied person, let alone a very ill man. He had little use of his arms. He signed several autographs for me, but I would like to add, What is a man like this doing in prison? This was called British justice I guess!

It was very difficult for me to sleep at nights because some of the inmates, I found to be total fruitcakes (mad). I saw a young man, once, cut his arm and pulled his vein out. It was almost unbelievable. I was amongst these people for a whole month because I was depressed and tried to commit suicide in the cell at Lewisham police station?

I have met an interesting character that went by the name Roland. This inmate appeared to be very much like a rat. During socialising and feeding times, when the cells were always left open, Roland would strike just like a rat nibbling on everything edible! I guess I would call him "Roland Rat." This was my opinion as he had all the characteristics of a rodent, hence the name, Roland Rat.

Another person I met was a young man aged seventeen years old. He was known as Denzel, housed in a padded cell. All night, he shouted and screamed from the window of his padded cell at the top of his voice, "Your mom sucks cock for a living," and all the abuse you could think of at its lowest form. During meal times, he would go past my cell that housed six men and guarded by four huge wardens. I always wondered, "Was this young man so dangerous?" But then, in this society, as long as the person was a black man, he will always be with six or more wardens. I was sure that a lot of brothers could relate to this, but why do some of us call the police on our own? The society we live in today—it was a known fact—is a police state, and the police got extra pleasure, as I happened to notice, when they break up a black or mixed-race family. Oftentimes, the police got their way with women from these broken families preying on the vulnerable, e.g., D. C. Duffus and co. One day, Denzel was shouting his usual expletives. I shouted back, telling him to shut up. He paused, and then said in a soft voice, "I can see you."

He was approximately four feet, eight inches tall and slim in built, but the words that came from his mouth were bigger than a mountain! Another interesting character that I had met called himself Count Dracula. I could not understand his reason for having such a name, but then, his appearance was rather Gothic. He appeared to be very friendly with all the prison officers, which I thought was a good thing. Apparently, he was transferred back to the hospital wing from house block three (HB3) because he was caught drinking blood. Whose blood? That was the question. This bloodsucker was released from prison. At the time of his release, I wished that it was me who got released. Lucky blood-sucking bastard, I thought to myself. He was released on a Friday, and believe it or not, the sucker was back in prison on the following Monday, after three days of freedom!

As he entered, the six-man bang-up, as they called it, he shouted, "Home sweet home."

He walked like a celebrity as the other inmates cheered and shouted, "Welcome back, 'Drac." The next day, I had the opportunity to speak to Count Dracula.

I asked him, "What are you doing back inside?"

His reply came back almost like a shock. He replied, "Have you ever tried living on the outside?" He appeared to have become institutionalised.

One day, an inmate came into the six-man cell with his throat half-cut. I took the opportunity to ask him what had happened. He told me he felt depressed after living in house block three for too long, so he tried to commit suicide. Apparently, HB3 was known as the worst block in the prison. He told me that one day, I would be sent there, and that really scared me. This inmate called himself "Ace of Spade." He was a white male with a black "A" tattooed on his forehead. He said, "Call me Ace, or don't call me at all."

One day, Ace attacked Mohammed; he almost killed him. Apparently, Mohammed went into Ace's cupboard and took a nude picture of Ace's pregnant wife. Ace told me he caught Mohammed masturbating whilst looking at the picture. I was shocked, but then, I was in a place that housed all categories—murderers, thieves, people with mental disorders, etc.

My transfer to HB3 came through. One morning, I got up. An officer came to me and said, "Today, you will be moving. Pack your stuff."

I nearly pissed myself with fright.

I packed my stuff into an HMP transparent bin liner. I was taken across to house block 3 where all the induction courses were started. Then from there, inmates were distributed to their appropriate blocks. House block 3 was also known as "Beirut." To me, HB3 was like the gates of hell itself. I was not saying I have been there, mind you, but I was sure, in everyone's mind, there was a rough idea of what hell was like. I was thrown into a cell where two inmates were waiting for a third person. I looked at the surrounding, and I suddenly went cold. I was literally walking in the valley of the shadow of death. I did not speak to the two inmates. It was obvious that I was on the top bed because that was the only bed that was available. The mattress had bloodstains and sweat patches (That is what I would like to think; the thought of sleeping on that bed makes my blood run cold) on it. Also, the walls were covered with pictures of nude women. I stood in the corner, looking through the oblong window that was approximately two feet high, six inches wide, and with bars parallel to each other. The gaps between each bar was two inches wide.

The two inmates stared at me, and I knew what they were thinking. One of them was Afro-Caribbean with dreadlocks. The other one looked like a vagrant; he had black teeth. I despised these two characters, but what choice did I have? I was locked up with them. I began staring back at them. The black one uttered these words: "What is your name, brother?" I replied, "My name is Ray, and I am not your brother."

The other inmate tried to join in by introducing his self. He stretched out his dirty hands, with black fingernails towards me as if he wanted to shake my hands.

He said, "My name is Rupert."

I replied, "I guess you are not the bear." He thought I was really funny.

Rupert said to me, "So what are you in for, bro?"

I said, "Would you really like to know?"

He replied, "Cheer up, my old son, this place is paradise. I have been in and out all my life."

Little did he know that I had a life. Looking at him was like associating with the living dead. I made the bed and climbed up. I lay there, thinking, What the hell am I doing here? I must have fallen asleep because the next thing I knew, it was the next day. Apparently, I have slept a good eighteen hours. All I wanted to do was just to sleep and sleep and sleep (sleep my prison life away); I was extremely depressed. After three days with these Muppets, I decided that I could not take any more, so I asked for a transfer, which I got. However, do you think the cell was any different from the previous one? What do you think? The cell was not any different, but the characters were. The new characters I met were very different; they both tried their best to make me laugh. Believe it or not, it was another black and another white inmate. They tend to mix them like that. The black inmate was of Jamaican origin. He was truly a character. In fact, he was a joker. This guy would do anything to make you smile, and if you didn't, he would get upset. I was not really interested in exchanging names because it was always in the back of my mind that I would be gone soon. The other inmate was white, and he did not say much. I got to know them after two months in a three-man bang-up. The black inmate was known as "Yardie," (I wondered why!) but the reason for his incarceration baffled me. He told me he was stopped in Brixton by a Black policeman. He was asked his name. He replied in a Jamaican accent, and that was the reason for his arrest. I nearly died of laughter when he told me. He said he was arrested because of his accent. Apparently, it turned out he was also an illegal immigrant with several aliases. He was put in prison until his true identity was revealed. I really could not believe what this young man had told me. We became mates briefly. He left for court, and another person was thrown into the cell. I never saw "Yardie" again. Prison worked this way—when you went to court, you got to take all your possessions with you because you never knew if you would be set free or would be returning to your cell. It was a horrible situation to be in. Nine times out of ten, you would lose your cell. However, I was quite lucky to be in the same cell for two months, not forgetting that I spent one month in the hospital unit.

I had several attempts to make bail, but each time I went for bail, I happened to see D. C. Duffus, the officer who was sleeping with my wife at the time. Could you imagine? If all the British police force were armed with guns, D. C. Duffus would have shot me in the head and ask my corpse questions after. As far as he was concerned, without investigation, I was guilty as charged. However, as we know, he was wrong, and you, my dear friends, would have not had the pleasure of reading this book because I would be dead! He always appeared at the court to make sure that my bail application would be refused.

On February 2003, this information was made known to me by one of my visitors: My wife was out of the United Kingdom, and my daughter was left with a friend. My daughter was not allowed to be taken by any member of my family. Could you imagine a four-year-old child who witnessed her father being dragged off by approximately twelve police officers with his hands cuffed behind him, knowing that I was bathing her at the time of my arrest? Just think for one minute, my dear friends, the trauma that my child suffered. I really do not think that any child should go through that, and I do hope that my dear daughter, Rochelle, would get over this before she became an adult. I, myself, would do everything possible to prevent the trauma entering into adulthood with her. At the end of February, I was informed that my wife was back through her cousin who visited me on a regular basis.

He said to me, "You will not believe what you are about to hear. Carol is back. She landed on Friday (this visit was on a Sunday). She called me from the airport to tell me she was back. But I went into a state of disbelief when she said, "where is Raymond?"

He said he paused for a while to catch his breath before he could reply to her question.

He told her, "He is in prison where you left him. Where else do you think he would be?"

He said she replied, "Why don't they release him? Why are they keeping him?"

Her cousin, George, said she seemed quite confused. He then said to her, "The allegations you made against him were quite strong, and the police are holding him based on that even though the allegations are false. You have to continue with it because the police will not let it go." He believed she wanted to put everything behind her, but the pressure from the police was too intense. She did not know what she was doing. A letter was written by Carol and was given to a friend to pass to me, but I simply was not interested in the contents of whatever she had to say. In fact, I had terminated my friendship with this so-called peacemaker. During my time of suffering in prison, I made myself a vow never to have any communication or contact with Carol for as long as I live. Although she is the mother of my child, to me, she was simply like a cancerous tumour that was removed. Failing that, I would have my right arm removed. So far, so good. It was five years later, and everything remained the same after my freedom.

However, in March 2003, an offer was made in exchange for my freedom. It was entirely in my power to accept this offer, but if I had done so, I would have gained a criminal record. It was arranged by my solicitor at the time (Ewing & Co) whom I believed was working in conjunction with D.C. Duffus, not in my interest, but in the interest of my ex-wife. I did believe it was an act of conspiracy. The offer was for me to plead guilty in exchange for my freedom, which would be nice and tidy for D. C. Duffus.

What about me? I thought for a moment, Criminal record? No, thanks! Favours for sex is a system that works very well in Jamaica for the police. I was almost horrified to find out that this system was operating in Britain where the law should be upheld.

I wrote several letters to my daughter to be kept on my file until the day when she was old enough to understand them. The letters were quite personal. I explained the circumstances about what her mother had done to me and that she must never forget her daddy. The letters were given to Ewing & Co in confidence because I wanted my daughter to see these letters in the event I did not make it out of prison alive. However, believe it or not, the contents of these letters came back to me in prison through my ex-wife's cousin! Do you see the picture? The letters themselves had somehow reached the hands of D.C. Duffus, and obviously, he passed them on to his floozy who was now my ex-wife. At this point, I was extremely upset because on top of making me an offer in exchange for my freedom, I discovered I was about to be stitched-up again!

The offer that was made to me was to plead guilty and go free. "Your job is there, waiting." "Your daughter misses you," said the solicitor from Ewing in a cunning voice. Little did they know I was wise to the fact that D. C. Duffus had the solicitor in the palm of his hands! Now, after three months in prison, for no reason, that is what the police and the solicitors wanted to do: I was offered a plea bargain. Freedom was nice, yes, but a criminal record for life was so much worse. Don't get me wrong, I missed my daughter so much, my heart hurt. The police wanted to tidy things up to cover up their mistakes, but I could see further than they could. I rang a dear friend and asked her advice. What should I do?

She said, "My son, if you are innocent, why plead guilty? Get a new solicitor and start again."

This lovely lady was the wife of my boss at the time I was working for Medway Precision Engineering in Kent. This tragedy happened to me after three and a half years of service with the company.

Jean said, "Ray, you are a very trustworthy person. I remember your honesty. Several times, I loaned you money up to £200 until you get paid at the end of the month. And even when I forget, you always repay me. This kind of honesty is hard to find. So get a new solicitor. Do not plead guilty for something you did not do."

I took Jean's advice, and I changed my solicitor to Ashley & Co in Lewisham. When I appointed the new solicitor, I rang Jean and told her. She was quite pleased. She offered to write to them to give me a character witness that indeed she did.

I was visited by Ashley Smith from Ashley & Co. He was my newly appointed solicitor. He took a statement from me and reassured me that he would definitely get me out of the dungeon I was placed in. A week later, I attended court for another bail hearing. On my way to the court, I walked approximately one to two miles underground. This was known as the Belmarsh tunnel, well equipped for executing escaping inmates. There were small gas valves above for releasing nerve gas. Each section had a cut-off point. The main exit from the tunnel to the court itself had a three feet thick steel door that had a code that changed every hour. Thus, my plan to escape was impossible! On the other side of this extremely thick door were security guards. Most of them appeared to me to look like Dykes, as the manner in which you were searched was almost as if you were being manhandled. I was glad when I got into court because walking under the tunnel had put me into a depressive slope. I arrived at the court where I was interviewed in a cell downstairs. This barrister appeared to be a nice person. We spoke, and we appeared to have got on well. After the interview with the barrister, I was called up in front of the judge for the sixth time, and behold! Who was in the court room trying to outstare me? Yes! D. C. Duffus.

I guessed the sex with my wife at the time must have put him on cloud ten! But then, to compare him, to me, the sex with Carol before my imprisonment was like humping a blown-up doll, not saying I have, I found masturbation much more arousing and pleasurable.

However, with a man like Duffus, a twenty-stone blubber, I doubt if he could do better for himself. He had no choice but to prey on vulnerable women. Sex had never been a problem for me. I had experienced extremely great sex and the wham-bam-thank-you-ma'am sex. I didn't have any problem getting it. Neither was I ever told of a disappointing moment. Don't forget, as I said before, during my marriage, the best sex was the ones outside, and yet, I was framed as being a sex monster by Carol. How dared her! Cheeky bitch!

D. C. Duffus looked at me as if he had some form of regret, but all I could do was to return a blank look. My barrister put the request for bail forward, and yet again, it was denied. Duffus and the system coupled together were trying hard to weigh me down, but the strength that I grasped from my inner being kept me going.

I was taken down back to the cell where my barrister came to see me once more. She had enlightened me that due to the strength of the statement from my beloved wife whom I loved dearly, and with Duffus in the picture, it was almost impossible to get bail.

"But by talking to you, I can see that the allegations against you are not true. I will make sure that you will be set free."

"Is that a promise?" I asked.

She looked me in the eyes and said, "Yes, you bet."

At this point, I started to feel almost human again, although every scrap of humanity had been extracted from my being. My barrister assured me that she would contact Ashley Smith, my solicitor, and arrange a hearing date for me as soon as possible.

I waited approximately two hours to make the journey back to the prison. Then it was announced that there were not enough officers available to take the prisoners back. We had to wait for a high security van to take us back. The prison van had finally arrived, and each prisoner was handcuffed to a security personnel and escorted to the van. The van was now full and ready to depart. We finally arrived at the main prison. We were now escorted off the van in the same manner in which we boarded. Now, for the bit I despised, we were led from the van into a holding room with three armed guards by the door. We were told to listen for our names in alphabetical order. Several names were called. Each time a name was called, an inmate would respond. Then, it was my turn. I heard a very loud voice said, "FRANCIS." I stood up as I always do and went to the desk.

"You are not standing on the yellow footprints," shouted the guard. Then he shouted, "FRANCIS, NAME and NUMBER." I was really getting pissed-off.

Then he uttered, (to make matters worse and to get me even more upset) "Do you love your wife, FRANCIS? Where does your wife live, FRANCIS?"

I could feel the volcano inside me erupting slightly, but somehow, I kept my cool because I knew he was trying to provoke a reaction. I responded that I do not have a wife. I then said my name, "FRANCIS, NUMBER HP6441, Sir."

He replied, "Well done," in a sarcastic manner.

I was raging with anger inside me, and I was truly exasperated. I was then placed in another holding room until two officers from HB3 came to collect all the inmates from that block. I arrived back at the cell with all my possessions. Then I discovered I had lost my space in cell twenty-two. I was now placed in cell two, on the ground floor. During the morning break the next day, I went to the cell to see the occupants. They were all different people from the ones I knew. There was a particular inmate in this cell that almost looked like a young lady, if you looked at him from behind. At first glance, he had a feminine appearance. He came over to me and introduced himself. His name was Rajah, and as usual, we exchanged our reasons why we were in the dungeon called Belmarsh! My spirit had taken to this young man. We became acquainted over the one-hour break. Also, in this cell, I saw a black and a white inmate who also spoke to me. They had London accents. The next day, it was all over the house block that Rajah was raped by his cellmates. I asked at the "bubble" (the information desk) for Rajah from cell twenty-two, and I was told that he was transferred to the hospital unit. I never saw him again, neither his two cellmates.

    I was riddled with disbelief by what was going on around me. The next day, my name appeared on the visitors' board list. I wondered who could that be as I had made no arrangement for anyone to visit me. All inmates who were getting visitors were placed in a holding room. At this point, there were no guards, the door was locked, and suddenly, there was one man down in seconds, cold as ice, lying on the floor. There was an inmate of Mediterranean appearance known as "boxer." He was very loud and arrogant, an egotistical man. Whenever we had a break, you would always hear his voice like a megaphone over all the others chattering. He was always jumping, skipping, and shouting, "Float like butterfly, sting like a bee." It was Mohammed Ali's famous words. I do believe that this inmate was most feared by the other inmates, but I always prepared myself if or when it was my turn to face him. This inmate went around as if he owned the prison and if he liked you, he would pat you on the back and say, "Hello, mate." He actually patted me on the back and said, "Hello, mate." The inmate who got knocked out in the holding room was a part of a gang, which on the outside was known as a "super grass" at the time. That day, it so happened that we had lost almost all the visiting time because when the screw (warden) came back, there was an unconscious inmate on the floor, and within no time, there were screws over the place like flies. The unconscious man was bleeding from his nose.

The boxer uttered, "That is what happens to super grass." The screws began to question us as to what had happened and asked if anyone saw anything. No one saw anything, including myself. The silence was deafening!

I was able to see my visitor, although my time was shortened by the incident. It was a surprise visit from Marion. I questioned her about life outside. I tried not to discuss anything about the affairs inside due to CCTV. Two weeks later, Marion came back. We talked about sex in deep explicit description. She had drawn it to my attention that she has had an orgasm whilst speaking to me due to the intensity of the conversation, but I did believe that this was brought on by boredom and sexual starvation.

When the visit was over, I went back to my cell, thinking, Was this for real? Or was she trying to cheer me up? Quite frankly, I think she was trying to cheer me up. I had never spoken to a woman about sex so intensely that she had an orgasm. How bizarre, I thought! On the other hand, anything was possible due to her situation concerning self-pleasuring.

One week later, a strange thing happened. I was walking in the yard during exercise. This time, I was by myself. All the inmates were walking in a group. I heard a strange voice that brought shock waves to my system, and indeed, to the other inmates, too. The voice said in a feminine tone, "Stop. Stop, you are not having me now. You've had me twice last night." We all stopped and looked in the direction of the sound. I asked a screw why those inmates were not on a break.

He replied, "That is the gay section, man on man if you know what I mean. Son, get my drift?" they didn't mix the gays with the straight as this would cause problems. Believe it or not, it was a black face that appeared at the small window that made matters much worse. I could not believe my ears; I was disgusted! But then, I guess everyone found a way of relieving frustration in prison. I could not believe the amount of drugs that was at hand.

In fact, I had never seen so much drugs outside. Although I am not a user, it was there, on sale in abundance.

It was used as a trade for anything. In prison, there was no money, but if you had something to trade, you would always get by. I, too, had things to trade. I traded clothes, and believe it or not, as a non-smoker, my biggest trade was tobacco.

On the day I was arrested, December 23, 2002, I happened to have £300 in my pocket that was transferred into the prison account. I also got myself a job that paid £5 per week. My spending in prison was quite minimal because there was not much to buy apart from toiletries, food, and tobacco. I did not care much for prison food, so I bought my own, which, to me, was quite reasonable. I bought a lot of tobacco. It was the best currency to have. You can trade it for almost anything. In fact, I almost seemed to be top man due to my trading ability. I always got my head shaved at any time in exchange for tobacco.

It was with the exception of Sir Ronnie Biggs, a man whom was well deserving of the Queen's honour of knighthood because he was the only living escapee from Wandsworth prison. However, I did not think he would escape from Belmarsh! I would have gladly joined him, but I knew that they could not keep him there forever. Although he was bound by chains and handcuffs—on top of his illness—he was a free man. His spirit was outside. Hail Ronnie Biggs.'

I also met some other characters such as Abu Amsar and a few well-known killers, murderers, and rapists. You name them, I have met them. I also met another Muslim brother who had no arms, yet charged with bomb making. I was with all these hopeless misfits of society in Belmarsh AA category prison. I was also an AA category prisoner. This meant all my phone calls—incoming or outgoing—letters, and all forms of communications were all intercepted. I could not understand why I was an AA cat prisoner. In fact, I could not understand why I was a prisoner at all. The question was, "What did I do to find myself in such a place paid for by the Queen and the country and treated like royalty with such diligence? My dear friends, don't laugh too much. I guess that's British justice. If the British police wanted to have their way with your wife, trust me, they would get it. They would do anything to get her. Policemen such as D. C. Duffus were an insult to the crown on the Queen's head, knowing the crown did not belong to England anyway—stolen goods all over again!

By now, you might be asking yourself how I became a Muslim. You might have guessed I changed my faith purely accidentally, but for the best. On Fridays, I attend a prayer meeting. On a Sunday, I tried my best to keep out of the cell as much as possible by going to the chapel. I booked in for the morning service with the Church of England, and then at midmorning, I go to the Roman Catholic service. After lunch, it was time to exercise in the yard, and then, if one was really lucky, one might get to go to the gym afterward. Then, it was dinnertime, and after that—you guess—"Lights out, you fuckers."

I discovered that visiting all the various denominations at the chapel was a means of keeping out of the cell, even if it was only for a few hours. By doing that, the Friday prayers start to appeal to me in a big way. I found it rather ironic that I was in a relationship with a Muslim woman for four years. She would have done anything for me to convert to Islam. In fact, the break up was based upon me not being a Muslim, and now, look at me. I did consider myself to be a Muslim, although praying five times daily was quite difficult due to my work. I visit the Mosque when I could after work, and I did consider Allah to be my God. You might find this ironic, but it was true; my prayers were always answered whenever I pray.

Back to my interesting characters. My dear friends, those of you who reside in South London, you might know this to be true. There was a killing of an estate agent in the Brockley area. "A gunman by the name of Lenny and his troops had gunned down an innocent man," that was front page news in the local paper (South London Press). Lenny was one of the characters whom I had the displeasure of meeting. He walked around with several crucifixes around his neck. He also attended the Church of England's service every Sunday. I oftentimes wondered why he bothered because I could see in his eyes that he was a killer. When an inmate told you the reason of his incarceration, and he could not look you in the eyes when speaking to you, then the body language spoke for itself. There you have it. Lenny and his troops got ten years each for the brutal murder.

I did hope that one day, the crucifixes he wore around his neck would take him home peacefully as simply a mockery of God. I met another interesting character by the name of Adam. This character was of Somali origin. We shared cell thirty-four. He told me of his beautiful sister whom he believed would like me. I had no doubt of her beauty based on Adam's features, but I was not sure of her name. He called her Eva. So here we had "Adam and Eva." I thought he was having a laugh.

I told him of the pains I suffered, and he appeared quite sympathetic towards me. He asked me if I wanted some phone numbers so I could make a call and sort things out from the inside. I told him it was the wrong time. We grew closer as the days went by, and he told me of his imprisonment in France and Germany. He said that when we got out, we should both team up, go across the channel, and do business. I told him I would give it some thought.

One day, he asked me if I really wanted my wife dead. I said, "For doing this to me, she deserves to die." However, it was not in my nature to kill. Don't get me wrong, I had thought about it. Adam drew me a map of a cemetery in Hackney, marked with an X on the spot where a gun was hidden. He said that when I got out, I would be welcomed to take it. Two weeks later, Adam went to court. He lost his space in cell thirty-four. I never saw him again until November 2003 at a car auction in Deptford. I could not believe my eyes. Strange enough, most of the faces I became familiar with in prison, I came to see on the street, even today. Adam and I met up on a few occasion, but our friendship had no substance, so it phased out.

Still in cell thirty-four, HB3. After Adam lost his space, a Rasta inmate joined the party. This Rasta appeared to be very much like a lion. His locks were very thick, shoulder length, and his beard reminded me of Moses. This inmate appeared to be somewhat mixed-race, with very dark skin. I found out that his mother was a very dark-skinned Indian, and his father a very dark-skinned West Indian, so that determined his complexion. For three days, I did not speak to him, but I listened to him talking to the other inmate. The other inmate whom I had mentioned very little of was a white male, slim built, with a northern accent. We did not have much in common. He was quite withdrawn and kept himself to himself. However, on a few occasions, we spoke. He told me of his depression in prison, and believe it or not, he was there for a traffic offence. During a few times in the exercise yard, we spoke. I gave him some free tobacco as a gesture of friendship.

One day, I saw the Dread putting up different pictures of Rastas on the wall. Amongst those pictures were Bob Marley, Peter Tosh, and many others unknown to me. The wall were covered. At the top of all these pictures was Haille Selassie, with a crown on his head. He was wearing a golden robe. I found these pictures quite interesting, and I stared at them for a long time, almost as if I was hypnotised. The Dread then uttered in a Jamaican accent," What are you looking at?"

I replied, "Your pictures are quite interesting."

Also among these pictures was a beautiful Indian girl. However, this picture did not add up to the rest. I started a conversation based on all the pictures; each of them had a story. I asked him about Haille Selassie, and he looked at me, saying, "That's the Almighty King, the God of Israel, the conquering Lion of Judea."

I found this quite amazing, and I burst into laughter. I then asked him about the beautiful Indian girl.

He said, "That is my empress."

I was quite amused.

A week went by, and the three of us became acquainted, telling each other our reasons for being inside and what crimes we had committed in the past and got away with. I do believe that the police or the screws would look upon this as "cell confession." The discussions that inmates had in the cell were often used as evidence at their trial due to bugging devices or super grass amongst them. Information was leaked back to the police in that manner. If a super grass was found amongst inmates, he was simply erased from the face of the earth. All one had to do was to tell boxer, whom I had previously mentioned. It was customary that super grass shall die, must die, and will die."

The Dread told me of his crimes, and I was totally shocked. These crimes that he had committed spanned from Jamaica to America then back to the United Kingdom. My opinion of him was that he was a dangerous man but very funny. He told me of his gunfights with the British police. He said that one day, he went to deliver some guns, he and a co-defendant who was residing in another prison. They were approached by the police, and there was a shootout (Sounds like the wild, wild west?). He said a police was shot. This happened in the countryside. He tried to escape, but he did not know the area. So he ran back to his girlfriend's mansion. Unknowingly to him, he was followed. The police called for backup, and his girlfriend's mansion was searched; they found machinery which was used for converting replica guns into real guns. That was almost unbelievable!

Believe it or not, the lovely Indian empress was living at her parent' home. Both of her parents were doctors. The empress was now in HMP Holloway Female Prison where she gave birth.

When I looked at the picture of this young lady and the picture of the mansion, I asked myself, "Why would a woman of this calibre get involved with a gun hustler?" That was a total mystery.

The Dread asked me, in case I got released before he did, if I could go and visit her in prison to offer her moral support. However, I was afraid to accept this invitation to help because a beautiful woman was my weakness, and I knew that one day, I would be hunted by the Dread. It was obvious that I would vacate HMP Belmarsh before the Dread. I had never seen a real gun nor had the opportunity to shoot a police, but the day may come when I could face D. C. Duffus.

One month went by. I was walking in the exercise yard with the white inmate whose name I would not mention. He spoke of being bullied by a prison officer whose name I also would not mention.. This particular officer, in my opinion, had no regard for human life. I found him very cold and calculating.

One day, I was extremely depressed. I waited until it was time for exercise. At this point, I wanted it all to end because it appeared that there was no way out of Belmarsh Prison. I started to think about the life I used to have, and I decided to end my life.

I was in the cell, alone. I tied a pair of prison trousers onto the metal frame of the window and put the other end around my neck. I tied it into a noose, and I tried to hang myself. As I was doing this, somehow, I was caught by Mr. Lemon. Mr Lemon should have acted professionally by speaking to me and giving me some form of counselling, but instead, he threatened me by telling me that he would strip me of my clothing and put me in the segregation cell naked. This, in my opinion, was grossly unprofessional.

This was not his real name, but whoever might relate to this might guess his real name. I still believed up to this day that Mr. Lemon was highly involved in the beatings and intimidation of several inmates. My friend, Charlie, succeeded in hanging himself two days after telling me that he was being intimidated by Mr. Lemon. Cell thirty-four of HB3 was closed due to forensic investigation, and the Dread was moved to house block one. I was moved to house block two, and the only time I saw the Dread was on exercise, when we both went into the yard. We had no close contact because HB1 and HB2 had different exercise yard, divided by a fence and a road through the middle. However, we shouted at the top of our voices to greet each other from a distance.

One day, on March 2003, I had a visit after trying for several months to get my daughter to visit me. I tried everything I could from inside prison to get someone to bring her to see me, but all my efforts failed because D. C. Duffus was on the outside, making sure that I never see my daughter as a part of his vindictiveness toward me. Rochelle was placed on the "at risk register." At risk from what? I may ask, my dear friends. The only risk that Rochelle faced was given by D. C. Duffus. The only risk was of losing her dad, but I could tell you one thing, my dear friends, at this point in time, D. C. Duffus could never stop my daughter from loving me although he had tried. Reflecting on the day when my sisters came to visit me, something strange happened that brought me to tears. There were quite a few children visiting on that day, and there was a little girl that looked almost identical to my little Rochelle. This little girl came over to me, put her little hands on my shoulder, and said "Hello." I responded by saying "Hello." Then her mother called her over. At this point, when the little girl touched me, I knew that my daughter was with me in spirit, so although D. C. Duffus was stopping my daughter from seeing me physically, it was impossible to stop her spiritually.

My sisters came over, and I started wiping my tears from my eyes. They asked me what was wrong. I told them the truth. I also requested of my sisters to access my mobile phone, get Anita's phone number for me, and I would call them to get it. One week went by, and Anita's number was at my disposal. I called her several times, and we had pleasant conversations. What I did noticed was that each time I spoke to Anita, I seemed to get extremely strong and confident. I really had no idea where this power came from, but it was there.

On reflection, I was at the time dating Marion when I met Anita. Also, it was the same time that I was separated from the evil witch I had married. I finally found myself drifting back to the old days of the old school when I used to have four women on the same night. Those were the days!

Although I was dating Marion before my imprisonment, it so happened that each time I went to visit her, I always saw this Indian woman with long hair down to her waist, and I just had to meet her. I kept on thinking about her even when I was not in the area; she was always on my mind. However, it could have been an escape from the reality of my life because I was not having a good time, separated from my wife and living at my brother's home. It was not exactly the best time of my life. I found that the more women I met, the better I felt within myself. However, deep down, I was very unhappy. I made myself a promise that the next time I saw Anita, she would be mine. That day had come when I saw her walking down the road again. Since that day, I visited Plumstead more than I ever dreamed of. Yes, by now, my dear friends, you have probably guessed that I chatted up Anita successfully. It was a Wednesday night, and I remember it so clearly. I asked her to accompany me to a party on the Saturday, prior to meeting her on the Wednesday. She agreed. I took her for a meal early that Friday evening. Then we went to a party afterwards. That was all I needed. My friends, the host of the party had offered me a room for the night if I wished. I accepted this, and Anita and I spent all night together after staying at the party for a short time. That night was beyond all my dreams. The next day, my head was above the clouds. I found myself falling for her; I could not believe the impact she had on me. It was nearly time for me to pick up my daughter as I usually did on a Saturday afternoon. I took Anita with me at the meeting point, at the SavaCentre car park, Sydenham. Rochelle's mother—my wife at the time—appeared somewhat upset, which I could not understand. Several weeks went by, and I always had Anita with me when I pick-up my daughter. Each time she was seen with me, Carol would get upset. One day, Anita asked me how I could have married such an old-looking woman. Anita was twenty-three at the time, and I was very happy with her. One month after meeting her, we got on so well, communicating daily by text messages and phone calls. It was all I needed to soothe my aching heart.

We decided to take a trip to Paris. We jetted off on her "magic carpet." It was the best week I had ever had since I met the mother of my child.

It suddenly dawned on me that my reflection had me so far from reality; I almost forgotten where I was—I was still in prison. I really wanted to see Anita after speaking with her for so many times on the phone. I wanted to see her in person. I rang her and asked if she could visit me. At first, she declined, saying she had never been in a prison before, and it was just not her scene. After pleading with her for several times, she agreed to visit me. I told her to arrange a visit with my sisters, and it came to pass. She came to see me, and I was overjoyed with her presence. My sisters left a little early to give Anita and I some quality time together. Although I was surrounded by other inmates, it felt as if we were in our own private world, just the two us. I was very happy to be with her that moment I would never forget.

I went back to my cell after the visit, feeling refreshed and strong, almost as if I was walking in the desert for a long time and found an oasis.

One of the inmates from my cell, cell twenty-two of HB2, had to go to court, and as per usual, when one went to court, his space was lost and was replaced by a new inmate. The new inmate now occupied the top bunk. Each night, the new inmate tended to relief himself on the bed. I was on the bottom bunk. It was very difficult to get any form of sleep because of his sexual antics. Apparently, this inmate, I was told, was known as the masturbator. I could not understand why a man would masturbate every night in such an environment, but one day, I found out why he did this. We both had visitors the same day he sat four tables away from me with his girlfriend. She was extremely beautiful, almost as beautiful as the Dread's empress. With a woman like that in his thoughts each night, well, there goes the reason for his action. Nonetheless, it was quite disturbing for me. One morning, all three inmates, including myself, had a discussion about sex in the cells. I was told of how to make a prison pussy. I found it quite hilarious. It was said that you had to wrap a towel around a very small bottle and then pull the bottle out, leaving a hole. Wet this hole with soapy water, then you place this so-called vagina between two pillows, and, excuse my French, fuck it! I had never tried it personally, but I was told that it was very close to the real thing. I dared say that I had no desire for this kind of pleasure; it was just not me. I found this quite ridiculous, but then, it explained the shortage of pillows in the prison.

 I finally began to enjoy myself in prison. I began to go to pottery class, music, art and design, and English. All these activities had taken me out of the cell each day so that I only went to the cell to sleep. In pottery class, I began to design a memento for my daughter. I was making this from clay. I found music lessons to be interesting because before I got married, I was a budding musician. It was just like the good old days although I was in a cage. I found English lessons most enjoyable because I used this time to write letters and anything I wished to write. One day, I was writing about the event that took place in cell thirty-four, HB3. My tutor came to view my work. When she read what I had written, she took the paper away from me and put me in a corner by myself. She gave all the other inmates strict instructions to get on with whatever they were doing as she wanted to speak to me undisturbed. She sat down, facing me at the table, looking me in the eyes. She asked me, "Is this true? What you have written?"

I replied, "Yes, miss." She had tears in her eyes. Apparently, she was a close friend of Charlie's parents. It appeared to be quite a serious situation because I also mentioned the person called Mr. Lemon, the intimidator, in my writing. In art lessons, I surprised myself because I did not know I had the ability to draw so well. One day, I was rather bored, so I decided to draw my tutor. His name was Enrico. He was Spanish and had a big nose. I had also heard that he was gay, and I could tell that by his body language. I drew two cartoon characters. I wrote his name next to one of the two whilst it was being humped by the next character. He came over to me to see what I was drawing. I tried to cover it up, but he insisted on seeing my work. When he saw what I had drawn, he told me with his strong Spanish accent to get out of the class. I never returned to that class again.

Nevertheless, it was to my advantage; I disliked art anyway. I used this extra time to double-up on my music lesson instead, which did me the world of good. As I might have mentioned previously, I had my own band and record label, so the extra music lesson was in my favour. With each lesson that I disliked, I always tried to get myself kicked out of the class to enable me to use that time constructively to attend music lesson; it was so rare, I did not give a damn! I quite enjoyed the computer and pottery lesson. I had improved on my computer skills, which helps me today. Now, I could actually read the notes on a musical keyboard, which I was unable to do before as I was self-taught. I was teaching myself without a book, and I could still make a good sound! I must admit really that the jam sessions, when all the rapists, murderers, thieves, and pimps got together in a musical jam and when everyone forgot what they were in prison for and just jam, those sessions were really kicking—hell, they were hot. If only one could get those sessions on a disk, one could make a bag of money. I could make enough money to buy the whole of Belmarsh prison, free the prisoners, and execute the prison officers with it! Serious shit!

One other thing I enjoyed was the pottery lesson. Inmates were making stuff from clay. I had never seen something so constructive in my life. I stood back, sometimes, and looked at the money that could be made, and these guys were making things just to pass the time. I also got my hands dirty. I made something for my little angel, Rochelle, which she might not appreciate now. However, when she's in her twenties, she might look at it and become a little tearful; it was made with all my love.

I had my work of art delivered to Rochelle upon my second week of breathing fresh air on the outside. Six months later, I requested it back. I was told that it was nowhere to be found in the house where my daughter lived with her mother. I kept on requesting for the return of my work of art, but I was told that it was, as I suspected, in an outside cupboard, amongst unwanted relics. Indeed, I had retrieved it, but the frame that cost me £30 on my release from prison was damaged beyond presentation. Believe it or not, when I was released from prison, I had no money or any insight of where to obtain some quick cash, but I still spent £30 on a frame for my work of art for my daughter because it was something I had to do; it had sentimental value.

The day had come. My first trial had been scheduled on May 7, 2003. It was my first journey to trial, not that I had not made this journey several times before. When I got to Belmarsh Court after travelling through this hazardous tunnel from the prison, I had to go downstairs to the prisoners' interview room to speak with my barrister. She asked me several questions, and then she said, "Mr. Francis, I know you are innocent. I will get you out of here."

Then she asked me, "How long were you married?"

I replied, "Seven years."

She also asked me, "How old is your daughter?"

I replied, "Five." Then I asked her, "Why do you ask me these personal questions?"

She replied, "I just want to get a picture of your situation." Then she asked, "How long have you been away from the marital home?"

I replied, "Since April 2002."

Then she mentioned, "There's a loan that is a joint between you and your wife for £1,000. This was taken out in October 2002."

She then said, "Mr. Francis, what did you do with the money?"

I replied, "My wife wanted a new car, so I borrowed the money to purchase the car for her. The money was given to Carol with the agreement that she would make the monthly repayments."

"Well, Mr. Francis, I am pleased to tell you that the loan has been paid back, and you are in prison. But your wife is lucky because I, personally, would not have got the loan due to the circumstances." She then told me that I had to go back to the cell and wait to be called back for the trial in about ten minutes. Twenty minutes later, I was called up to go to into court where I was faced with judge, jury, and prosecutor. Although I was innocent, I was extremely nervous. At this point, I felt as if I was crunched between the jaws of death. D. C. Duffus looked me in the eyes and shook his head. I knew he was ashamed of himself. Well, let's face it, was this not a human emotion? I ask you, my dear friends, D. C. Duffus knew what he was doing, but did he not know what he was up against—the force that comes from within?

In came the judge. "All rise. May the court begin."

I stood up with my knees knocking. I was sure that the jailer who stood next to me could hear the knocking of my knees, but I was also sure that he could not smell the steam coming from my pants. The sweat was dripping from my forehead, and I heard the sound as it splashed on the floor. That was my own experience. I heard a voice, deep in the background, said, "Mr. Francis, you may be seated." I then caught myself because for some strange reason, it was almost as if a seventh sense had kicked in. I sat down, then I started to see clearly again. D. C. Duffus was still glaring at me.

I sat down and glanced around. I could feel the eyes of everyone: the twelve members of the jury—two of Afro-Caribbean origin, three Asians, five Caucasians, and two Chinese. They looked at me as if I was a condemned man. But then, it could have only been in my mind. Carol Francis was called to the witness box to give her statement.

Questions to Mrs. Francis from my barrister:
"Mrs. Francis, what date did you have your husband removed from the marital home?"
"I don't remember," she replied.
"Mrs. Francis, what did you do on December 23, 2002?"
"I don't remember," she replied.
"Mrs. Francis, how long have you been in the United Kingdom?"
"I don't remember," she replied.
"Mrs. Francis, are you able to remember anything?"
"I don't remember," she replied.
"Mrs. Francis, why did you come to England?"
"Life in Jamaica was too tough," she replied in her strong Jamaican accent, finishing the sentence with Madam!
"No further questions."
Carol requested to leave the courtroom.

I sat riddled with disbelief because my wife, at the time, seemed to have lost her memory—convenient indeed! Or perhaps she was intellectually constipated? I found it quite strange, but then, D. C. Duffus was determined to get his pound of flesh. He was called to the stand after Carol had left the courtroom. He was questioned by the prosecution barrister and then by my barrister. After approximately one and a half hour of vigorous questioning, D. C. Duffus had requested that he wished to change his statement—in the middle of the trial. When a police officer caused a trial to stop (This was known as spanner in the works.) it often meant that a police officer saw that he was losing the case. He would then use this tactics in order to obtain a retrial. (On reflection, I found this act by D. C. Duffus quite pathetic because they got their retrial, and they lost anyway). At this moment in time, there was a deafening silence in the courtroom. However, I did not know that this was a ploy used by police officers in order to obtain a retrial, and it worked. The trial was stopped, and a retrial was requested. D. C. Duffus looked at me with a slight grin on his face as he left the courtroom.

This was heard by an eyewitness who also gave a statement that D. C. Duffus got on his mobile phone in the lounge area of the court. He was heard saying these words: "Hello, Carol, it's me. Where are you? I have managed to get a retrial. Let's do it right this time. Get Maggie and Christine. We need all the ammo we can get; we are going to get him this time. I will come round, and we will arrange something."

It came out in court that the night before my arrest, Carol called the police and asked them to pick up Rochelle They replied, "We are not a taxi service."

Question I may ask: Why didn't the police assist her that night due to the fact that she was in fear of her life and also of Rochelle's safety? Why did D. C. Duffus come and arrest me the next day? To me, my dear friends, it was quite simple. The night before, the police had no doubt in their minds that Carol was in any danger at any time. However, due to the fact that Duffus was having his wicked way in bed with her, it was quite a personal issue for him. The fat bastard! How could she go with such a man? It was a disgrace, not that I cared.

My dear friends, at this point, the only thing I could say was D. C. Duffus and my present ex-wife were in conspiracy. I would go on to say that body language and telephone manners would always give the game away, e.g. "Hello, Mrs. Francis, this is D C Duffus." That manner of speech meant something totally different from "Hello, Carol, it's me." I do believe that this was personal and not business. We expressed ourselves with our speech both professionally and casually. My dear friends, forgive me if I am wrong.

I was dragged back down to the cell as usual, where I had to wait for all the cases to be tried before we could make our way home back to Belmarsh prison through the tunnel. At approximately 3:00 P.M., it was time to go. Six of us left in the morning, eight returned, and another two brothers joined the chain gang. But it was not always like that. Sometimes, less returned, sometimes more returned. Unfortunately, when I got back to house block two, there were no room in the inn. All the returnees from the court that day had to be distributed throughout the prison, and unfortunately, for me, I was thrown into house block one with the most unhygienic men I had ever come across. I was thrown in a cell which housed three men. I started to think I was in hell because I did not know that humans could carry such an appalling stench! But did I have a choice? . . No! My new friends happened to be from Africa. This cell, which I assumed measured two meters by two meters to accommodate three people, was quite disastrous. The air was acrid, and breathing was an effort. The stench of the body odour was suffocating.

The memory would stay with me for the rest of my life. I had complained several times, but I was told by Matumba, who was approximately six feet, five inches, that Joshua did not like to wash or change his socks. In other words, I was not the one that smelled. After a week of this, I began to drift into a state of depression once more. I regarded myself as an extremely hygienic individual, and seeing what I had to endure in prison was having a profound effect upon me.

I received a letter from Ashley & Co Solicitor who was representing me. The letter stated that a second trial date was set for July 7, 2003. I put up with whatever I had to tolerate with because Allah told me that on my next appearance in court, I would not be returning to prison again. I had faith, and that was the light at the end of the tunnel. July seventh came so quick that I did not notice my undignified surrounding. On the morning of the July 7, I got up at 5:30 A.M. I prayed to Allah to protect me from the evil that got me into this place (D. C. Duffus and Carol), to take me through the day, and to protect me from the evil that I might face in court. At 6:00 A.M., the cell door was opened, and a voice said, "Francis, court today. Pack your stuff.'

I packed my bag as usual and waited for the prison officer to come to take me and a few other inmates to court. This had now become routine for us. We were bundled into holding rooms at every stage of the trial. At one point, there was an orange sitting on the window ledge which happened to tempt a prisoner, and he went for it. I would understand if it was an apple, the fruit of temptation. He started to peel this orange, and suddenly, he was attacked by another inmate. Apparently, the orange belonged to the attacker. Could you believe a big brawl over an orange at seven in the morning? As Allah promised me, I would be free from this, the journey through the tunnel had started at the other end as usual. We were met by butch-looking women with masculine appearances, dressed in yellow shirts and black trousers.

There was one that was a bit more feminine who always tried to speak to me whenever she saw me. I had a hunch she liked me. She always walked with me from the end of the tunnel to the courthouse cells, trying her best to get a conversation going, but on this day, I told her that she may never see me again. She placed me in cell and said, "Good luck, if I see you again, it will be on the outside."

I was visited by my barrister at the court, in the private chamber as usual. We discussed all aspects of my case. I was then sent back to the cell. At approximately 11:00 A.M., I was called up for trial, but strange enough, I had no feelings of fear or fright; I just wanted to get this over and done with. I went into court. I sat down. There was a prison officer next to me. Whether I was being guarded against the public or the public against me, I hadn't a clue. On reflection, I believed I was being guarded from D. C. Duffus.

In court was D. C. Duffus, my wife at the time, Carol, twelve new members of the jury, and a new judge. My barrister had explained that a new set of jury and a new judge had to be appointed because of D. C. Duffus's performance at the last trial. I was told that this judge was sent from the Old Bailey specifically for my trial. She also explained that the judge and jury would have been in a confused frame of mind if they had appointed the same group, so this had to be done.

In the courtroom, a voice said, "All rise." In comes the Judge. "You may be seated.".

"First, we call Mrs. Carol Francis."

"Take the stand please, Madam," said the usher.

"What religion are you?" asked the usher.

Carol replied, "Christian."

To my surprise—she had never been a religious person—she was given a Bible to swear on. She was sworn in, taking an oath.

My barrister had questions to ask her.

"Mrs. Francis, would you prefer me to call you Carol?"

She replied, "Call me Carol.

For some reason, my barrister never once called her Carol. She always referred to her as Mrs. Francis. I was really getting annoyed as the woman in front of me had no qualifications to be referred to as Mrs. Francis. My barrister continued with her questioning. Although I disagreed with her using the term "Mrs. Francis," I just sat there and listened.

"Mrs Francis, how long have you been in England?"

"'Six years, Madam," she replied.

"Mrs. Francis, how old is Rochelle? It is Rochelle, isn't it, your daughter?"

"Rochelle is five, Madam."

"Have you any other children, Mrs. Francis?"

"Yes, I have another daughter who lives in Jamaica, Madam."

"Mrs. Francis, in October 2002, do you remember what happened? Can you tell the court?"

"It was his birthday."

"Whose birthday?"

"His birthday, Madam."

"I take it you mean your husband, Mrs. Francis."

"Yes, Madam."

"You bought a new car, didn't you, Mrs. Francis in October?"

"Can you tell the court how you got the deposit?"

"Yes, Madam. From my job, Madam."

"Mrs. Francis, I have a document in front of me with your signature. If Mr. Francis was the person that you portray him to be, why would he get a loan in joint names, with a verbal agreement for you to pay back? Do you remember how much the loan was for, Mrs. Francis?"

"Yes, Madam. It was £1000, Madam."

"And when did you receive this money from Mr. Francis? This £1000?"

"I can't remember."

"Mrs. Francis, I do believe you are lying. Mr. Francis was not living in the marital home when he took it upon himself to borrow a £1000 to give to you to try and rebuild his marriage, but you simply abused him. No further questions."

My dear friends, Carol tried to project to the court that this money was a loan that she had previously given to me, one year prior to this case. But how could this be? If I had acquired a £1000 loan from Carol, should it not be the case that I would have to make the repayments to her? The loan in question was taken out by myself to aid Carol's car purchase, with a verbal agreement that she would make the repayments. I had never had a loan from Carol. My dear friends, just take one step back and look forward as far as you could. Would Carol be paying a loan for me whilst I was in prison and in my present predicament? Somehow, I do not think so. I dare say that she was extremely transparent or perhaps just an old fool. On reflection, I could remember it as clearly as if it was ten minutes ago. On October 23, 2002, I was living at my brother's apartment due to the fact that I was driven out of the marital home by Carol, her cronies, D.C. Duffus, and his friends. Carol wanted £1000 to pay a deposit on a Renault Clio, but I did not have this cash sum of money available. Carol suggested that I get a loan and she would make the repayments. Although we were separated, I still found it to be my duty to do whatever she asked at the time, with a view of getting back together (On reflection, what an old fool I was indeed). So I went ahead, and the loan was approved by the Black Horse Bank. The money was promised by the creditor to be in the account by midday on Friday, October 25. Carol rang me on my mobile phone at 1:00 P.M. At the time, I was working for Precision Engineering in the Medway Town. I was horrified by Carol's behaviour. She began shouting, "Where is the fucking money? It is not in the account. I know that you stopped it, you fucking bastard. I don't need your money. Go and suck your mother's pussy."

I gasped for breath as I shouted back, "Calm down, you fool. I did not stop the money going into the account; it is the bank's fault." I tried to explain. I dared say I called her a fool, but I was the fool. She hanged up. On Tuesday of the following week, I contacted the bank to make confirmation that the money had been credited into the account, and indeed, it was! I then rang Carol and asked if she had checked the account. My dear friends, what do you think she said to me? I would tell you if you promised not to laugh and think I was a fool though indeed, I was.

"That money was spent from yesterday she said you batty sucker." She then hanged up the phone. I could not believe this was the woman I marry. The sin that brought me to my knees— I took another man's wife—Mrs. Woodburn. May God forgive me.

Back to the barrister's questions…

Prosecution Barrister:
"Mrs. Francis, do you love your daughters?" he asked.
"Yes, Sir," she replied.
"Mrs. Francis, how do you find the United Kingdom?"
"It's a nice place, Sir," she replied.
"If you should get the opportunity to return to Jamaica, would you do so?"
"No, Sir. Jamaica life, too tough."
"Mrs. Francis, I want to ask you something, but I want you to think before you answer me, understand?"
"Yes, Sir."
"Mrs. Francis, do you hate your husband?"

At this point, for the first time during the trials, I had looked at Carol. She was facing the jury, and I was sitting at the far corner, so she had to turn in order to see me. She then glanced over her left shoulder. We made eye contact, and then she started a performance that was beyond my belief. Quite shocking "In fact," to the Judge and Jury. She began to stomp her left foot in approximately three seconds intervals while she stared at me. Her cat-like grey eyes rolled, and stared at me, changing colour to red. She continued stomping her feet. She then screamed with tears running from her eyes, "I hate him! I hate him! I hate him!" Stomping her feet whilst she screamed, she then fell to the floor and lie there for approximately thirty seconds, motionless. At this point, I thought she was dead. I gasped for breath as I watched the drama unfold! Two ushers rushed to her assistance. She was placed in the recovery position as they fanned her with sheets of paper. She was then placed on a chair, still on the stand. She was offered a cold drink of water and was asked by the ushers if she felt well enough to proceed.

I sat there, applauding to myself. I had never seen acting of such high calibre off-screen! I thought, at that point, Why did Catherine Zeta-Jones get so many awards when there was a much better actress right in front of my eyes? She deserved an Oscar award made from solid gold. She was taken off the stand and led out of the courtroom. With such a performance by Carol, there was the doubt in my mind that I was totally destroyed. Seven years in prison rang in my head like a bell, if found guilty, but the act was too transparent. The jury saw through it as if it was plain glass.

<u>Prosecution Barrister</u>:
I took the stand, and the questioning began.
"Mr. Francis, have you ever beaten your wife?"
"No."
"Mr. Francis, have you ever thought of killing your wife?"
"No."
"Mr Francis, I am sure you are capable of killing somebody."
"What made you think that?" I asked.
"You have a bad temper, haven't you?"
"I suppose we all have a bad temper at times, depending on the circumstances," I replied.
"Mr. Francis, I believe you are an evil vicious man. How did you feel when you phone the marital home, wishing to speak to your daughter who is your pride and joy, and found that another man was bathing her? How did you feel? Mr. Francis, did you want to kill him, rip his face off?"

I replied in a composed manner, "I was quite concerned about my daughter." At that point the prosecution barrister looked at me as if he had seen a ghost. On reflection, the prosecution barrister expected me to explode with anger, but his questioning failed to show a violent side to my character.

He replied, "No further questions."

The judge gave the jury his summary and then gave them two hours and ten minutes to decide whether I was guilty or not guilty.

At that point, I was taken back down to the cell whilst the jury deliberate on my execution. I felt pretty tired of the whole situation, but then, do or die, I was ready for anything. I had already made my peace with the world, so if I had died, it would not have made any difference. I got down on my knees, prayed to Allah, the God of all men, and then I lay down on the hard wooden bench, thinking of my daughter. I suddenly felt extremely calm and peaceful, almost as if it was all over and I had met God. I suddenly heard keys being pushed into the lock. I had a fright because the peaceful moment had been broken. Then a loud voice screamed, "Up, Francis. They have reached a verdict." Believe it or not, this was within ten minutes from the judge's decision to deliberate. I was paralysed with fear because I thought that if they had made a decision so quickly, I was doomed. But then, I was ready for it. If I was found guilty, I would have had seven years to contend with. I journeyed back to the court room along with a prison officer. On the way back, I asked, "What do you think my chances are?"

He then said, "Son, I have been doing this job for the past ten years, and I have never seen anyone being called back so quickly. The only thing I can say to you is be strong, and whatever comes, take it on the chin like a man. I can also say to you that the jury had made their minds up before the judge sent them out, so it can be good or it can be bad. Let's hope it's good for your sake."

"Alright, Gov," I said.

We went into the courtroom, the usual procedure

"All rise." In comes the judge. "You may be seated," a voice uttered, and everyone sat down.

Then a voice said, "Mr. Francis, please remain standing."

My heart started to palpitate, bursting from my chest to the momentum of the beats. I started to sweat, and for some strange reason, I drifted off into another world for a brief moment. Believe it or not, I was in the ring with Mike Tyson. As he punched me senseless, I drifted back into the courtroom. I could not explain this strange pattern of my mind. I heard the voice of the judge, "Members of the jury, have you reached a verdict?"

"Yes, your Honour."

"Have you selected a foreman?"

"Yes, your Honour."

"May your foreman stand? What is your verdict?" asked the judge.

"Not guilty, your Honour."

"Was this a unanimous decision?"

"Yes, your Honour."

The judge knocked his hammer, and said, "Mr. Francis, you are free to go."

D. C. Duffus looked at me. His face went bright red as his hair stood on ends, as if he was being electrocuted. He crunched his fist and walked out of the court room. My sisters were jumping for joy upon my release. My barrister gave me a big hug and a kiss on the cheek, and said, "I believed in you from day one."

I never saw D. C. Duffus or my barrister again, but I was still fighting to get compensation for the injustice that I suffered at the hands of the British justice system. The law was an ass. Allah had kept his promise to me. All praises be to Allah.

Freedom Freed From Prison July 2003

On July 7, 2003, I was discharged from court, a free man with no criminal record. My first taste of real food was in the restaurant of the courthouse. My barrister and my sister took me for lunch. Somehow, the food tasted very different from what I had just left behind. I actually enjoyed it. I asked my barrister what she thought of the relationship between D. C. Duffus and my wife. She replied, "It is rather obvious that they are seeing each other because I have never seen a policeman go so far out of his way to help a total stranger. It appears to me that they are having something far more than a business relationship. My advice to you is to stay as far as possible from your ex-wife, but you should never forget your daughter."

After we had lunch, my barrister said her goodbyes, and my sister and I went back to her place where I spend the rest of the day. In the evening, I went back to my brother's place, the same place where I was arrested in December 2002. I was extremely traumatised, I kept on getting flash back of my arrest. I went to the bathroom where I saw my daughter, the same way she was on the day of my arrest, standing in the bath, covered in soap. I burst into tears. I covered my face with my hands, but it was just the past that was haunting me.

I took a bath and went to sleep. I thought about my daughter all night. It was almost as if she were there with me. I heard her little voice calling "Daddy, daddy.' I would never forget what happened to me in December 2002, but at the same time, I had to live with it. Perhaps, if I had a memory erased, somehow, I think it might have done me some good. Nonetheless, I would still be carrying the burden of the British justice system.

On my second day of freedom, I had to see my daughter no matter what. I rang George, the cousin of my ex-wife, and asked him to make some form of arrangement for me to see Rochelle. He said it had already been discussed between himself and Carol that it was forbidden for me to see my daughter, but he said he would try a bit harder. I went to a solicitor (lawyer) in Lewisham to see if they could get some form of agreement drawn up through the court to give me access to see my daughter. When I was in prison, I learnt that Carol was trying to get a non-contact order against me to stop me from seeing Rochelle, my only child, I might add. The court refused this order because they could not see the monster in me that was projected by Carol. The solicitor made a one off arrangement with the mother for me to see my child through the help of a mediator, George. The arrangement was made for me to see Rochelle on the Saturday of that week. I was overjoyed to know that I would see my little princess again whom I so loved. Saturday came, and I had to go and face my daughter, which I did, at George's workplace—a local mental health institute. When Rochelle saw me, she screamed and ran towards me almost as if she was shot from a cannon. The impact of her excitement almost knocked me to the ground. I settled on my feet, and then picked her up. She locked her arms tightly around my neck, with her legs locked around my waist. At this point, my little girl was crying. She asked in a tearful tone, "Where were you, Dad? I missed you so much." I would never forget the look on her face when she saw me for the first time after seven months in prison. That moment would stay with me forever.

At that point, I could not hold back the tears. We both cried as we embraced each other tightly. I wiped my tears and tried very hard to compose myself; this was not very easy. I told my little girl the truth, "Rochelle, baby, daddy was in prison."

She said, "What? Mommy said you were on holiday. You went to America."

"I wish I was," I replied.

After two hours, my daughter and I had settled down, getting to know each other again. I kept her overnight. We had a lot to discuss. Although she was a mere five-year-old child, I felt comfortable talking to her. The next day, I took her back to George's workplace in order for him to return her to her mother. It was almost impossible because she refused to go. All I had was non-stop screaming and clinging to me as if she would never see me again. I looked at my suffering child, but I was helpless.

I said, "Don't worry, my little pet. Daddy loves you."

She asked, "When will I see you again dad?"

I said, "Soon, Rochelle, soon."

She said as I watched the tears rolled down her face, "Dad, don't leave me again."

I kissed her, and said, "I will never leave you, Rochelle."

Fortunately, for me, I had a good solicitor who believed in me. She had fast tracked my case through the Bromley Family Court where I had a hearing, and the judge did not hesitate to give me joint custody of our child. The question I would like to ask was how could a judge give custody of a child to a man like myself after looking at past allegations? I guessed the Judge knew that all the allegations were lies. My dear friends, was it not obvious? Either that, or the judge was drunk! It was arranged for me to collect Rochelle from the Welcare Contact Centre in Catford operated by the government. Collecting her from the centre was great, but the problem rose when I had to return her to her mother. An arrangement was made to give her to a friend or a family member so that her mother could collect her from wherever I dropped her off. Thanks to Peter Bonner & Co Solicitors for believing in me after reading Carol's statements that claimed Rochelle's life was in danger. What danger, I asked myself?

After six to twelve months into this routine, it appeared that the mother had fallen out with most of the people who were helping with Rochelle's return. So my means of returning her got very slim. At one point, I took her to the police station where I left her. She was collected from the station that night by her mother. I got fed up with the situation, so I decided to drop her off myself. Rochelle lived in a cul-de-sac; I knew that if I drop her at the entrance of the road, she was able to walk to the door by herself. This had continued for a period of one year. I became worried when she disappeared around the corner. I had no knowledge of what happened after I drove away. I was always very worried about this situation. Rochelle was now seven years old. I decided to give her a mobile phone to talk to me after dropping her off. She called me every other day, and this made me very happy. Although I paid the phone bill for her, I dared say that it was well worth it.

During my struggle in the picking-up and dropping-off of Rochelle, I was also busy integrating myself back into society. Upon my release from prison, I went back to my previous workplace before I was arrested. They were very glad to see me, but, unfortunately, I was given my P45 and all my holiday pay that was due to me. This came in handy, but at the same time I did not have a job. The temporary staff who was employed in my absence had gone over the three-month period wherein his employment could not be terminated upon my return. He had actually been in my post for six months. Therefore, I had no job, but still I had no ill feelings against the company.

I had managed to find myself a job in London with Volkswagen; it wasn't a bad job. I worked as an engineer reconditioning engine parts and re-boring engine blocks for bigger pistons to the required specifications. But believe it or not, the highlight of working for Volkswagen was that the workshop was near the street, and I could see everything that went on in the street. It was great fun. Although I worked in the machine shop by myself, I was never bored because there was always something going on in the street to take the boredom away from me, and best of all, when the sun started to shine, my main activity became bird watching (females)! There hadn't been a day that went past that a woman had not been seen by me. I flirt with every woman that went past the place. It actually became too much because they started to visit me at work, bringing me cakes, drinks, and all sorts of goodies. I began dating a few of these women just for fun. However, I oftentimes got into trouble when there was not enough work done for the day because I was so distracted.

At the time, I was living with Marion in Plumstead, but she had no hold over me. She always told me that a man should be "free" to do whatever he wanted to do. Marion was not a great believer in trapping a man or dictating to a man, which was very good for me. As long as the bills were paid, she had no problem. On the weekends, when the centre was closed, I had no other way of gaining access to my daughter except via this route. I often used these weekends to my advantage because Marion had no idea if I saw my daughter or not because I spend the weekend with my daughter at my brother's home. So when the centre was closed, I still spend the weekends away—in a hotel room down the coast. I did not love Marion. The only woman I had feelings for was Anita Patel, the Indian girl who saved me from heartbreak during my separation, and I still feel for her now, in 2006. We were not lovers, but we spoke on the phone regularly.

I had developed a taste for flirting over the years, which sometimes got out of control.

I was a member of a health club in Deptford where I visited religiously every weekend. There, I also flirted with lots of women. I also dated a few, which led me into problems.

One day, a young lady came in whom I thought had the best legs I had seen in a long time. Once again, my habits had taken me over.

I said to her, "You have a lovely pair of legs." She looked at me and laughed but remained unresponsive to my compliment. I told a close friend who was using the same health club that my next target was in view. For several weeks, I have watched this lady, trying my best to open a line of communication with her, but she always seemed to ignore me when I tried speaking to her. I asked her, "What do your friends call you?"

She replied, "None of your business."

Nevertheless, I kept on trying until one day, I said, "Those legs are really nice," and she responded by asking me if I would like to stroke them. I was really shocked by her response. All the lads were staring at me, and this fit woman was standing in front of me with her legs in my face. So I did what a man had to do. As I stroked her legs, I became aroused. I was quite embarrassed as I could not stand up to walk back into the sauna, so I had to sit there with my towel on my lap for a while.

One of the lads shouted, "You're in there, man," and indeed I was; he was right.

The following week, I asked her once more, "What is your name?"

She replied, "My name is Felicia, and your name is Raymond."

I replied, "How did you know my name?"

She said, "A little birdie told me so."

Three weeks went by, and I did not see Felicia. I was very interested in her. I wondered what had happened. Have I offended her? Or perhaps she was embarrassed due to the fact that all the lads knew the effect she had on my third leg because of her sex appeal. Her composure was non-flirtatious; she was a sensual woman.

During the three weeks of her absence, I started flirting with someone else, just being myself, of course. My sight was set on a Chinese girl who always took a bottle of milk to wash her face and her private part. My eyes were focussed on a certain part of her anatomy in her swim wear. I was hungry for her and felt my mouth salivating, ready for some action! Her name was Anning. We went on a few dates that were quite enjoyable, I must say. She claimed that she was better than me at sex, but she found out that she was wrong.

However, when Felicia returned back on the scene, I had to cool things down with Anning, although I was falling in love with her. Was I really falling in love? Or was I indulging in plain unadulterated lust that I was feeling, the result of my carnal mind because of the pack she was carrying?

I rekindled my liaison with Felicia again. We started having fun, but I had no idea where this was leading, Don't forget that I was living with Marion at the same time (Unknowing to her, she was kept in the dark.). Felicia asked me if I was living with a woman or if there was someone else I would rather be with than with her. She asked me this for several times. Each time, I denied everything, and professed that I was single, not living with anyone, and that I did love her. Evidentially, this was a lie. I assumed that she asked me these questions because she wanted to make it clear to me that she was not prepared to play second fiddle, to be the other woman, and to be my part-time lover: When it came to her feelings, she did not play games; "no one plays games with my emotions" she said. "I have been through too many traumas, too many emotional roller coasters, and enough was enough." As far as she was concerned, her mother did not give birth to her to give men the pleasure of abusing her. "Treat others the way in which you would like to be treated" was her motto. She wanted an honest committed relationship with a man she could trust with her heart. She wanted love and respect in its entirety. Obviously, if I was honest with her, the fun times we were having would come to a grinding halt.

There was no way of finding out if I was going to wake up to find her legs wrapped around me—my new body armour! When a man was having fun, it was not right for him to reveal his true status. Whether he was married or single, it was irrelevant to whoever he was flirting with that she was just a part of his game plan.

Thank God, I was not married at the time. On my release from prison, my ex-wife had done me the greatest favour a woman could ever do for a man, and for that, I was eternally grateful. But this favour was not even logged because she had no idea she was doing it. What was this favour, you may ask, my dear friends? She had issued me with divorce papers! I didn't mean papers asking me for a divorce, I meant papers informing me that I was divorced! Hassle free, problem free, and I was at last free from her. I must say that it was the only day that Carol had brought me happiness. Thank you, Carol, for setting me free…until I got a bill from the solicitor (for £5000). Unto this day, the bastards had not got a penny from me. What did they take me for?

I must have been the happiest divorced man on the planet. I was finally released from the bucket of cement that turned into concrete around my ankles before being thrown into the sea. You bet. I was as free as a bird, and I lived to tell the tale. I classed myself as a good man, and to quote my daughter's words, I was "the best dad a girl could ever have." Women in my life always fall for me, but little did they know the love that they desire will not come from me—women to me were just there to pass the time! Falling in love was taboo. I always made a woman think that I was falling in love with her, which she always believed. Sometimes, I tell a white lie that I was in love, but little did they know that it was total bullshit. I loved only one female in my life, and that was my daughter, Rochelle, my only daughter (at present) that I cherish. She is my world and would always be until breath leaves my body. But who knows what is around the corner! I might fall in love, but at the moment, I took what I could. Wham bam, thank you, Ma'am.

I was getting frustrated having to juggle all these women on my case. Believe it or not, Anita, my Hindu friend, was living on the next road from Marion, and she did not have a clue up to now that I was living with a woman on the next road. Yet, Anita and I had the most wonderful time and shared the greatest sex. My relationship with Anita, as I may have mentioned previously, had taken a back seat, although we still communicate by telephone. I always kept her sweet until I was ready to reclaim what was mine.

One day, I was washing the car outside Marion's house. Anita came walking down the road. I turned my back towards her, watching her in the wing mirror. As she got closer, I pulled the bucket of water across the front of the car, stooping down as she went by, and she never saw me. Or did she?

I rang her one hour later and made arrangement to go out that evening, and it was all good. She did not suspect a thing. I must have been born to be a player. As I said before, the good thing about Marion was that she asked me no questions about my comings and goings. But she had started to upset me now. At weekends, I disappeared; she knew that weekend was for my daughter and me. Rochelle and I always spent the weekend at a seaside resort, staying in hotels. She found it very enjoyable because she had endless fun with her daddy. But of course, when Rochelle was not with me, I use that weekend for my leisure. It all came to an end when Marion decided that she would not have me staying away at weekends anymore. So I had to make a choice to deal with my situation. It was very boring staying at home at the weekends, because all we do was to watch TV or sometimes have a barbeque. Rochelle always complained about being bored. I started spending time away from home again, but this time, we were spending time with my family. This continued for about six months, and then we continued again with the seaside resort routine. To entertain my daughter was all that matters. Apparently, I was getting fed up with Marion. One night, during our pleasuring session, she had mentioned that she had bought a toy. I was in a state of shock when she revealed to me what the toy was! It was approximately twelve inches long and two inches in girth, with veins all over it. It looked positively life-like and felt real. I had never seen anything like this before. She had demonstrated its use whilst I watched, and then she demanded that I use it to pleasure her, following her instructions, which I did. It appeared that this was indeed what she wanted (Was I not man enough for her? I wondered). As I inserted this artificial instrument into her orifice, I was in denial, wondering how deep inside it would go. She then switched to the highest speed. The vibration was a little too much for me as I held it. She commanded that I pull it out and smother it with the lubricating gel. I did as I was asked, but I got no pleasure from this. She, on the other hand, was in sheer ecstasy. Believe it or not, this instrument had disappeared. All that I held on to was the battery cap, right at the very end! I had no choice but to make a drastic decision after pulling it out. I looked at her, but I could not perform, although I tried. I was extremely embarrassed when I compared the sizes. She had asked me to do this several times, but it was inevitable. It was time for me to leave her and end the relationship. I guess, somewhere in my mind, I knew that Felicia and I would get together, although she had no knowledge of my current situation.

One morning, I got up and went downstairs. Unfortunately, that morning, I was quite upset by what I had encountered the night before. Nonetheless, I had already made up my mind. For several nights and mornings, when I went to the toilet, I always stepped into dog piss, and I was pissed off with it. The morning that I had made my decision to leave, I went downstairs, and I stepped into the dog piss again! The dog was not trained to use the toilet!

I said, "Marion, may I have a word please? (It was a Saturday morning. I remember it clearly). Here's some money for the bills, and I am leaving you today."

She replied, "What?"

I said, "I am leaving you."

She replied, "You can't do that."

I replied, "I have made my mind up." She looked at me with tears in her eyes. I said, "Don't worry, you will be okay."

She said, "After all I have done for you, you are going to leave me?"

I replied, "Yes."

She asked, "What have I done?"

I replied, "Nothing."

I went upstairs and packed my bags. In every trip I made to the car, she stood and stared. When I made my final trip, I said, "I have left the TV and VCR for you. You can have them." I went through the door, closing it behind me, and I never returned.

I set up home with Felicia, trying to make a life. She was a lovely person, but she had no idea what was lurking in the shadows (Another of my victim, unknowingly).

No matter what I did or how hard I tried, my appetite for womanising always overcame me. I guess it was just me. One day, I was at work, looking out as usual, watching the women as they went by. I saw a nice, fit-looking woman. I shouted out, "Hey, sexy." To my surprise, she came over to me, and we started to talk. We hadn't actually dated, but we always had a good chat. Whenever she went past, she always came to visit me. Her name was Elaine. Elaine and I became very good friends until one day, she mentioned that there was party at the weekend. She asked if I would like to go with her, and I agreed. The next day she came to see me again and said that she needed to go to the hairdresser to get her hair done. She asked if I could give her £50 to pay for it. I was quite surprised because at this point, I had not even slept with her, and she was already asking me to give her financial support. Nevertheless, I obliged and gave her the money. I remember it very clearly. It was a Wednesday. The following day, she passed by my workplace but did not stop. Then she came to visit me on Friday. I asked her, "Why did you not get your hair done?" She came up with an excuse that was totally irrelevant to me. The weekend went by, and she did not phone me as promised. On Monday, as she passed by again, I called her over. I asked her, "What had happened? Did you not promised to call me on Saturday?" She gave me a sad story about family problems. I was expecting to get the money back because she did not get her hair done. It was plain obvious to me that she needed quick cash, hence, the hairdressing story! Elaine had two daughters whom I have no connection with, apart from waving to them as they pass by and, sometimes, when they visit with their mother. Although she lived next door to my workplace, I was never invited in for lunch or afternoon tea. In my eyes, she was just seeking someone to use and abuse. She also told me that she had erased the children's father out of their lives, as he was not giving them any financial support. At that point, I thought, Don't look at me. As it continued, I awaited the next time that she would approach me for money. However, before that happened, I had met someone else who was walking pass my workplace as usual. This happened to be my pick-up point for meeting women; a great job, indeed!

    The next person I met was a young lady called Jackie. She lived five minutes away from my workplace. Jackie invited me for lunch on a regular basis and sometimes dinner. One thing I did like about her was that she had big breasts and long legs. She also had a child. She was married to a young man, but it was strictly business, purely to stay in the country (Where have I heard that before?). I told Elaine that I no longer wanted us to be friends. She appeared quite upset by this. The next day, she came to visit me, and she was in tears. I asked her what was wrong, and her reply hit me like a bullet. She said that the children were upset because they saw me as a father figure, and they were traumatised, so I dismissed this as madness. I do believe that Elaine herself was upset because she could no longer ask me for money, so she used the children to play on my emotion. But this was a typical trick that women use; it did not work on me. At that time, I was living with Felicia. A man was just a man. Jackie and I got friendly. As time went by, we did not get intimate, but I found out that she also wanted to use me. What could I say? She was just another Jamaican woman. Jackie's visits to my workplace became too frequent, and I was not getting much work done. I work on my own, as mentioned previously the Boss had noticed that my production level was a bit low. He knew that I was a hard worker. She began to borrow my car frequently, like every other day. I got really fed up with this, but I never said "No." My car happened to be a black Mazda 2.5V6. I had no idea of the type of insurance she had because she drove a Honda Prelude, which was always breaking down. I did have a bad habit of leaving my important documents such as my passport in my car. Jackie had no idea of what my name was, but she knew me as Ray, and that is all she knew. Since I came from prison, I had never used Raymond. New people who I had met always got the name Ray. My friendship with Jackie ended a few days after she returned my car, handed me the keys, and addressed me as Mr. Francis. I was shocked because this told me that my car had been searched. Important documents were left on the floor in the rear of the car. She claimed that her son went into the rear pocket on the back of the front seat where I kept important papers. Believe it or not, my brand new British passport was gone. I asked her of the whereabouts of my passport, and she denied the facts of ever seeing it. I had reported this to the police. Now, three years later, I had not replaced it, nor was it found. But someone out there was using it, thanks to her. I wondered how much it fetched in the illegal market! Associating with the wrong people could be fatal to one's existence or even to one's health, I might add. But such was life.

That was the end of my friendship with Jackie for what it was worth. Believe it or not, several times on Sydenham high street, I had seen Rochelle's mother almost as if she knew when I was coming out for lunch. Although, she was there clearly in my view, I had the ability to walk past with my head held up high, and although the sleeves of our garments had touched a few times, I still couldn't tell what she was wearing because I did not see her, if you knew what I meant.

One day, a strange thing happened. I happened to be driving up Sydenham high street, and I spotted Rochelle and her mother on the other side of the road. The traffic was very heavy. I was rolling at approximately five miles per hour or less. Rochelle's mother saw me, to my disappointment, but then, this was a free country. She used this opportunity to put herself even more in my view. Whenever I saw Rochelle with her, I really didn't see them at all because to me, the mother was invisible. As a result of this, I regarded my daughter to be invisible as well. At this point, whilst driving, Rochelle's mother shouted very loudly. In an attention-seeking kind of manner, she shouted to Rochelle, "There's your dad." Rochelle then bolted across the road, which was very dangerous. By this time, she was standing next to my car because the traffic was at a standstill.

I greeted her with a kiss on her forehead and said, "Hello, my little pet." By this time, her mother was standing alongside her. It was Friday; I remember this day clearly. The traffic suddenly started moving, and I said to her, "I have to go, Rochelle."

She asked, "Will I see you tomorrow, Dad?" I always picked her up from the contact centre every Saturday.

I said, "Yes, you will see me tomorrow." I then drove off.

I would never speak to her mother for the rest of my life, as I made a promise to myself that upon any exchange of a dialogue, I would amputate my right hand. So you see, my dear friends, how serious this was. But don't get me wrong. I didn't hate her. She's the mother of my child, the little girl whom I love more than myself. What she did to me was what I hate, although it was simply a survival mechanism that was built into her genes. At the time, I did not know that it was totally ungodly to take another man's wife for my own, and in fact, someone who just had a face and no form of education. I did believe that if Carol was as educated as my present wife, it would have worked, but for two people with different levels of education to make it was almost impossible. One would feed the other. In that context, it would not be true compatibility. Also, the different worlds clashes. The British and the Jamaican way of life was always in conflict of each other, but thank God, it was something I called ancient history. However, I have to add that when someone tried to mimic you or become you, sometimes, they would find it very difficult because of their education standards or their living standards. There was no way Carol could become like me, although she tried very hard. I was just too advanced for her to keep up with. When she failed to become like me, she tried to destroy me. If there was one thing I regret very deeply, it was the day when I shook Mr. Woodburn's hand (her husband) and accepted the fact that his wife was going to be mine. The sin that brought me to my knees. Nevertheless, I had a lovely daughter as a result of this, and to me, that was, perhaps, a natural blessing in disguise. My daughter is very special and dear to me. She was the end product of a disastrous relationship, but at the same time, she deserved to be loved, and I would never let her down. Some fathers would turn their backs on the child in a situation like this, but I would never do that to Rochelle.

Sometimes, I sat and thought of the day that I was arrested; I was then bathing my little girl. The question that always came to my mind that never got answered was: D. C. Duffus and his cronies entered my brother's apartment on the day I was arrested. At the time of the arrest, it was alleged by D. C. Duffus that I had barricaded the front door. I found this accusation quite ironic because my brother's girlfriend entered the apartment freely by using her keys, and she was followed by ten or twelve policemen alongside the big chief, D. C. Duffus. This was a total mystery to me. I did believe that he had a wild imagination. The arrest that took place on December 23, 2002 had a heavy impact on Rochelle and myself; we are both still traumatised by the event. I still have a strong hatred for the police to this day. Whenever I saw a police, I would suddenly get in a rage. To calm myself, I count to ten. I knew that it was the trauma which I had suffered through the hands of D. C. Duffus. Occasionally, when I got stopped by the police whilst driving, I would automatically become enraged. That gave the police the reasons to suspect me, but they had no form of understanding of my situation. Not many of us had experienced a policeman who gave himself automatic authority to take over one's life and family as I may have said before. Duffus took my human rights away from me. Could you believe it? He had the power to prevent me from seeing my daughter whilst I was in prison, but her spirit was always with me, and that he could not stop. One day, I went on a visit. Whilst waiting for my visitor, a little girl came over to me, and I had an extraordinary warm feeling inside. She looked at me, smiled, and said, "Hello." At this point, I was driven to tears because the little girl looked like my Rochelle, and I would always believe that it was Rochelle who came to visit me spiritually. My visitors came. It was my two sisters, and they saw me in an emotional state. I then explained to them what had happened. I did believe that the personal issue with D. C. Duffus had gone way out of hand, but when you think of his rewards, you may not think so. His payments were always in kindness by my ex-wife, if you knew what I mean!...

...Now, I am a free man as I always had been, although I was in captivity. Whenever Rochelle and I were together and she saw a police or heard a siren, she would go into a strange protective mode towards me. Whether or not she demonstrated this behaviour when she was with her mother was unknown to me. However, she tried her best to protect me for some strange reason, e.g., Rochelle and I went to Liverpool Street Market one Sunday. In this crowded place, we saw three officers on the beat, strolling along observantly, coming towards us face-to-face. They were simply going about their duty. At this point, Rochelle jumped in front of me, stretched out her arms in a protective manner, and screamed, "Leave my daddy alone." The officers showed concern. They asked me why she behaved in such a way, and I told them what had happened. They suggested that Rochelle and I should seek counselling. I do believe that the incident in December 2002 had caused great damage to my daughter and myself, and I do believe that D. C. Duffus was wrong to execute the act of arrest in such a manner that left my daughter and I traumatised. Although, to Duffus, it was a personal vendetta on behalf of Carol who paid him in kindness. Not often did a big, fat, perverted-looking man had access to black pleasure of such quality! I guess a slut was a slut by any other name. The spots of a leopard never changed, if you knew what I mean!

However, you might ask, my dear friends, "What's been done about it?" The answer is simple—nothing. Perhaps, one day,

Rochelle and I would forget what had happened to us that day. That would be the day when someone stood over my grave, saying the words, "Ashes to ashes and dust to dust."

It was quite frightening, when I look into my daughter's life, and I saw my own life reflected in front of me as a child. I wish there was something I could do to change the course, but apparently, there was not much I can do. Rochelle happened to develop all my childhood ailments. Sometimes, I looked at her when she was in pain. Only I could feel the pain she was going through because I felt it as a child growing up. I, too, suffered from inflamed tonsils, especially when I had a cold. My ears used to hurt as a child. Sometimes, I held my nose and blew. This always had an effect on my eardrums; it was a very painful thing. It was similar to having mumps for several times. My poor little girl was exactly the same. During my suffering as a child, I had no parents to cuddle or comfort me, but thank God, I am there for Rochelle. I would never let her down, nor forsake her in any way as long as I am alive, and I am 100 percent certain that when she become an adult, she would always remember her dad, unlike myself. I do believe that at this point in time, I must give up the ways of my teenage years.

Four women in one night at this age was not for me to brag about, as I did when I was a teenager. On reflection, during the infancy of my turbulent marriage on 1994, I was always looking for an escape. Sadly, my escape was always through women. I must say they gave pleasure better than alcohol. Women had been called users but if I were a woman, what would I be called? I guess a woman was very similar to a man. If she was unhappy in her relationship or her home life, under normal circumstances, she would seek satisfaction through a man, and if she didn't find what she was looking for in a particular man, then she moves on to another man. At the same time, she would carry a label with her that was quite derogatory, the label that a man whose behaviour is of the same nature is somewhat of an ego booster—a Casanova!

Carol had to return to Jamaica in 1994, and although I was not happy with my life, I had an incredible experience. I looked through the window, and I was in total shock. I saw my neighbour with a sizzling hot Indian woman. I could not believe my eyes because my neighbour was an old boy, almost ready for the grave. I watched from the window on a daily basis, hoping to see her again, and indeed, I did. I went to knock for my friend. On this occasion, his woman answered the door. She looked at me in a seductive manner as she invited me in. I chatted with my friend while she served cold drinks to us. She had appeared quite friendly, but I could see that he had her under heavy guard. I couldn't say I blame him. This woman would make a dead man come. I visited my friend for approximately one month intermittently, and his woman became friendlier with each visit. Her name was Margaret. One day, I knocked at my friend's door, and Margaret opened it. She was wearing a bathrobe, and to my utmost surprise, she opened the robe and gave me an incredible view of her assets—a sexy body, I may add. Her breasts were voluptuous and firm. In fact, her whole body appeared to be to be quite athletic. She then closed the robe and giggled. I was extremely turned on, and I had a hard time controlling myself in the presence of my neighbour after what I have just seen. To think that she was only two doors away from me! I was quite surprised by her action. However, I had to curb my arousal and leave my neighbour's apartment in a hurry. I could not enter the apartment due to my embarrassment. Two weeks later, Margaret's daughter, Indra, came on a vacation from the United Stated of America to visit her mother for three weeks. Indra and I had become friends. One night, she knocked on my door, crying. I asked her what was wrong.

She replied, "It's the first week of my vacation and I can't take the arguments between my mother and her boyfriend.'

She asked if she could spend the rest of her vacation in my apartment. I agreed without hesitation because Carol was away in Jamaica with her ex-husband, and I was sure that he was not the only one who was keeping her satisfied during her stay. So I welcomed Indra into my bachelor's pad where she found happiness. That night, we went out, had a few drinks, returned home, and then went to sleep. I found myself drifting into a deep slumber, but it appeared that Indra was masturbating me. It did not take much time for me to wake up, and surely, I made a meal of the situation. However, she complained of deep penetration, finding it uncomfortable. She was only four feet, ten inches tall, a very petite woman. I did not get a chance to use all my gears because of her complaint, but if only she knew, all six gears were in motion when having sex with her mother previously. Dared I say, Margaret could take a beating! Indra enjoyed her three weeks, and I was certain that she returned to the United States of America happier than when she came. She told me that she might be pregnant, but that, I would never know. We communicated for months, but our lines of communication broke down when she changed her address. I had enlarged photos of her all over my apartment, almost as if we were lovers.

In fact, we were lovers in a way, but I didn't think it would have lasted. Don't forget that Carol was in Jamaica and due to return shortly.

Nevertheless, Margaret kept coming to see me regularly. I had not disclosed to her any information regarding my liaison with her daughter. One day, Margaret came to see me, bringing a large envelope, which she handed to me. She was giggling as she did this. I opened it, and put the contents on the table. To my surprise, they were nude photos of herself. She looked just as good in the photos as she did when she revealed her body to me the day she gave me a flash of her hidden assets. I complimented her on her amazing physique, and she replied, "I am glad you like it."

I was extremely aroused at this point. Then, the inevitable happened, but it was truly an awesome experience. Can you believe it? A ménage-a-trois! Yes, it was both mother and daughter. It was good fun, and I was quite happy with the situation because Carol was away for six months. It was almost like déjà vu. I was wearing the same underwear, the same shorts, and I was wearing the same cologne when I scored with mother and daughter within one week of each other. Mother and daughter—can you believe it? Was this a miracle, or was I just lucky? A bit of both, I may say, old chaps. Not many men were so lucky! I made the most of it, realizing that I did not love Carol at all, but I did not know how to reverse the process of getting her out of my life. All she wanted from the marriage was a bit of paper to say, "I am a British citizen," which indeed she got. She showed me signs that told me that there was no love, so I returned to my teenage attitude—fuck without fear and never watch a tear! She had more to gain than myself from the marriage.

To become a British citizen—that is the dream of people in the third world. The British Government is a fool; it allows people from all other countries to flood this little island called England. Now, it is overcrowded with foreigners, including myself. The people from these poor countries that flood Britain knows every loophole to gain residency or citizenship. They are also misled by the misconception of thinking that the streets of London are truly paved with gold. How naïve they are! When I walk down the street or in the park all I see on the pavement is dog shit. The average thug who owns a pit bull dog does not walk with a bag to pick up its shit. Therefore, you step on it. It was black gold, I may add!

However, for some strange reasons, foreigners seem to think the streets are really paved with gold. How pathetic.

In fact, Margaret had told me several times that she have had close encounter with third world gold (dog shit) as she walked down the streets of London. She complained of stepping onto it. It had been three and a half months since Margaret and I started seeing each other on a regular basis, almost day-to-day, in fact, and I sensed that she had been developing feelings for me. Her boyfriend was a close friend of mine, but still, due to my kind-hearted nature, I let it flow. I was simply doing her a favour as with all my other women. Nonetheless, I know that one day, I would hang up my gloves, go into retirement, and dedicate myself to one woman, and that was just a dream! Dreams are for fools.

It came to pass that my suspicions of Margaret's feelings for me were true at the time. I was running a small business, renting rooms from a large house that I had bought verbally from my dad. This was a very large house with six rooms. Each room was individually rented. I was paying the mortgage quite comfortably from the rental income. Whenever a tenant vacated, I always decorate the room and replaced any damaged furniture (if there was any). On rare occasions, I had supplied new beds. Once, I had prepared an empty room again for renting. That room became a love nest for Margaret and I until it was once again occupied by a new tenant.

I was never in a hurry to rent a room because I always have five rooms occupied, which easily paid the mortgage. Having a spare room was always welcomed, especially with my current predicament. It had gotten to the point where Margaret would ask me to take her places, as well as visiting family members to whom she would introduce me as her boyfriend. This introduction gave me feelings of great discomfort because the truth of the matter was that my relationship with her was only sex. Five months after explicit sex sessions with Margaret and her daughter, believe it or not, my dear friends, Margaret became pregnant. At this point, I was in a jam because Carol (my wife at the time) was due to return from Jamaica. I gave Margaret a fist full of dollars to have an abortion, which was carried out, and we continued having sex with protection. Carol arrived back in the United Kingdom after six months in Jamaica. At the airport, she was stopped after baggage reclaim and her suitcases were searched for contraband substances. I waited over one hour for her to come through the gates that would make her free on British soil. She was a touch upset but nevertheless walked through like a Goddess unlike the times when she did not have right of abode in Britain. The journey home was long but she was very excited to be here once more. I don't think her excitement was due to the fact that she was with me, but to know within herself that one day she would execute the devious plans that lingered beneath the face that smiles so gracefully. One week later, she began to spread her wings beyond her boundaries I got home from work one evening.

As I entered through the front door, she said, "I am really pissed off because every move I make in this house, I feel watched by an Indian." She then took all photos of Indra and smashed them to pieces as I stared helplessly. There were broken glasses and torn up pictures of Indra everywhere. Her behaviour, I guess, was inevitable because she was meant to be the woman of my life. I had never experienced anything like it. I just stood there, speechless. She was only jealous because Indra's picture had covered all the wall space. I simply began clearing up the debris caused by hurricane Carol whilst she sat on the sofa, sipping ove-proofed Jamaican white rum neat (undiluted) as if it was water.

After two hours, my mission was completed. The bottle of rum that was full was now past halfway. I decided to go out to get a Chinese take-away meal. She insisted on coming with me, but I refused her company. Believe it or not, after her alcohol consumption, she showed no sign of drunkenness. But then, it was in her blood. Her father was known to be a hardcore drinker who showed no sign of having any adverse effect caused by his drinking habit. I watched her return to the apartment; she walked in a straight line without staggering. I stopped around the corner and rang my friend (my neighbour), but really and truly, I wanted to speak to Margaret. He answered the phone, and I could hear Margaret's voice in the background, enquiring who was on the phone. We spoke for a short while. Then he called her over to speak to me, much to my delight. I asked her to come out using our coded language. She agreed and met me around the corner. We drove to our love nest, which was waiting to be rented.

At this point, I was having serious thoughts of keeping that room vacant for myself for emergencies! Margaret and I decided to stay there for the night. She called her boyfriend (whom I dared not name) to let him know that she was spending the night with her cousin. I left in the morning and went straight to work. When I arrived home that evening, Carol had cooked my favourite meal, acting as if nothing had happened previously. But I was one step ahead, knowing what I know. She would never get the opportunity to feed me spiked food again.

Six month later, it came to me as a great shock when Margaret announced to me that she was pregnant again! At that point, I was totally confused. I clearly remembered the night when it could have happened. Unfortunately, a condom had split on me due to the power and the speed of the strokes I also remembered her saying to me in a Jamaican accent you are like a machine that doesn't stop (smoking baby!) I could not confide in my friend (my neighbour); I was stuck. However, I have tried using my persuasive skills on her to convince her into telling her boyfriend that it was his child. She responded by giving me a few factors as to why she would not get involved in this bizarre triangle.

    i. She replied, "I have no love for him"
    ii. "He is not capable."
    iii. "I would hate to mislead him because he may believe that I love him, and furthermore, we are not having sex."

The only decision I could come to was to suggest the inevitable. Although it hurt me deeply, it had to be done. As the daleks (robots) in Dr. Who says, "Exterminate, exterminate." The operation cost me a small fortune, but it was (due to my carelessness) inevitable for the sake of my friend, my neighbour.

Margaret returned to Jamaica, and believe it or not, one year later, I went to Jamaica to find her, even though I had just become a dad. I had no success in finding her, but I had learned that she went to the United States of America to join her daughter there. Thinking about it, I wondered if Margaret and her daughter are carrying hatred for me after exchanging notes about their sex lives. Can you imagine mother and daughter having a conversation about sex? I wonder, did they? Could I have been a topic of conversation? If I was, I am in real shit.

To this day, my neighbour and I are still friends, although I no longer live next door. Carol and I moved to a new house due to the birth of our daughter, Rochelle, on December 16, 1997.

The new house was situated in a very quiet neighbourhood, not far from the apartment I had vacated. I still had the business, but I also got myself an engineering job in the Medway town of Sittingbourne to escalate my salary as it was combined with the income from the business. However, I still had a thirst for using the spare room, so to speak. I was back on the road again, occasionally returning to the love nest for some unadulterated fun due to the fact that my home life was non-existent. I was overworked, and I had to look after the baby and keep everything together. My regular snacks at the love nest were now cut down to a minimum. My dear friends, please do not look upon me as a beast because I am a good father who at the time had no home life.

At present, I believe that I was doing okay, although I was still being overworked by the women on the side. Felicia happened to think that I was a good man (that was what I think), not by telling me so, but by her reactions to the things I say and do. I knew I have treated her unkindly; she did not deserve this. She was a wonderful caring person. Looking back on the situation, I could have handled things a lot better, but I repeated the same selfish behaviour over and over again. I knew that she saw me as a heartless, inconsiderate beast, but deep in the back of my mind, when the voice in my head said "Go," I have to go. Nonetheless, the old habits still lingered. I guess, I was still trying to catch up on the sex I missed out whilst in prison.

At this point, I had enough to last me a lifetime. However, the women were still there, cracking the whip and counting the strokes.

I met up with Yvonne one day whilst shopping in Woolwich. I said to her, "I told you we would meet again," so I did not hesitate to get straight to the point. Each time we meet during my imprisonment, she was always saying she liked me, but she was a prison officer, so nothing could happen. I said to her at that point, "Do you still see me as a prisoner?"

She said, "I have never seen you as a prisoner."

I arranged to meet her on the same evening. We met up and went for a meal and then a drink as the evening wind down to night time. I went back to her place, and she insisted that I spend the night with her.

She asked, "Where are you staying at the moment?"

I replied, "At my brother's. (This was my usual excuse, and it always worked. It was the same story I told Felicia!) It is not possible for me to take you back there."

Her apartment was very cosy, a bit like a parlour. She was the fly, and I was the spider!'

She said, "Have a seat, and I will change into something comfortable." She came back to the living room. At this point, I dare say, I was in a state of shock. She was dressed in black leather attire, wearing knee-high boots, cupless bra, and crotchless panties. Her exposed clitoris was hanging through the opening of the panties and protruding downwards. Believe it or not, she was the hottest thing I had seen since I was discharged from prison. I almost ejaculated on myself when I looked at her with excitement! She cracked the whip and said, "Are you ready for me, big boy?" She joined me on the sofa and sat across me. We began to kiss. I placed my hand on her pussy, and I swear, it was like a river that had burst its bank; she was dripping. The sex we had was wild; I had scratches all over my back. She was like a wild animal on heat, dying to be cooled down. As I was about to shed my load inside her, she screamed, "Wait for me! Wait for me!" I could not hold out any longer, and I released my load inside her. Seconds later, she screamed, "I'm coming. I'm coming." She held on to my head and buried it into her huge bosom. That experience would stay with me forever. Occasionally, I still used that memory to get aroused when I am with a woman who was boring. Dare I say, that was a night to remember!

Yvonne and I carried on, meeting every other week until the guilt got the better of me. Oftentimes, when I got home, it was difficult for me to look Felicia in the face and tell her another pack of lies. The trouble was that the harder I tried to go on the straight path of becoming a one-woman-man, there always came something to lead me astray, which I found uncontrollable. Women were always making me offers which I dared not refuse (Got to keep up with my reputation!) At least I know I would die happy!

A dear friend of mine goes by the name of Lady P. I had not seen her for at least one year. I decided to call her. Strangely, someone else answered the phone.

I asked, "May I speak to Lady P please?"

The lady on the phone asked, "Who is Lady P?"

I replied, "She is a very close friend of mine. How come you have her number?"

She replied, "I have recently obtained this phone number from my service provider."

I replied, "I am sorry for disturbing you. I will not call back again."

She replied, "What is your name? I like the sound of your voice."

I told her my name, said goodbye, and hanged up the phone. One month later, my phone rang. Lady P's name flashed on my screen. In my thoughts, at the time, it was an old friend, trying to get in touch with me, but to my surprise, it was the same lady who had recently obtained Lady P's number.

I said, "What can I do for you?"

She said, "I was just calling because I like the way you sound the last time we spoke."

She asked me if I would like to go for a drink.

I replied, "I don't know you. Neither do I know what you look like. So how can I agree to go out for a drink?" I asked her, her name.

She replied, "Lillian, but my friends called me Lil."

I said, "What do I call you then?"

She replied, "Lil."

I said, "Are we friends then?"

She replied, "Yes."

I said, "My goodness, I have a friend, and I don't even know what she looks like.'

She said, "Are you coming for that drink, now that we are friends?"

I said, "What area do you live in?"

She said, "Near Gatwick Airport."

I arranged to meet her at her workplace where she was also a resident. She lived and worked in a hospital near Gatwick Airport. I decided to go on a blind date. When I got close to the landmark, I discovered that I was somewhat lost. It appeared that I have taken the wrong turn. I rang her for directions, and I was given directions leading to the hospital where she worked as a nurse. I asked her for a description of herself. At this point, she started laughing.

I said to her, "What's the joke? Please share it."

She said, "Just drive down to the outpatients department, and I will be waiting outside. What car are you driving?"

I described my car to her in every detail possible. I then said, "All you have to do is look out for a black sports car with orange fog lights." As I drove towards the outpatients department, I spotted a lady standing outside. This lady was approximately six feet, five inches, with the body of a sumo wrestler. I said to myself, This could not be the person. Let me ask her if she knows the person I am looking for. I said, "Excuse me, please, I am looking for a young lady by the name of Lillian." The twenty something stones (in weight I may add) woman looked at me with her eyes shining like a light bulb, she then said, "I am Lillian."

At that point, my brain was saying to my legs, Accelerate and get out of here. I ignored what my brain was saying to my legs and said to her instead, "Pleased to meet you." She sat in the car, and I heard the car screamed, Don't do this to me! She took me out for a Chinese meal, which I enjoyed very much. All expenses were paid for by her, of course!

On the way to the pub, I tested the water to see what this lady was all about. I said to her, "I have to go back to London, and furthermore, I do not have any condoms." At that point, I found out exactly what her intentions were.

She replied, "Don't worry, we can get condoms in the pub."

I knew at that moment that I was in for a hard night.

We arrived at the pub. I had a soft drink. She disappeared into the ladies. She came back with a packet of three latex diving suits and said, "I have them." I guzzled down my drink, and we then headed back to her apartment at the hospital campus. Upon entering, she showed me to the bedroom. I got undressed and laid on the bed, thinking of the course of action I had to foretake as I lay there.

She said, "Just let me go to the bathroom to freshen up." I watched her as she walked to the bathroom door. I was certain I was looking at the back of a bus! She returned. As she began to get undressed, I watched her closely with a strange feeling. Obviously, it was simply a favour that one could never call upon to be returned (as in a favour for a favour). In fact, she had one more crease than the Michelin Man. I counted them, and I did not say a word. I dare say that she had the largest breast I have ever seen in my life. In fact, they were much larger than Yvonne's. As she climbed into the bed, I watched her side of the bed sank. I closed my eyes and saw a cartoon image of a mosquito having sex with an elephant!

I rolled over. Her heaving bosom were like mountain peaks and boy, didn't I have fun with those twin peaks! I buried my head into the valley of the twin peaks, slapping my ears with the two mountains. It was good fun and a new experience for me. I was exhausted by the end of the night. I collapsed into a heap and fell asleep.

She woke up early in the morning and prepared breakfast whilst I was asleep. I felt someone shake me, saying, "Wake up. Wake up. Time for breakfast." I could not believe the breakfast I was served. To put it mildly, I thought I was a king!

I said to her, "I must leave early because I have to go to collect my daughter from the contact centre." I ate breakfast and showered, and then it was time for me to leave. She walked me to my car. As I started the engine, I noticed tears running down her cheeks.

I asked, "What is wrong, young lady?"

She replied, "I have a feeling I will never see you again."

I said, "Don't worry, you will."

She replied, "I am in love with you."

I thought this woman is truly crazy. I enjoyed the experience I had, but LOVE? No way!

We communicated, and I saw her a few more times since our liaison. Whenever the urge of feeling like a king came over me I always retreated to Lillian. A close friend of mine worked for a Mental Health Institute. I visited him one day when he introduced me to the manageress. Her name was Camilla. I thought she was stunning, so just to see her, I visited my friend frequently. I invited her on a date, and she accepted. Since then, we had had a few dates, wined and dined. One night she invited me back to her place, which I agreed to. Her apartment was not all that flash. It was not what I expected anyway, but I knew damn well what I was there for, so that really did not matter.

We sat down in the living room and had a few drinks. Then she indicated what she wanted by putting on a blue movie which did not impress me at all. Nonetheless, I went along with whatever she was doing.

We managed to climb the stairs to the bedroom where she produced two wine glasses and a bottle of champagne from her bedroom refrigerator. I dare say that it was a bit like a Venus Flytrap. We started a bit of shenanigan. Then things got really serious. I then asked her if she had a diving suit. She asked me, "What are you talking about?" I told her, and she then produced a packet. I took one, placed it over my third leg and rolled it down, watching the seven inches throbbing. Immediately after doing this, she jumped on me with no mercy at all. I was lying on my back, and she rode me as if she was trying to tame a wild horse. After one hour of intense work, we paused and had some more champagne. She then got out a pair of handcuffs and cuffed my hands to the headboard of the bed. She then sought my permission if she could tie my feet round the ankles. I was rather curious, but I allowed her to proceed with her fantasy. She started performing as if she was a pole dancer. When I finally rose again, she was away once more. I do believe that she was trying to see if she could give me a heart attack. In fact, I almost had a heart attack by what she was doing to me, but it was quite enjoyable.

We were brutally interrupted at around 3:00 A.M. by a loud bang on the front door, which was repeated several times. I asked her if she thought we were disturbing the neighbours.

She said, "I don't think so." She went to the window overlooking the car park. She said, "Don't worry, it is my boyfriend."

Apparently, she had a boyfriend who was a black cab driver (unknown to me).

She said, "He will go soon."

My problem was my car was parked in front of her garage. Would the boyfriend wonder whose car it was? Or would he simply go away? The banging eventually stopped, and we carried on till the early hours of the morning, doing what we do best. I was really shocked indeed to see that a woman would do such a thing all night to a man who was working hard to bring home the bread. But obviously, sexual pleasure meant more to her than the bread that was being brought in. If a woman treated me in that manner, I would be deeply hurt if I found out. One night, at a party, Camilla's boyfriend looked at me as if he knew that something went on between his girlfriend and I, although he had no idea. I guess his sixth sense was kicking in, poor bastard!

I was getting a bit tired of my playboy lifestyle. I did believe that, at that point, I must make some changes in my life. It was time for me to leave Felicia to save her from suffering due to my disgusting lifestyle (I had my sight on Zora), although I know for a fact that if I ask her to marry me, she would consent. Unfortunately, since my release from prison, I have not found a woman that bowled me over and won my heart.

I was still looking at the girls passing my workplace at Volkswagen. There was a young lady that went past that I found attractive, but believe it or not, I hated this woman purely because she appeared to be like another Jamaican, and I know nothing about her. Each morning I arrived at work, I happened to see her; it was without fail. Some mornings, I would drive past and blow the horn just to get her attention, but she never took any notice of me. One lunchtime, she drove past in a gold-coloured Nissan Micra, and there went my chance of meeting this woman. She drove past my workplace several times, but I knew it would be harder to meet her whilst she was driving rather than walking. One day, I sat in my car during my lunch break, relaxing in the heat of the summer. As my break came to an end, I got out of the car and crossed the road (I was parked opposite the work shop). I pressed the button to lock the car. Without looking back, I heard a voice with a very strong French accent saying, "Excuse me, Sir." I turned around, and to my utmost shock, it was the woman I hated because I thought she was Jamaican.

She asked, "Can you fix cars?"

I replied, "It depends on what's wrong."

She said, "My boot cannot lock, and it needs repairing."

I told her it would not be an easy job, so she asked me for a quote.

I said, "Meet me on Saturday, and I will try my best to fix it for you." I went into work that Saturday, and she came by as requested. I started to work on the car then I had a break to go and pick up my daughter. Afterwards, I returned and finished the job. I charged her £30 for labour. She said she had not got any money but, would pay me as soon as she got some.

I asked her if she would like to go for a drink.

She said, "No, I am a Christian, and I don't drink."

I then said, "Do you eat then?" She giggled and said, "See you later," and drove off.

One month later she came to see me on a Monday. I asked her for my money.

She said, "I haven't got it as yet."

Yet, she was still asking more favours of me.

She said, "My car is in a garage, and I don't know if they are charging me the right price. Could you come and see if I am being ripped off?"

I asked her, "Which garage is the car in?"

She replied, "East London, near West Ham."

I said, "I beg your pardon. It will cost you if I go that far on top of what you already owe! Have you got money for the petrol?" I explained that my car was a drinker

She said, "What do you mean?"

I explained, "A 2.5 engine uses a lot of petrol. Do you understand that?" She giggled. I then asked, "What is your name?"

She replied, "Zora."

I took her to East London as she asked. I looked at the work carried out by her mechanic, and it was way below standard. He tried to explain to me why the job was not well done, but to be totally honest, I had no interest in what he was saying. She paid for the work done, and we both left the garage. She followed me because she did not know the way back. When I got to an area which she knew well, I simply accelerated and disappeared in front. I did not even say goodbye. I had other things on my mind, and besides, she knew where to find me. What was on my mind? You may ask or even wonder. It was time to return to prison for a day in my opinion anyway. The inmate whom I mentioned previously that committed suicide in house block three, cell thirty-four, had somehow came back to haunt me.

I received a letter from the coroner's court demanding my appearance as a witness to my former inmate's demise due to the fact that whilst I was imprisoned, I was taking notes of events for my book—the book I hoped to write when I was released and now, my dear friends, you are reading it!

I went to the coroner's court as summoned. I did not see exactly what had happened. Nonetheless, I had to go. I was accompanied by Felicia, purely for moral support. Believe it or not, on that day, I was definitely back in prison. I had never seen so many uniformed guards, just the same as when I was in prison. In fact, a few of the faces stood out in my mind even today, especially the face of Mr. Lemon, incognito.

I was questioned by the judge, and I was asked to explain conversations I had with my previous inmate before his death. The dreadful day had passed, but I don't think I was very helpful in the findings of the cause of his suicide. All I could explain was that my former inmate was depressed when I last spoke to him, and the next day, he was dead. The real truth of the matter was, in Belmarsh, no one heard when you screamed for help. But I did believe that my friend committed suicide because he was intimidated by an officer.

Six months later, in my local area, I kept on seeing faces of residents in Her Majesty's Hotel where I stayed rent free! Life went on.

I was still enjoying the fruits of my successful education. One thing I know between Carol and D. C. Duffus who both have tried to destroy me was that they were able to take away my liberty, but they could not take my life or my engineering skills which was why I am writing this book today; I am here, kicking. Revenge was not necessary because self-destruction was in place. They tried to destroy me; little did they know they were destroying themselves.

My dear friends, please look into this and view it carefully. I may ask you this question: If someone tried to destroy you and failed miserably, was it not soul destroying to see the uprising of the subject who was meant to be destroyed? Can you imagine having a child with someone who you tried to destroy and failed miserably, and on top of that, having to deliver that child to a contact centre in order for the child to see the person whom you tried to destroy and whom the child was highly fond of? I think, my dear friends, that it was in itself a self-destruction because I personally could not stand the pain of delivering that child knowing what I had done. Think about it!

Believe it or not, nearly seven months after helping Zora, she turned up at my workplace out of the blue with a huge apology. She claimed that I drove off without saying goodbye, so she was under the impression that I was upset and kept away. Nevertheless, something was driving me towards her, and I could not understand what it was. We had lunch together a few times, but she had no knowledge of what or who I was. I guess, at the time, I was just a happy, carefree, bed-whoever-came-along kind of person. But I know that someone would get hurt because I have always lived a life in a love triangle or even a square, sometimes! It was two women and myself that made it a triangle or myself and three women that made it a square. But I guess I was never the one to get hurt because love causes too much pain. The only pain I would feel was if my daughter told me that I was not her daddy. The love I have for my little girl is enough to tear down buildings and move mountains. So you see, no one could hurt me mentally, but if anyone tried to come between my daughter and myself, I guess that would be an unbearable phase of suffering for me.

After several luncheon dates with Zora, I found myself breaking down the barrier that I had put up to stop me from falling for someone. I never thought that I could think this way, never in a million years. I found myself drifting into a problematic situation. I did believe that I was falling for her, and I had no control over it. What on earth was happening to me? At the same time, Felicia treated me like a king, as well as giving me 100 percent love. She always ensured that my dinner was ready when I came home after work. She wanted me to relax, have a rest after a long hard day at work, especially because I am standing all day, and to enable us to spend quality time together. My wellbeing was very important to her. She cared deeply for me; that much, I knew. I had never had to go home and cook after work. She felt it was her duty to take care of me and were prepared to do whatever was necessary to fulfil my needs and ensure that our relationship would be an outstanding one. She would also pamper and made me feel special. She truly believed in looking after the man she loved. I knew she would make an excellent wife. I knew Felicia loved me, but I asked myself, Do I love her? (I had feelings for her, but because I was in love with Zora and plan to marry her in the near future, I had to leave regardless of her emotional trauma.) It is very difficult when someone loves you, and you could not return the love equally because of being involved with someone else. Felicia still does not know why I left her. She wondered if she has done something wrong unknowingly. Only time would tell. The greatest embarrassment for her is that I went to meet her parents and promised her mother that no matter what, I would care for her daughter, especially since she had disclosed bad experiences from her past to me. Felicia's daughter and her parents were fond of me at the time. I wonder what they think of me now. Whenever I visited her parents, her mom would always tell us to look after each other. Empty promises, I guess! On reflection, I had to ask myself the question, Have I ever loved anyone? It appeared that I have no recollection, but was I lying to myself?

When I was eighteen years old, I was dating a Greek girl by the name of Maria. She became pregnant whilst I was still at college studying my engineering course. We were very close. I guess, after ordering her to have an abortion, the way I felt at the time could have been love. But then, we separated. So how could it have been? Believe it or not, the aborted child still lives deep within my soul. After all those years, even now in 2008, I still have regrets! Sometimes, when I think about it, I get somewhat tearful. Stop being so soppy, old boy! The same thing happened with Sue whom I met soon after separating from Maria. She was a most beautiful Arab girl. We were together for four years. She wanted to get married, but I was only twenty-five. Who wants to get married so young? When we separated, I cried for three days nonstop. Even my mother cried. I guess she loved Sue more than I did, but I got over it. The fourth day, I was having sex with someone else, a young lady by the name of Rita. She was also beautiful, a fashion model with a lovely figure, and I was ready to marry her. After six months, we grew very close. I thought I was what she wanted, but she dumped me for someone else, so I was back to square one. I was once again heartbroken, and since then, I made myself a promise that I would never go down that road again and became a man of leisure, a playboy until today.

I finally made up my mind to leave Felicia, although I know she loved me. I started seeing Zora on a regular basis, telling Felicia all kinds of lies about why I was not coming home. But because she loved me so much, she never questioned me or became possessive.

I spent all my free time working at Zora's, getting the apartment ready and bringing it up to date because I knew I was going to move in. I promised to help refurbish Felicia's home as I was living with her, but she did me a favour when she asked me to put the plans on hold (It gave me the opportunity to refurbish Zora's apartment instead.) until after Christmas because she wanted us to have a new beginning for the New Year (2005). This was very important to her. She believed that she had found her soulmate and life partner in me. I did not want to wait; I just wanted to leave, as the guilt was becoming overbearing for me, especially knowing that she was very good to me.

When I first met Felicia, she told me of her past, the tragedies in her life and how she could not endure anymore emotional destruction and heartache. She was honest with me from the onset, she asked about my feelings for her, and told me that if my intentions were dishonourable, it would be best if I stayed away from her and not set up home with her.

She asked me several times before I moved in with her if there were any other women out there that I would prefer to be with or want to be with. If so, then this would be my opportunity to go before laying a foundation, but I told her no. I wanted to be with her because I loved her. I recalled telling her one evening, whilst we were having a conversation in the car, that each time I leave, I felt like a piece of me had gone. She thought I was talking about my daughter. I was not! Then she suddenly realized I was telling how I felt about her. But look at the situation now; I have a new love and a new life with someone else.

My dear friends, perhaps you are all wondering what she did to me and why did I treat her in this manner. I had no answer to these questions because she did me no wrong. Prior to this, I took it upon myself to meet her parents who became fond of me, her mother in particular. One evening, we both went to visit them. I had a heart-to-heart talk with her mother, and she told me of her daughter's past disappointments, etc., more or less what Felicia told me. She asked me not to put her daughter through anymore anguish because she did not know if Felicia would be able to cope with more heartache and pain. I assured her mother of my honourable intentions for her daughter whom she loved very much. I told her of my plans for the apartment, that my first job was to start refurbishing the living room, and at the completion of the decoration, she would have a beautiful place that would become our home.

In January 2005, Felicia and I left the health club. Whilst walking towards the bus stop on Sydenham High Street, I told her it was over. She did not take it very well. She was shocked by what I had said to her and ran straight out into the street, in front of oncoming vehicles. I knew she wanted to die; she was truly in emotional agony and was very distressed, with both her heart and spirit broken, but I did not care because I wanted to be with someone else. Nonetheless, I would like to take this opportunity to apologise to her, knowing that this apology could never quell her pain and the betrayal. This had no meaning to her, but it helps me to feel better by acknowledging what I had done. My dear friends, I know that this act would still not heal the wounds I have left behind and that she would never forgive me for what I had done to her. One thing I can say is that she was truly a loyal woman and is also a sincere friend to me to this day. She cared deeply for me in a way that no one else did, but that was insufficient for me.

On Christmas 2004, all my wounds from imprisonment and being divorced were healed. I had no fear, although the love of a woman did not mean anything to me because women were simply toys that get old and then get thrown in a corner. It was time to leave Felicia. Each time I planned to leave, I kept putting it off. At this point, there was no question. I was definitely in love with Zora. It was unbelievable to me; I fell for somebody who was totally different from my usual type of women. She was a Christian from Guadeloupe and spoke French, while I am Jamaican. She had no understanding of my well-being, and communication was very difficult between us; she spoke a little English.

I was pushed into a corner during the festive season when my Christmas plans were up and running, and suddenly, destruction hit me. Zora had made arrangement to spend Christmas in France with her relatives whilst I was left alone to finish decorating the apartment. I had planned to spend Christmas with Felicia, although I had left her. (She still had no knowledge that I had actually left her.) It was painful for me to think that she was by herself, and I was also by myself. She asked me earlier in the month what my plans for the holiday was, as she would like us to spend our first Christmas together. She wanted me to meet other members of her family. Her daughter was fond of me, a well-mannered young lady, I may add. I told her that for Christmas, each member of my family would cook a dish, and then we would all go to the elected family home to get together for the day. I arranged to spend Christmas with her, but my plans went up in smoke because Zora rang me from France one week before Christmas and told me that she couldn't be without me and was coming home. I could not believe what had happened, so Felicia had to take a backseat. I knew that not being with me was killing her, but I wanted to be with Zora and was happy to have her back. Christmas came and went, and the only thing I could do to try and make some amendment with Felicia was to continue to pay her health club subscription for four months until February 2005 when I had it terminated without informing her. I promised Zora that I would give her Felicia's membership. This I felt I had to do. She had now had it for over two years, and it would continue for the duration of our relationship.

Felicia was very distraught over the break up and wrote a letter to Zora and myself. The contents of the letter were somewhat distressing, and I dare say humiliating also; leaflets about sexual transmitted diseases were sent to us. It was hard for me to understand the mind of someone who would send something like this (I could only say she was traumatised by losing me, and this was just a reaction to the situation). Whether it was caring or asking to get myself checked out because I had been promiscuous, I would not know. Nonetheless, Zora and I did attend the health clinic, and we were both okay. I counted myself lucky so far. One day, my luck could run out.

On the day I told Felicia it was over, it appeared to me that she refused to accept the fact. She cried hysterically, screaming, and dashed into the road in front of the oncoming vehicles, which gave me a nasty fright. The drivers began to sound their horns, but she just carried on, walking. I dashed after her and dragged her back to the pavement. I tried to calm her down to resolve the situation, but she wept profusely. She became a broken suicidal woman that night. I took her back to my friends' home as she was in no fit state to travel home on her own. He was shocked when he saw the state she was in and wondered what had happened. "Why is he leaving you?" he asked her. So she told him. He was disappointed because he knew she was a good woman to me, and I spoke highly of her to him frequently. Eventually, she settled down a little. I borrowed a friend's car and drove her home. Her state of devastation was due to the fact that I ended our relationship in public on Sydenham high street. She also said that it was devastating because I did not give the relationship a chance to develop; I was simply using her to test my feelings for Zora whom I was having the affair with whilst I was still living with her.

I did find it hard at this point—to be as promiscuous as I used to be. It appears that the tip of cupid's arrow had gotten the better of me. Zora and I have been enjoying the fruits of love. We get on well, but we also have disagreements when she is struggling with the English language.

During the spring of 2005, I had a telephone call from Lillian. We chatted for a while and then she mentioned she needed a favour from me. She wanted me to drive to her sister's place in Edgware in West London to collect a few things from her sister's place. I agreed to do this favour. I arrived at Lillian's place at approximately 8:00 P.M. and drove to Edgware which took me two hours. I packed the car with heavy objects including a huge television, which was rather heavy and nearly broke my back when I lifted it. At the time, I had a borrowed vehicle—a large estate car, the same car I borrowed to drop Felicia home on that turbulent night. At approximately 11:00 P.M., I was on my return journey to Gatwick where Lillian lived. I arrived there at approximately 12:30 A.M. As I drove back, the thoughts that was going through my mind was that I dreaded to do the lifting once more; I was exhausted. Nevertheless, it had to be done. I had to take all that stuff up three flights of stairs to Lillian's apartment. It almost killed me. At about 1:30, I told her that I was going home. This was after making the biggest mistake. I gave her a hug, and she read more into it. She said she was turned on, but I was dying from exhaustion. She took her top off, and her huge breast bounced in front of my eyes. She asked if I wanted sex, and I said I could do with a beer. She left the bedroom and returned with a couple of cans. As I sipped a can of beer slowly, she carried on, undressing. I looked at the body with the resemblance of a sumo wrestler. I could not take that on in my present state. She whispered in my ears, "I want you to take me now." But all I wanted was to escape through the front door.

I said to her, "Just wait a while. Let me go to the toilet." Instead, I made my way to the front door, but she had locked me in and removed the keys. I could not get out. I was very upset. I told her that I wished to leave, but she refused to let me out. She started to shout at me, saying, "When will I see you again, if I let you go? I need you now, not tomorrow."

I replied, "Even if I was going to please you, my mood has changed, so let me go." It was now approximately 2:00 A.M. in the morning. She eventually let me go. When I got home, Zora was lying in bed, waiting for me.

I asked her, "Why are you not sleeping?"

She replied, "I was waiting for you to come home."

I told her of my horrifying evening in full details. She was not upset.

She replied, "I know you love me because you turned down sex." We both went to sleep.

The temptation was always there, but somehow, I was not the stud I used to be. For the first time in my life, the desire for other women simply disappeared. Perhaps I had found the right person, but only time would tell.

I kept in touch with Anita via the telephone. I still have deep-rooted feelings for her that I could not forget; it comes to the surface occasionally.

During the summer of 2005, I could not believe my eyes. I saw someone from my childhood in my local area. I saw a girl by the name of Celia at the bus stop in Sydenham, and damn, she looked good. The last time I saw her was in 1993, when I went to Jamaica. I could not believe my eyes. Celia was a very close friend to me. I was dating her sister when I was nine years old. We greeted each other and then we began a long conversation. Believe it or not, Celia thought it was a miracle that we met that day because her sister, Joy, my childhood sweetheart, was coming to England a week from the date we met. We exchanged phone numbers. Two weeks went by. I contacted her, and Joy was really in England, someone I had a soft spot for at such a young age. I spoke to her over the phone. She then gave me her telephone number, so we could communicate directly. She told me she was visiting for one month. We met a few times, but the chemistry on my path was not there. I took her to the health club one evening. It was very quiet. She was wearing a cotton t-shirt and cotton underwear. As she started to sweat in the sauna, all her private parts became visible under the transparency of the material. We went into the Jacuzzi, and I had to try very hard to restrain myself. Somehow, the sight of her erect nipples through the wet t-shirt had aroused me. I was in a state of arousal, but I managed to control myself, although the hairy patch almost knocked me out. I was sure that Joy would be the winner of any wet t-shirt competition. Beneath the bubbles, she started to stroke my truncheon. I was at breaking point. Then I remembered, weeks before that, something similar happened. Unfortunately, the young man, at the time, had gushed. The Jacuzzi was closed for a few days. I did not want that to happen to me! My self-control had kicked itself into action.

 That evening, after a refreshing visit to the health club, I decided to drive her around London, showing her some interesting sights. She particularly liked the statue of Eros at Piccadilly and the unbelievable London Eye. It appeared to me that she seemed to like London. It was time for me to take her home to Crystal Palace where she was staying. I pulled up outside her home, and I said to her, "Enjoy the rest of your stay. I will call you." She stood there with a glare in her eyes. I asked her if she was okay. She did not respond. She opened the car door and came back inside. She looked at me with tearful eyes and began to kiss me. Her tongue had practically went past my tonsils! I could not believe what she had done. I was meant to be in love with Zora, but I could not stop myself from responding. We both played tickle my tonsils for a moment or two. The feelings to satisfy her was bursting, but I somehow stopped myself. We began to talk to calm down the situation. She explained to me that she was feeling quite wet and needed a mop and a bucket to clean the car seat, but I simply took it as a joke. She told me about the pain she felt when

I left for England as a child and asked why I did not communicate with her. She said she waited for eleven years after I left, but she heard nothing. Someone persuaded her to give up on me, and he then took her virginity. At this point, she wept.

I said I was sorry, but that was life.

I went home, and Zora was waiting there as usual. She asked me where was I, and I told her I went out for a drink.

The day when Joy was leaving for Jamaica, she rang me to say goodbye. She asked me to get her address from her sister and write to her. I had never seen her sister again.

I lost my job at Volkswagen, which in a way was quite sad because I was no longer being paid for watching the women went by—a most pleasant view from my workshop!

Unfortunately, I had an accident when machining a crank. The crank caught my sleeve and pulled me into the machine, almost severing my arm from the socket. It was very distressing, and the pain was excruciating. After two weeks off work, with very little sick pay, I went back to work; the sick pay I was receiving could not support me with my numerous expenses. During my time back at work, the management claimed that my work was substandard due to my in ability to perform my tasks, and I was unfairly dismissed from my post as an engineer. Fortunately, for me, I was a man of great skills and not lacking of self-confidence to approach work. I immediately found another job, paying almost twice the wages that Volkswagen was paying me.

However, I did not like the environment I was working in, so after two weeks, I was ready to move again. I gave in my notice to quit and left. However, a man of my integrity walked straight into another job. So you see, survive, I must.

As I had stated previously, my ex-wife and her police cronies took everything from me, but my skills remained untouched. So how could they conquer me?

My new employment happened to be just what I was searching for. I worked on my own initiative to the British Standard. At this point, on reflection, I had no regrets sweating my balls off in college to gain my qualifications. Believe it or not, my dear friends, I almost forgot about you. So sorry, old chaps, sometimes I get rather saturated into myself. I do hope you are enjoying the story.

I took Volkswagen to court for compensation, and after the court case, they walked out with their tails between their legs. Yes, I won the case and was compensated handsomely, if I may say so.

I was still enjoying the fruits of my new employment. My new manager whom I thought was dissatisfied with my performance showed me his appreciation in a gratified manner. On Christmas 2005, he had greased my palm with a bonus of £400. I say, old chaps, I was rather shocked. I literally walked out of work that Christmas with a total of £1100, very little for a man of my ability, but hopefully, next time round, it would be much more substantial, providing I did not change job.

I had a rather wonderful Christmas and also a splendid New Year's celebration. Yes, I had another year in front of me. With so much things to do, I doubt if I would be able to complete them all before another Christmas was up on me. I should use 2006 to clean out the closet and get my act together.

The month of January crept past me like a mouse sneaking upon a piece of cheese on a trap. The early part of February promises to be fulfilled were dawning upon me as the time got closer. I had promised Zora that I would get engaged to her on St. Valentine's Day, 2006. Sometimes, I said a lot of things, but really, there was no meaning behind them, so the comforting promise I made came back and bit me. It was engagement or goodbye. A man has to do what a man has to do—that was what I always said. I found getting engaged was a difficult task for me to carry out due to the fact that I had someone else in mind, and I guess, my dear friends, you would have no idea who this person was. It was also a shock to me. I knew I like this person a lot, but it appeared to me that it was more than just liking her. I guess, by now, you were quite puzzled, trying to work out who this person was. My ex-wife? No, you could not be more wrong. The woman in question was my old favourite, Anita. She happened to take a place in my soul that was non-erasable. Before I got engaged, I rang her. Perhaps I wanted to play the last game. We arranged to meet, and I rang her a few times before our rendezvous. At one point, a male voice answered her phone, and this sent me into a state of wobbly knees. She was unable to speak, which she apologised for. The next day, she called me and tried to explain the whole situation to me in detail. She mentioned she had a boyfriend who becomes very jealous whenever she got a phone call from any male friend. Although she and I were more than friends, out of fairness, I had to explain my position also. I told her about my engagement plans. She was shocked; she had no idea I was seeing someone. I told her this just to get even, but deep down, inside my heart of hearts, the feelings of bereavement almost killed me. At this point, I decided to set her free. I rang her, and we both agreed that one day, in the future, we would get back together. This promise was somewhat like lighting a candle on a windy day, although occasionally, the small flame still flickered. We still send text messages to each other, but to me, the flame had gone out, leaving a slight trail of smoke.

Valentine's day 2006, my engagement became public. As time went by, the women in my past went into a faded memory. I had gained a lot of weight, I had no stress, no financial problems, and I dare say I was almost back on my feet, not to mention I had the reset of what all men needed to survive—the love of a woman and the love of his daughter. Without these two elements, a man would be unhappy.

One day in May 2006, I received a strange text message. The reading was quite disturbing. It read as follows: "How do you feel to go with someone else's wife? Can't you see that it is very dangerous?" This text message had me shaken. Although there was a contact number, I was baffled as to who had sent it. Approximately ten minutes after receiving the message, my phone rang, and there was a male voice. This man appeared to be crying. I said, "Hello? Please calm down and speak slowly."

He said, "my wife is in love with you and I want it to stop."

At this point, I burst out laughing and I uttered, "Who may your wife be, my friend?" Apparently, this young man was suffering because, I dare say, his wife was in love with me and that she was also in a dream to think she could have someone like me.

Early in February, the boss was away and I was rather bored at work, so I sent Lillian, the woman with the physique of a sumo wrestler, an erotic text message just for a laugh. Her reply was even more erotic. We must have gone through over 100 erotic text messages between us; it was great fun, and purely by reading the replies to my messages, I could tell that this woman was on heat. I had no knowledge she was married, but she had mentioned his inability to perform and satisfy her. I do believe that this poor man had painfully read all the text messages of his wife's in and outboxes. I could now see why he contacted me. I gave him some advice and told him that if he wanted to obtain further advice from me, there would be a fee. Lillian rang me and asked me if her husband had contacted me.

I said, "Yes, simply for some advice."

She asked, "Did you tell him to tie me to the bed?"

I said, "Yes." She had never rang me again.

My dear friends, it appeared that I was struggling to keep on the faithful path. Having one woman had never been my way of life, and it sure was a hard fight to keep it that way. In fact, as the weeks passed, in the sweltering heat wave that we were currently having, the temptation to use my dipstick elsewhere grew stronger and stronger. I have not done this yet, but I knew I have failed already. The desire to lust after women apart from the one I called my own grew stronger and stronger. It was approximately eight months ago, at the infamous meeting spot where I always seemed to meet women—the good, old, local health club. I couldn't be too shy to mention. One night, I went to a spin class, and I came face to face with a woman whom I swear I know from a previous life. This woman stared at me in a seductive manner that pulled me over to her like a magnet. I was then engaged in conversation with her. I asked her name.

She said, "My name is Susan. What's yours?"

I said to her, "You should know my name because I know you."

She started chuckling, and then she said, "You know what, I know you, too."

I said, "I know you do, so what's my name?"

She said, "I can't remember your name, but I know you."

I started to play mind games just to test the water. I said to her, "Don't you remember the night we had?"

She then covered her face with both hands, peeping through her fingers riddled with embarrassment. I then said, "I guess the night we spent together was not very good because you have forgotten."

She said, "I can't remember having a bad night. It has always been good sex."

I then said, "Two hundred positions in a one-night stand—that is almost unforgettable." At this point, she began laughing hysterically. I watched tears of laughter rolled down her cheeks as her glossy eyes stared into my face.

She said, "You are one funny guy."

I said, "Not really, I like women, too.'"

She said, "I don't mean that way," as she continued laughing, covering her nose. We exchanged phone numbers, and indeed, we had many juicy conversations. Each time Susan and I met at the health club, we always seemed to drift off into some type of sexual conversation that always led into a chemical connection, which was unseen but was felt by both of us. I really had no explanation for this chemistry which flowed between Susan and I. It was just one of those things. This led me to say that I couldn't understand why some men could not find a woman. Women were so easy; all you have to do is to make a simple conversation that would escalate beyond the imagination. I met another young lady at the same place. I was watching her for a few weeks. She had what I would say was almost the perfect body. This person was approximately six feet, and her legs were extremely long. However, I never found the courage to approach her for fear of rejection. I dare say that in the world of picking up a member of the opposite sex, rejection could be very damaging to one's self-esteem. Once this had happened, you were fucked.

One evening, Miss Long Legs came in to my surprise. She said, "Hello." She broke the ice. I left it for a few weeks; later, it was quiet that evening in the sauna She sat in front of me in the extremely hot and sweaty atmosphere. She was one of two women amongst eight of the lads. At this point, I jumped at the opportunity to do what most women said I do best. I started massaging her shoulders without her permission. She began making erotic sounds, which was driving all the lads crazy. I worked my way down to her waist, and the noises became even more intense. At this point, she said, "Can I ask you something?"

I said, "Go ahead."

"Are you a professional?"

I started to giggle, and all the lads started to cheer.

I said, "I am just a natural. Whatever I do comes naturally."

She said, "Last week, I was treated to a massage by a professional who worked in this club, and it was not a fraction as good as what I am getting now. I don't know what it is, but your hands are special."

Little did she know I was in a bad state. I could not get up because it almost appeared I had an eight-inch bottle of massage oil in my pocket.

She said, "Next time, you will be massaging me all over at my house."

I started to blush. I could feel myself losing faithfulness. That day, I had an extremely great boost of self-esteem.

Two weeks after that memorable moment, I did get the opportunity to go and massage Ms. Long Legs at her home, and indeed, it was much more than I set out to accomplish that evening. After massaging her for two hours, I was getting rather tired and hungry, and believe it or not, the bottle of massage oil re-appeared in my pocket once more! At this point, I became embarrassed to massage her shoulders as she lied face down. I then commenced the massage. She began to make erotic groaning noises. At this point, I was extremely aroused; it was beyond my control.

I believed she suspected I was aroused. Her arms reached down to my legs and began stroking up and down, and then I lost control of myself. Suddenly, it was my turn to be massaged, but to my utmost shock, she began to massage me with her lips. This was not an unpleasant feeling, I may add, but very enjoyable indeed. She knelt across my chest, and I suddenly felt droplets of her body fluid. I took the opportunity to seek out where it was coming from. It was very exciting because at this point, the palm of my hand was filled with fluid. I then stroked the cat and then realized that all the cat wanted was some milk, so I let it pour.

This experience was extremely great, and I hope that I would get the opportunity again in the near future.

She asked what was my fee, and I told her that to have this treat on me was enough. Also, that the next time would be free. She gave me a big kiss.

On my way out from the apartment and as I approached the front gate, a BMW pulled up outside. I got into my car, and the driver opened the gate I had just closed. I then drove off. I got home, and Zora was waiting in bed as usual. I went and had a shower, then climbed into bed. For the first time, a feeling of guilt came over me, but I managed to fight off that feeling.

One month after the Ms. Long Legs episode, Zora and I had a huge argument. This led to no communication between us. I called Susan, and we went out on a date. I had explained to her in the past that any action had to be at her home, and this was agreed. I was back in business as usual, and flames were blazing. I was back to my old self. Jack the lad had reclaimed his ground. That evening with Susan was almost as good as my time with Ms. Long Legs. Susan scared me by telling me that she was in love with me. I didn't believe I would want to see her on a regular basis because I was only having fun and love did not come into it. Why do women always tell me that they love me? How ridiculous!

I recently rang Felicia and requested that we meet for afternoon tea. Seeing her again was great. We exchanged stories, how we have progressed since parting. I told her of my engagement and my pending marriage. The question she asked was, "Are you really happy?"

I paused and then replied, "I guess so." But good old Felicia, she knew me more than I knew myself. She told me that she did not believe I was happy, but as usual, I never listened to what she told me. There were times when she told me things, and I was amazed as to how she knew. I was now married to Zora. I had given up being a player, and I was now no longer a playboy.

I recently saw my friend, Frankie. He was a close friend of myself and my ex-wife in the early years. He was riddled with disbelief as his eyes gazed upon me. He said, "Damn! You look good. It is almost as if you were born again. What happened to that long face and hunchback you used to carry? You used to have a stressful face. It has now disappeared. I heard about your divorce. If that is the look of divorce, I think I want one.

"You have put down the globe that was resting on your shoulders. It is almost as if you were carrying the world on your shoulders. Damn! You look good."

I said, "You know something? I feel damn good. They can't stop me now because I am solid as a rock!"

On reflection, as I sat in the glass cage, watching the case proceed through the darkness, I remember clearly the prosecution barrister asking Carol, "Do you hate your husband?" She took a deep breath, and I could see her bubbling like a volcano, waiting to erupt. She glanced around, rolling her catlike eyes, as I watched them changed from grey to red.

She shouted at the top of her voice, "I hate him. I hate him." She then fell to the floor, motionless. That moment would stay with me until the flowers started to grow on my grave.

My barrister came to see me in the cell of the court. She told me that D. C. Duffus and Carol were seeing each other as a couple. Due to her code of practice, she was unable to testify or give a statement on my behalf.

When I was released from prison, I had nothing but the debts that I could not pay due to my incarceration—credit cards, bank loan, and a car loan. My life was worth shit, and now, three years on, I have a damn good job, a second wife, no debts, and a daughter who would give her life for me. Rochelle sometimes wished Zora to be her mother. I know they love each other, but for my dear little one to say such a thing, I found it extremely heavy to digest. In fact, it led me to believe that my little girl was not happy at home with her mother. Although I dare say that when I met Zora, my life had just began—at the tender age of forty-four!

Occasionally, Rochelle refused to go home at the set times on Sunday. I frequently said to her, "Do you want D. C. Duffus to take your daddy away?" I said this to show her the seriousness of her reluctance to go home.

She always replies, "D. C. Duffus is dead." I guess this a way to relieve herself of the trauma she had suffered at the hands of D. C. Duffus.

On the return of a two weeks holiday in Jamaica, the moment she landed, Rochelle rang me, telling me how much she missed me and love me. It was a Thursday, and I do believe that she could not wait until Saturday, the day I collect her. However, I had to encourage her to wait a few more days until she saw me. I went to collect her on Saturday, second week of August. I got out of the car. Upon sighting me, Rochelle dropped her bags and ran towards me like a bullet from a gun. She jumped on me, and I almost fell to the ground from the impact. She then said, "I missed you so much, Dad. I didn't know what to do." At this point, my little girl began to cry.

I replied, "Daddy is here, my little pet. Daddy is here." I comforted her just as I always did from her birth, using the same words. Believe it or not, my dear friends, one day, in the days of old, when Rochelle was just a mere toddler in her nappies, I was overjoyed to see this bouncing little baby. To satisfy my inner emotion, I uttered some words to Carol. Reflecting back on those words, I do believe I must have been somewhat intoxicated or heavily influenced, under hypnosis, as I told Carol that I love her. "Blast! What did I do by saying such inappropriate words?" I said to myself.

She replied in a sarcastic manner, using her extremely strong Jamaican accent, "Mi no want no love so strong. Them kind a love wi kill me." I was flabbergasted!

Carol tried to show Rochelle that I was the hater of the two parents by telling her that she loved me and she always would. I guess this was meant to be a joke. Rochelle was not a fool. She was a very clever and independent child, and I doubt if, for a moment, she would fall for this pathetic line of drama. I told Rochelle the truth like it was, of course. I said, "My dear child, I love you very much, but the only thing your mother would get from me is a silver bullet. That's the only way to get rid of blood suckers, and that's a fact."

"Are you happy?" asked Frankie.

I replied, "I am married to a woman who does everything for me, not to mention how much she loves me. I am still working as an engineer in the same area that I live, as well as the bonus of being loved dearly by my daughter, Rochelle. I have everything I want. You bet I am happy."

Just before my dear brother-in-law had passed away, I was feeling a little low, and I found a need for someone to pick me up, although I was happily married. I rang Lillian and arrange to visit her. When I got there, to my utmost horror, she had booked a room with the intention of having sex! We went out for a lovely meal, which she had paid for, as usual. She mentioned the room, although her intentions were miles away from my thoughts. I went back to the hotel with her. We sat in the room, had a few drinks, and talked. I then said to her, "It is getting rather late. I must go." At this point, she got rather upset and said, "You can't go because I have paid for the room and the meal, and there is nothing in it for me." For the first time, I told her that I was a happily married man, and I left. I rang her several times, but she had not responded to any of my calls. Nonetheless, that did not impede my happiness. Meeting Zora had changed my whole life. I had never planned to fall in love after my first marriage, but now, look at me—married again. Believe it or not, the total cost of the first wedding was the price of the train for the second wedding dress. How ironic! I guess I valued Zora more. Guests came from several countries to attend this special wedding.

On the day leading to my wedding in September 2006, I received a text message from Sabrina. She stressed that she could not allow me to marry Zora because she was so much in love with me. She asked me to make a choice between a cleaner (herself) and Zora, an educated French woman. Of course, I have already made my choice. My dear friends, never marry someone out of your class. Make sure the person is compatible with you and not beneath you because that person would always try to be like you or drag you down to their level. I dare say that I had made that mistake once, but I lived to tell the tale! Sabrina had the chance to be with me, but she blew it. When I was freshly released from prison, I wanted her to be my girlfriend due to the fact that we have a long history of seeing each other on and off. She had turned down my advances of a relationship with her because she claimed she was seeing someone, although we were still having pleasurable moments in bed. She often said that after intercourse with me, Steve would detect that she had been with me again due to the size of the undercarriage having been stretched to the max!! I would never forget the day when I visited her. She had just come out of the bath. She opened the door with a towel wrapped around her. As I entered the apartment, the passion started to flow. A man has to do what a man have to do. Shortly after, Steve arrived. He introduced himself to me, and they went downstairs into the bedroom. They left me for at least half an hour. I was in the living room by myself. I imagined Steve pumping fresh air not touching the sides, knowing I had just finished. I couldn't imagine the feeling Steve had as he entered her still slippery with my body fluid! Poor Steve!

One day, I was feeling hungry for some steam fish and West Indian food. Sabrina and I went to Brixton after a pleasurable session that led to my hunger. I bought two large fish, yam, bananas, flour to make dumplings, and breadfruit. Sabrina and I went back to her place to do some serious cooking. When the food was ready, she served the meal, but to my utmost surprise, she had the head of the fish on her plate, alongside a portion of food. I did not say anything, but I was quite curious as to why she did not have the body of the fish on her plate. Shortly after we have both eaten, Steve came home. At this point, I was in the kitchen. He said "Hello' and went downstairs to the bedroom as usual.

Sabrina took a serving of food from the pot alongside the body of the fish I mentioned earlier. I asked her, "Who was that for?"

She said, "It's Steve's dinner." I could not believe my eyes. I felt used. Steve was eating my food. But then, should we call it quits? Because earlier, I was having his woman! Fair enough, I thought. Was I not the lucky one? I asked myself.

My relationship with Sabrina had been going for over twenty years, but I had never found her to be marriage material. I was glad I did not marry her; several nights after having good sex with her, Steve always came home for what was left. Can you imagine? If I had married her, I would be coming home to what Steve had just left! I would not eat Steve's leftovers, thank you very much! One day, Sabrina asked if I could buy her a bag of Basmati rice because she had no money. I took pity upon her, and I fulfilled her wish. When I went to place the bag of rice in the cupboard, I discovered she had several ten-kilogram bags of rice inside. She walked into the kitchen, and I asked, "Why did you lie to me?" She was speechless! At that point, I thought Perhaps Steve wasn't just having what I left, but what other male friends have left. But then, it appeared that she gained a bag of rice. Or was she simply a rice collector? At least she would never go hungry. I guess I had a narrow escape. I was also HIV negative!

On my wedding day, I received a telephone call from her. She sounded tearful and asked me if I was on my way to the church.

I replied, "We are having the photo session now." She hanged up. Three months later, she called me. We are still friends to this day. How could she feed my food to her man? Damn cheek! Steve had left her, and she was still hopeful.

She asked me recently, "Aren't you going to leave Zora?"

I thought to myself, You are going to have a long wait!

Tears of joy flowed from my eyes as I exchanged vows with Zora. On reflection of my previous marriage, I give praises to Allah for helping me to escape from total damnation into the comfort zone of love and happiness, which canceled all pain and hate. My dear friends, you must always remember that the comfort zone of true love is a special place. If you could relate to my story, I share your pain; but I do hope you are also with me in the comfort zone of love and happiness. On reflection, before I married Zora, she had said to me that if she got a percentage of the love I have for my dear daughter, Rochelle, she would be very happy. I do believe that we both share the same comfort zone!

My Wedding Day

I must say, my dear friends, although Zora and I love each other like teenagers, my only complain is that her libido is overactive and that always leaves me extremely tired. But then again, on reflection, am I not the one that Carol claims to be a sex monster? I remember clearly, in the statements, she claimed that I have had sex with her whilst she was sleeping because she always wakes up wet! I guess her wet dreams were quite intense. Don't forget the ghost that sexually assaulted her when she lived at Laurel Grove. Was she a dreamer? Or was she a drama queen? Can you imagine having sex in your sleep? Would it not wake you up? I think it should. How pathetic. If I was a sex monster, would I refuse all the offers I was getting? No, I don't think so!

Thinking back, I wonder if Zora would have married me, knowing my playboy history?...Recently, I decided to try an experiment just to prove to myself that the female's urge for sex was the same as a male or even more. I decided not to have sex with my wife for almost three weeks. I stayed in a celibate state as I watched her reaction on a day-to-day basis. I was sure she was thinking why I didn't approach her for sex, but I stood my ground silently until she broke at the end of a three-week drought on her path. She then approached me for sex. That told me that females think about sex and want sex the same as a male—experiment successful. I guess Carol's sex monster was on strike. Pathetic fool.

When I was a DJ working for my father in a pub called the Rising Sun, we usually had strippers on a Friday night, and they always came in the DJ box. On one occasion, two strippers came to do a double act. But before the double act, they performed single acts, and whilst one was entertaining the punters, the other was entertaining me in the DJ box. I must say I found the experience very erotic and exciting, but then, I was a bad boy. Though I am not anymore.

Carol and I were married on paper only; anything else to say it was more than that would be horrific. When she heard of my wedding plans, she went to my brother's business place (also known as the one-stop-gossip shop). I do not think she really believed that I have found someone to take away the pain she inflicted upon me.

On my release from prison, it was ruled that Rochelle needed her father. How true, I dared say, old chap.

I love Rochelle more than any living thing on the face of this planet. Rochelle and I are very close. I recently went shopping into Asda Supermarket. I was in the queue (line) waiting to be served when Rochelle hugged me and said, "I love you, Dad."

A man behind us appeared very tearful. He said that it was a rare sight these days. I wondered what was going on in his head. Perhaps he had a child or children that he had no contact with, but that, I would never know. On reflection, on my release from prison, Sister Jane went to visit Carol, and she was turned away rather rudely with words to this effect, "It is too late. When I needed you in court, you did not help me." I dare say, my friends, I must say to Carol, "Sorry for robbing you of the pleasure of saying to your friends, 'He went mad because of me!'"

The trauma that Rochelle and I have suffered will remain with us forever. The day D. C. Duffus handcuffed me in the presence of my daughter was always in her conversation, even to this day. I am still confused as to how D. C. Duffus claimed in his report that the door was barricaded while at the same time, the door was opened with a key by my brother's girlfriend. How did he justify this? I am now free, as I always should have been. On reflection, for five years, leading up to the arrest, I was never happy to go home after work. Today, in 2007, I was always clock-watching just to see the time to go home because my life was in a completely different phase which I call happiness.

Myself and my dear daughter, Rochelle, at the end of the rebuilding of my life—my wedding day.

I was very bitter with my neighbour at Thomas Dean Road because in a cul-de-sac, everybody knew each other's business. The police visited number four Thomas Dean Road, 168 times in six years. Can you believe it? That was over two visits per week! In my present address where I have been living for the past three years, I had no visits from the police to do with marital problems. Carol was simply building a file. How ironic! My neighbour knew that Carol was seeing other men, especially on my days at work. I recently learnt that he knew of a man who would come to my ex-marital home each morning when I left for work. He also knew about D. C. Duffus's affair with her. However, he had failed to reveal this to me due to a silly trust violation between himself and Carol. He revealed to me that he was afraid to let me in on this secret because he was saving me from myself.

"I knew you would have killed her," he said.

Perhaps four to five years ago, I would have killed for what had happened to me, but today, I must say that it was simply a true experience, water under the bridge. During my time in prison, I was given a map, as I may have mentioned before, of a cemetery where I could locate a hidden gun. This information was given to me by an inmate who shared my pain. Today, in 2007, I dare say that I found it in my heart to forgive my ex-neighbour because I, too, was put in such a position. I had a very dear friend, with whom I was close to both he and his wife. I discovered that he was having an affair with a woman who was also a friend of his family! I had to keep quiet about this sordid affair because I did not wish to cause any problems, although the information caused me discomfort when I visited them. I totally understand my ex-neighbour's feelings now. On reflection, little did I know that while I was having sex with Mrs. Woodburn before I stole her from her husband, that the day would come when someone would be having sex with my wife ex-Mrs. Woodburn. Ironic, wasn't it? I dare say the spots of a leopard never changes. When Mr. Woodburn shook my hand on the handover of his wife to me, he said, "I love my wife. Take her, but I want you to remember, she will always come back to me." Little did I know that it was the handshake of death because he knew what lies ahead. Nonetheless, I lived to tell the tale. *The sins that brought me to my knees. My dear friends, what was worse than taking an old man's young wife away from him and left him heartbroken at the age of 200? The tears he shed for his wife at the time was like poison raindrops from above, falling on me.*

He lived not to see my downfall, but to see me rise again from a point that he was once at, divorced and heartbroken. Unlike Mr. Woodburn or shall I say Mr. Bojangle, as I remember him with silver hair and baggy pants, I am happily married. Words cannot explain the depths of my happiness. I find myself putting on a few pounds here and there. When Mr. Woodburn saw me in Jamaica in March 2007, he actually looked right through me, as in not recognising me. When I said, "Hello," he looked around, and he almost fell off his chair. He stood up and reached out to shake my hand as he did at the handover of his wife all those years ago. He still had the same tight-grip handshake. He said, "My God, you look well. You look damn well. Life must be treating you well."

I replied, "Oh yes, old boy, certainly," as I reached for my wallet, showing him my wedding picture.

He said, "I am glad to see you have moved on so quickly. I am so happy for you."

He replied, "Nice woman."

I said, "Oh yes, much better than the one before, old chap."

He asked, "How long are you staying?"

I replied, "Two weeks."

September 2007, six months after my journey to this forbidden island, I returned because the trip in March was not for pleasure. However, this trip was planned for pleasure. I wanted to show Zora where I came from and also to celebrate one year of our marriage. The journey started out somewhat hazardous. The flight on the local airline—Air Jamaica—was the worse flight I had ever taken, saying that the flight in March was fantastic with the same airline, believe it or not. This time the flight was delayed for five hours. I was told that this was a typical move for Air Jamaica. I was given different stories at the check-in desk, which I thought was ridiculous. I was scheduled to land in Jamaica at twenty-one hundred local time when I was told of the rescheduled time for landing. I had to telephone the taxi that was picking me up at the airport in Jamaica. The driver had arranged with my sister-in-law, dearest Pat, to travel into Kingston to meet me. I had previously explained to my driver that my flight would be arriving at approximately 3:00 A.M. To my utmost horror, when I landed, Zora and I were treated like stow-away; our passports were taken by immigration, our luggage were searched piece by piece, and we were left to repack our cases. I was riddled with disbelief and not to mention embarrassment. The question that I ask: Was it because of the passports we carry? Or were we picked on because we were classed as foreigners? I could not help but notice that Jamaican passport holders were simply going through quite easily!

On the return journey, (back to the United Kingdom) the boot was on the other foot. Jamaican passport holders arriving in the United Kingdoms were put aside and questioned almost like tit-for-tat strange, I may add. On the exit, I was to meet my driver in Kingston, but he did not appear at all. However, as I looked around, I spotted someone who had a crush on me for several months before I decided to travel to Jamaica whilst in England. Oh yes, my dear friends, it was the one and only Pat, the sister-in-law who knew I was married but still wanted a piece of me! Or was she just after some money? What do you think? Whilst she was here in the United Kingdom, I did treat her very well, I must admit. I gave her two cell phones, took her on day trips, in fact, that my wife felt uneasy about my kindness toward this young woman. I was actually rather pleased to see her at that time of the morning. Pat was at the airport for a reason. On the way to Mandeville, we spoke very little due to tiredness, of course, but we did speak about the fares because Pat had brought her own driver. She told me that the driver wanted £70. (I replied, "I beg you pardon?" Originally, an agreement was made with my previous driver for $4000 (which is the equivalent of £35). The fares with the new driver was doubled, and I was in total shock. We reached our destination at approximately 5:20 A.M. at my father's ranch, of course. The driver and I got out of the car, and we both went towards the boot to retrieve the suitcases. As this was done, I gave the driver the sum he requested—£70 English pounds, of course!

He replied, "Don't pay me, pay my friend." At this point, I smell a big rat! I gave the money to Pat. Zora got out of the car. My dad opened the door, and we both went in to the house that was our first rip-off. I discussed this with my dad, and he was rather upset because he could have got us home much cheaper. We went straight to bed. Later on that day, Father had arranged a vehicle for us. It cost $4,000 rental per day. However, due to the fact that the agent was Father's tenant, we had an incredible reduction, paying $2,500 per day instead $4,000 for a four by four jeep. That was a very good price. I paid the agent $3,500 for two weeks rental, and he took us back to the airport for free. Good deal. Beat that, Pat, you bitch! I acquired the vehicle on Sunday still tired from the flight. I took it for a test drive and was pleased with the performance.

The next day, we plunged head first into holiday mode we almost died for. First trip on Monday was the alligator pond, Little Ocho Rios. I was so excited about being at this delicate spot. I always told Zora about the seafood that was served there. I went to the bar and introduced her to my dear friend who worked there who was a friend of Carol Woodburn, or shall I say Carol Nembhard? I then ordered a meal that was very big to the eyes and dangerous to the stomach. I ordered a huge snapper fish approximately eighteen inches long, steamed with bammy. Zora ordered conk, followed by lobster. We sampled each other's meal, and we ate until we could not move. This meal was very expensive indeed, but I dare say that we did not want to waste our money, so we took the leftovers back home with us. When we returned to Mandeville, we had a shower and went to bed. My God! I started to feel sick. I asked Zora how she felt; she was also sick. I vomitted violently and felt rather weak afterwards. Believe it or not, whilst trying to sleep, I was kept awake by the continuous repetition of seeing the faces of dead people. I saw Mother's face. Then appeared Sister Jane's dead husband's face—John. They were both calling me for some strange reason. I told them I was not ready, and the faces suddenly disappeared. Perhaps, if I had responded the way they wanted me to and went with them, I am certain that I would be sent a wreath by all my friends and family, but I beat death once more! On the subject of death, an unbelievable bit of news hit me. In the newspaper was news of a young man working on the night shift in the same funeral home that Sister Jane's husband was kept. This young man was caught by his colleagues having sex with a dead woman. He was beaten close to death, and unfortunately, for him, he lost his job. He told the papers when he regained consciousness that the woman was so beautiful, he could not resist the temptation. In my opinion, I am sure that this young man needed serious psychiatric help. How bizarre!

I told Father about the turbulent night we had after consuming our meal at the restaurant. He then said that his dog had died because he fed to the dog the remains of the food we brought back with us. We were both in shock. The same day, Zora complained of stomach pains. I took her to the pharmacy, and they gave us some medicine. However, we both still remained unwell although we were taking the medicine. We were both walking in town, wondering what had happened to us. I saw a familiar face. I stopped and looked at this old lady, and she gazed back at me, pointing me out to her husband. I looked at them both and said, "I know you." They continued to stare. I then said to her, "Your name is Louise."

She said, "Yes."

I said to her husband, "Your name is David."

He said, "Yes."

They both asked in harmony, "Who are you?"

I said, "Look again."

Then Daddy said, "Of course, you are Raymond."

I said, "Yes." Believe it or not, these were the two people that raised me from the age of one year old! They now resided in America. Coincidentally, we were all on vacation at the same time. At that point, it was all hugs and tears. Aunt Louise is Father dear's sister, and Daddy is her husband, David. We planned to meet later in the day, and so we did. We told them about what had happened after eating the seafood. Auntie immediately started to get together numerous herbs along with a piece of ginger. She boiled this concoction. She then added a little sugar and gave it to us to drink. Zora went to the toilet and was vomiting violently just as I did the previous night. I was by her side in case she needed assistant. Apparently, it was the same thing that came up when I was ill. Auntie's old remedy had worked.

She then asked, "Who is the pretty girl?" I then gave her all the details. She was ecstatic when she knew Zora was my wife.

We left Auntie's house and went to Westmoreland, the border near St. Elizabeth. This particular area was called Border, several miles out of town, I may add. In this area, there was a lot of cooking going on. We tried the local cuisine. We ate well and then drove back to Mandeville. The next day, we were feeling 90 percent better in our health, and throughout the rest of the holiday, we never returned to alligator pond! Why do you think?

We went to YS Falls, but unfortunately, we got there a little bit too late. The last trip for the waterfalls was already in progress. We then decided to do an impulsive act. I said, "Let's go to Negril," as it was en-route. Although we had no toiletries, we proceeded on our adventure. When we arrived at Negril, we had to find some place to stay the night, so we spent almost two hours visiting guesthouses and hotels, picking and choosing as we went by. Only one hotel passed our hygiene test—Coral Seas Resorts. It had the cleanest environment that I had personally ever entered, fully air-conditioned, with swimming pool, restaurant, and bar; it was extremely posh, I may say. We went and bought some toiletries that we needed and booked into this amazing hotel. The next day, we travelled from Negril, stopped at Border and Bluefields beach, and then up through the hills to YS Falls. That day was a day to remember. From YS, we returned to Mandeville where we spent the night. The next day, we were off again, heading for Ocho Rios. The journey to Ocho Rios was quite hectic due to the damage that was done to the roads by the hurricane. Nevertheless, we plunged through in the jeep. In Ocho Rios, we did not waste time looking for hotels because I knew exactly where we were going. It was an unnamed guesthouse which I called Barratts's place, named after my friend Barratt whose dad owned the place. However, to my surprise, the cost of stopping there was more expensive than I imagined. In fact, it cost the same as the hotel in Negril. Talk about doing a friend a favour, but never mind. I guess, although it was my friend's dad, my accent was different. We visited Dunns River Falls and Dolphin Cove.

We also jet skied to the house where the James Bond film was made.. From Ocho Rios, we proceeded towards Portland, stopping at all the beauty spots along the way. We arrived at Annatto Bay at 9:00 P.M. I spoke to a local who insisted that I was crazy. "Travelling at nights is unheard of in these parts," she uttered. I must admit that I was scared, but I did not show it. We journeyed through Buff Bay and Port Maria, arriving at Port Antonio. We stopped at a petrol station and asked for the best hotel in the area. We were directed to a placed called Tim Bamboo. I do not wish to comment on it. The next day, we travelled to Manchioneal; I wanted to show Zora where Sabrina came from. We then turned around and travelled back towards the areas we covered during the darkness of the night. We stopped at a place called Summerset Falls, which had a lot of wild birds, including peacocks and talking parrots. Also, there was a huge cave with a waterfall inside. Inside the cave, some parts of the rock appeared like creatures due to the continuous beating of the water against the rock. The guide told Zora to touch the rock. She was terrified. I, too, was afraid, but I touched it also after seeing the guide played with it almost as if it was a living creature. I would hate to be in that place at night.

We left Summerset Falls and continued our journey around the island. We also went to the Blue Mountains and around Jamaica in approximately seven days. We spent the rest of the holiday visiting families, going to the places we overlooked, and most importantly, familiarising ourselves with Father and his new family. One day, Father's new wife and I were having a conversation. She seemed somewhat troubled. I asked what the cause of her troubled mind was. She started revealing to me some of her utmost secrets, which took me all the way back to my childhood.

She said, "Your dad is a disgusting old man. Several times, I have had to save him from prison because of his perverted lifestyle. Just before you came to Jamaica," she said, "your dad had lured a thirteen-year-old girl to go back to his house. His trap was telling the child he is a millionaire, and she can have anything she desires. The naïve child went through the shortcut that leads to the house. I was told by a neighbour that he was seen approaching the house after taking a different route, meeting with the child. At this point, I was taking care of the business. This was a big disgrace for me." Her family came to the business place, and there was a great scandal outside. The child was taken to the doctor next door to the business place. Traces of semen were found in the pubic region, but no sign of penetration.

I said to Doris, "You have my sympathies. All I can say to you is at the time when Mother was away in England for treatment of cancer, I remember the chef telling me that Father was having sex with a member the staff." I really do not think she knew that I knew that it was her. She looked at me as if she had seen a ghost! I said, "You are now the wife of my father. You and Mother dear were running a race. My dear mother simply passed you the baton so you carry on. What goes around comes around, as they say. Look after your daughter."

She said, "I have two daughters, and I will not encourage any of them to go with a married man." I guess she was ashamed. She also revealed to me that she knew all the so-called secrets of the family. She told me of the rape of Cousin Velma and also the rape that took place when I was attending Mandeville school at the age of eleven when my father was imprisoned. In fact, she told me everything I knew that I have previously mentioned in Chapter One - My Wonderful Family. Then she gave me the biggest shock of all. She had revealed to me that her last child who was my baby sister was not the only child she gave birth to for my dear father. That came as a nasty little surprise. She said that nine years ago, she gave birth, but unfortunately, the child died. I was totally shocked. The next day, I went to visit my dearest Auntie. She had confirmed everything in detail. She told me that the baby had a great send-off, almost as if it was royalty. Mother was alive at that point. I was told by Sister Jane that during the pregnancy, Mother dear was approached by Doris and said words to this effect, "I am pregnant by your husband, and you can't do nothing about it. Your husband is mine because you are finished. Done wife that's what you are. If you could fuck like me, your husband would still be yours, but now, he's mine." So, you could see, my dear friends, I do believe that God removed Doris's first child she bore for Father dear because of his lack of compassion for Mother during her terminal illness. However, I say that whatever happened to Doris was what she deserved. Nonetheless, Doris had a bizarre request of me. She had requested me to go to Father's doctor in the United Kingdom, try to acquire his medical records, and forward it to her so she could see if Father really had a perverted illness because as far as she was concerned, he was a sick pervert. Why are you with him? I wondered. I guess the life after his death looked bright, I dared say. For me, to have my medical record seen by my solicitor, I had to go through a lot of red tape. Why would Doris think that Father's medical record would be handed to me over the counter? I thought she had simply forgotten that I was not living in Jamaica, but in the United Kingdom. Father claimed that he and his new wife went to Mother's tomb on a regular basis to clean it. I dare say that Mother had missed the chance again to slap the bitch. The dead have no power. Rest in peace, Mother dear.-I was asked by a respectable member of the community and of the family, a cousin of Mother dear who was also running a business in town, "How does your father walk the street with his head up? The whole town knows what he is about. It is a disgrace." Father claimed that none of his five children who were employed and resided in the United Kingdom had ever given him a dollar. I was certain that he had a very convenient memory loss because the last trip to England that he had, I made a contribution to the begging bucket. I also gave him money in March to connect the emergency water supply, the rent from his luxurious apartment in London, and the joint pension, to name a few. His income far exceeded mine. Personally, I should be tapping him for some money.

Note to the British government: Sister Jane thought that it was a big joke, how Father could pass himself off as a millionaire when the luxury apartment that he was subletting was actually being paid for by the government through the benefit system provided by the United Kingdom. Personally, my dear friends, I had not really known a millionaire on benefit. Do you? British government nil returnee to Jamaica $$$! If I had his income on a legal basis in Jamaica, I would be crowned a king!!

He had revealed to Zora that the mansion in Jamaica would never be sold because that was written in his will. Doris, on the other hand, may live in that house as long as she had the ability to breathe. From my point of view, I do believe that Father was putting down a time bomb because what happened in March would simply recur on a larger scale. I mentioned this to Doris, and she replied, "I will not be moved. I know my legal rights."

But the trouble was there were family members who would kill to preserve Mother's honour, excluding myself, I may say, old chaps. My dear friends, the burning question was Doris knew what she knew. She was young—aged thirty-three. In fact, she revealed to me that she was the only living member of her family who was unhappy in a relationship. Was this not enough to make a woman walk away? I had personally seen women walk away after finding out less than what Doris had found out. The molestation of the young child would have been enough for her to walk out, but no, she was still hanging in there. The question was why? My dear friends, would you walk away from a profitable business in your name and the comfort of an eight-bedroom mansion in the sun? I don't think so. One day, Doris would own everything. Mark my words. Mother's honour was buried the same day as she was. Although Doris confirmed that she did not start seeing Father dear until way after Mother had died, she simply made a fool of herself. Mother died eight years ago while the first child she conceived for my dear father would have been nine years old. Ironic, wasn't it? She was simply a notorious liar. The next day, after hearing all these revelations, I decided to go walking in the town, showing Zora the market place, local shops, and gift shops. To my utmost surprise, while we were in Superplus Supermarket looking around and, comparing prices with other places, I looked across, and sitting down as usual—do you need to ask? Of course, it was good old Mr. Woodburn. He greeted us with great admiration and that same old tight-grip handshake once more.

He said, "Damn! You look great as always."

I said to him, "This woman is the reason for my great looks."

He said, "This must be the wife." He shook her hand.

"He held on a bit too long," she said to me on our way back to London. Looking at the way Woodburn held onto Zora's hand, it was clear to me that he had never held the hand of an angel. Then I guessed there was a first time for everything! He was quite pleased to see that the bottom of my shoe didn't have the residue that I picked up ten years ago in Jamaica whilst on holiday.

I would simply say he could have her back! If I did not visit Jamaica in 1992 and stole Carol from her husband, they would still be together and in love, although the image they projected were more of a grandfather and granddaughter. In fact, at first sight, that was my thought. I knew he loved her because you could see it in his eyes. I must apologise to the silver-haired old man once more.

Mr. Woodburn asked, "What brought you to the island this time? Business or pleasure?"

I said, "I am here on this island to celebrate one year of marriage and to bury the turbulent past once and for all."

He said, "Boy, the wife is very pretty."

I replied, "Better than the old one." I say, old chap, much better.

He had a look upon on his face as if to say "Why did you take Carol away from me?" However, that look told me that he still loved her. I remember him saying to me, "I will always love her, and she will come back to me." I hope it was not too late for Mr. Bojangle, as I remembered him.

On reflection, one day during the adventurous trip around the town, I had built up a passion for something sweet. I stopped at a cake shop that sold delicious cakes and other delights of the island. I ordered what I wanted. Whilst being served, a young lady with a group of friends walked into the shop. This particular young lady was staring into my eyes with a smirk on her face. As I paid for my order, she shouted to the shop assistant, "Have you finished serving this young man?"

Her friends gathered round, giggling like a bunch of teenage girls on heat, as she stared into my eyes.

She said, "I want two slices of chocolate cake please, and make sure they are big." She started to grin as she figured I was lusting after her. She reached for a banana from her bag. As I stared at her helplessly, she peeled the banana, and I watched it disappeared in her mouth. She was still staring at my face. I was absolutely speechless. I tried to speak, but my speech came out as a stutter. Her friends stared as if they were watching their favourite artist on stage. She retracted the banana from her mouth unscathed by her teeth. At this point, I do believe that she was trying to tell me something. I was blushing like a well-mothered teenage boy.

I uttered in my stuttering voice, "My wife is in the car."

To my utmost shock, the shop assistant shouted, "What's your wife got to do with it? Deal with her." I do believe in my innermost heart of hearts that if Zora was not with me on this island, I would have committed the same sin that brought me to my knees all over again. Even writing about it, just remembering it, had got me into a state of arousal. Her face always appeared into my mind at the wrong time, and I had to use my inner strength to dismiss this state of fantasy. Nonetheless, saying all that did not stop me from thinking, Will I ever see her again? The chance was a million to one. Or was I thinking, What if, or If only I had.... But I know the consequence of seeing her again would be too great.

On the subject of lust, whilst walking in the market looking at all the fresh fruits and produce of the land, I heard a voice saying quite loudly in a Jamaican stylie, "Angel face. How did you get here? What was heaven like when you left?" At this point, I turned around to see what was going on. This local hustler was hovering over Zora as if he had never seen someone of her appearance before. I did believe that she did not understand a word he said. She stood there with a grin on her face, as if to say "What is he talking about?" I thought it was rather funny because I understood every word he uttered.

Later that day, I happened to bump into a dear friend who was very fond of Carol and I, although he warned me of my friendship with her. He was saddened to know of my downfall, but I assured him that Carol did me a favour. He was rather bitter when he was explaining to me of his break-up with Carol's sister, Karen. He enlightened me that he caught her in his bed, having sex with his best friend who was grinding Karen whilst still wearing his working boots, so he had to break off the engagement. I guess it was in the blood of the Nembhard breed; they just could not help themselves. Don't forget, as I had said before, "If it smells like a fish and it has a hole, Eastan will ride it." That was how the Nembhard breed came about. Eastan Nembhard, alias "platehead," almost had a child out of every other woman in St. Elizabeth. In my opinion, the sperms that flowed from this vagabond were similar to the thorns on the red rose due to crossbreeding. Just imagine a lovely bunch of red rose looking so beautiful. Be careful, though, because the thorns would get you. Think about it! It was a very poor bloodline, almost like a generation cursed. Come to think of it, Eastan was an alcoholic, and Nancy was purely a mental person who was taken advantage of by Eastan. The poor woman was only earning a living by cleaning. Unfortunately, for her, the day she went to clean his shop, she was ravaged and became pregnant. The offspring of these two people surely must be a bad bloodline to get involved with.

I was made an incredible offer. "How about putting her to sleep?" says my angry friend. "What her sister did to me tells me that it is time for me to get even." I though about it for a while. "Putting her to sleep would be too good for her," I said to the angry young man.

He said, "You may be over what she did to you because you are happily married, but what Karen did to me will stay with me until the moment of my revenge." He insisted on me contacting him on Carol's return to Jamaica and he will fix it. But this I refused because I would never deprive my daughter of her mother, although to me she was a monster and I also didn't have the freedom that I have now for caring for my sweet little angel full time. I carried no bitterness nor hatred for the owner of the cocoon that carried Rochelle for nine months.

I stressed again to my angry friend, "One day, you will feel just the way I do. Peace be with you, my friend. Although revenge is sweet, sometimes, it is not the only way. Think about it.

"Whoever tries to destroy you, my friend, you must not try to destroy them in return. You must do nothing but let them see that they were unsuccessful in your destruction. Let the pain the enemy inflict upon you make you strong, that way you will always be laughing at the enemy. An old Japanese proverb, which I use quite frequently, says, 'Never do what the enemy expects you to do.' Always do the opposite because the enemy will always self-destruct. Time is the master."

On reflection, I rang Carol and asked her why was she confusing Rochelle by telling her that Michael was her daddy. She knew that I would end up at Savacentre, her place of work, to sort out this matter. She also knew that if she fled from Savacentre, knowing that I was on my way, I would end up at the marital home at 4 Thomas Dean Road. She was ready and waiting for me with D. C. Duffus and his cronies because she knew that when Maggie, her work colleague informed me that she was not at work, I would have gone straight to the house where I would be arrested by the police for breaking the injunction. But I denied those bastards of the pleasure. I simply held my daughter by the hand and left Savacentre. My daughter and I spent that weekend at Southend-on-Sea, and we stayed in a hotel. I guessed that D. C. Duffus did not fuck Carol that night because the trap had failed yet again! "Never do what the enemy expects you to do!" Get my drift?

I must say that I have deep hatred for the police because of what D. C. Duffus did. He abused the power given to him, disgracing the Crown.

My dear friends, please forgive me for what I had done. At this point, you may be thinking that I am a so-called softie because I knew that Father dear thought that I was back in the fold. Christmas 2007 was upon us, and as you knew, the world gets hungry for money during this time of year. It appeared that the trip to Jamaica in September had caused the whole family to think that bygones would be bygones! But they were so wrong. I did not carry bitterness, but the memories of what was done and what was taken from me always haunted me. In fact, it was quite traumatising, and no matter how hard I tried, the trauma that I suffered from the family would not let me be. Father rang me four times. At one point, I told Zora to tell him that I was not at home, referring back to when Father visited Brother Malcolm's shop. I was told that he also gave word that he was not around. At the time, I could not understand why, but now, I could simply relate to it. I got fed up of hiding, so when the phone call came through again, I answered it. Father claimed that he was down on his face and penniless. Christmas was fast approaching. He said, "And all the houses surrounding mine have a new paint job, and mine looks totally disgusting." He also said, "I was wondering if you could give me a loan."

I replied, "I really can't help you at this point, but I am expecting a bonus for Christmas. I will then see how much I get, and then I will know if I can help you."

Three days passed, and the phone began to ring again. I never answered the phone; I always leave it for Zora to answer if she was not too busy. It was Father again. I was not in the mood to talk to him so he had a forty-five minutes conversation with her. After, she filled me in with the details. She said Father was asking her if she knew anything about the money that I promised him. At this point, I was very upset. He also mentioned to her the house in Jamaica that belonged to his children in England. You see, my dear friends, it seemed that I was back in the fold. It sure looked that way. A few days later, I got paid, the bonus was included, and you know what? I sent him some money, but I tell you, I prefer if I did not do this because the pain of sending the money was simply cutting me like a knife. I told a family member of what I had done, and she was in total shock. In fact, she said she was disgusted with me, but I was even more disgusted with myself. I guess the kind-heartedness of my dear mother had simply rubbed off on me. How sad. I knew that any money that went in the hands of Father by any family member was what they call dead money! Days after lending him the money, I learnt that it was not used for repainting the house. He lied to me. Instead, the money was used for medical fees due to the fact that he was adding another extension to his siblings. I dared say, "Bang goes whatever inheritance would have been left for the children of the previous marriage." As mentioned in chapter one, my wonderful family, the old man has done it again, still firing live ammunition at his age! Hey! So, there was still hope for me at age forty-seven. I wonder what he was taking! A close friend had revealed to me that while Father was here in England on holiday, he asked my friends' girlfriend to meet him whilst my pal was at work. Some people claimed that I resembled my father, but I will not replicate his lifestyle! My faithful messenger who alerted me through the wonderful communication path of the Internet also informed me that the biggest joke in the small town of Mandeville was that a frail-looking old man walking the street with a thirty-three years old man-eating woman, who was pregnant. The question was who for? It was plain to see that it was a "jacket" or perhaps a "raincoat!" But I do believe that Father dear would not take the test to prove his paternity (or to simplify, the DNA test). Nonetheless, whether my name was on the scribbling of a will handwritten by Sister Judy or not, I am in the same boat. Whether the will was made with or without a lawyer makes no difference at all. In fact, all the five siblings who resided in England had fuck all to get. So why bother to fight? Father's new family had everything to gain, and you know what his so-called floozy of a wife knows that her future was bright, whether he wears a jacket or not. Think about it. I wondered how many times Mother turned in her grave, looking at the situation from above, hovering and looking down on her poor children, knowing she could not do anything to regain her loss. The dead had no power after all! Thirty-five years of working in snow and ice, not to mention the thick fog, had gone to someone who had no idea of work. Rest in peace, Mother dear. In our hearts, you are still alive.

On a brighter note, Zora's mother decided to go to France for Christmas, travelling from Guadeloupe. Zora decided to meet her there. She asked if I wished to travel with her. I consulted Rochelle, and she decided that she wanted to stay in the United Kingdom with me. However, I did not expect my daughter to stay with me throughout the whole of the festive holiday up to New Year because a little girl's place was with her mother. I made several plans for letting my hair down and to party my way into the New Year, but Rochelle refused to go home. We went shopping. We did everything together. I quite enjoyed watching her counting the £2000 pounds that I had for Christmas.

She said, "Dad, where did you get so much money?"

I said, "The bank, of course." She was extremely excited. I almost thought that she thought her daddy was a drug dealer. We went shopping, and I bought her everything her little heart desired; she never left my side. When I mentioned taking her back to her mother, she simply cried. Looking back, I really appreciated her being with me.

She made me a little tearful when she said, "I wanted to stay with you, Dad, because I love you."

How sweet, I thought. The feeling of having Rochelle with me over the festive season was simply unexplainable. The relationship I have with my daughter Rochelle was simply what Carol, her mother, dreamed of. Rochelle and I is a sealed unit.

Five years later and the trauma that I suffered was still fresh like a wound that refused to heal.

D. C. Duffus was guilty of misconduct in public office and, typical of the British Law, he got away with it. I wonder how many more cases were just like this, floating away with the tide. British justice is like a one-way street.

The amazing thing was that D. C. Duffus was seen on CCTV locked in an embrace with Carol within the court building on the upper floor. The IPCC called this unprofessional behaviour and ruled out conspiracy. I must say, not one day had gone past that I did not think of what had happened to me. In the crime file that was sent to me, it was suggested that D. C. Duffus had spoken to me in July, five months before my arrest in December 2002. I had never seen or heard of D. C. Duffus until the day in December 2002 when I was arrested, so obviously it was clear that he was a notorious liar, the same as his counterpart. You may ask, my dear friends, if I was compensated for what had happened to me. Believe it or not, I would say "Yes," but not financially. I guess the unconditional love from Rochelle and the fact that I got divorced from Carol at no cost to me, also, the freedom to marry someone far better than the previous one, to me, all these are deemed far better than any financial settlement for compensation.

My dear friends, would you believe it? Six years after being handcuffed and dragged away from my child whom I was bathing at the time, the trauma of the incident is still with me as if it had happened yesterday. Some nights, I had terrible nightmares repeating the incident over and over. I always woke up on my side of the bed, soaking wet with sweat. My wife oftentimes asked me what the cause of my sweating and tossing and turning in the bed was, but it was something that I really did not like to discuss. This mainly occured when I see uniformed police or a police car. You could imagine what I was going through. Come to think of it, I wonder how Rochelle felt six years after my arrest. But then, she was only four at the time. She always said to me, "D. C. Duffus is dead." I guess she had dealt with her trauma. She never failed to tell me how special I was to her and how much she loved me. This always brought a tear to my eyes. My relationship with Rochelle was enough to keep me alive, but then, I cannot depend on the love of my child in order to survive. People still approached us whenever we were out and about, complimenting us on our closeness, but I don't think anyone understood. The British government, with its highest powers, stopped many fathers from seeing their children simply by listening to the lies of their mothers. Many children are suffering from not getting the love of their fathers. I believe, if every child were given the opportunity that Rochelle had, there simply would be less teenage crime and violence, not only in this country, but I dared say in the entire world, and that's a fact.

When I met Carol, I thought I had found gold, only to discover later on in life, after meeting Zora, that there is gold, and there is pure gold. My freedom had had a severe impact on Carol's life, knowing what she wanted the end result to be for me — ten years in prison. For what, may I ask? I was never able to put the news right until 2007 when I visited Jamaica. The imprisonment did not happen, to her disappointment! Apparently, it was sensational news in Jamaica in 2002 that "Wife stolen by Englishman is imprisoned by her!" With her newfound love, D. C. Duffus, coupled with his cronies, they merged in a pot of conspiracy and plotted to imprison me through false allegation. At the trial, Carol Francis.. Sorry, I meant Carol Woodburn. Oops! It was Nembhard. Carol Nembhard had lost her memory. I, today, stand as living proof of a resistance to destruction. I, Raymond Francis, the author, is proud to tell you that happiness is love, peace, and well-being of one's mind and soul, solid as a rock. They cannot stop me now!

My dear friends, would you believe that the playboy lifestyle was back, haunting me in 2008? It was very difficult to maintain the faithfulness that is required of me in a relationship, which is filled with love and happiness. Believe it or not, my dear Anita was single again. Also, to add even more pressure, I met a lovely lady in the usual place—the health club, of course. We've been friends for a while. She also knew of my predicament—being married, that is. A few weeks ago, I visited the health club just to relax and chill out in the sauna. The young lady was there. Her name was Rebecca. What she did send me in a state of shock, all the way back to Jamaica, in the incident with the banana. Apparently, Rebecca was drinking Lucozade from a slimline bottle. She held the bottle at approximately 45 degrees, allowing the last drop of drink to trickle down on to her tongue. At that point, she was staring me point-blank in the eyes. To my surprise, the bottle started to disappear in her mouth, just as the banana did with the young lady in Jamaica. Now, I wonder, was she trying to tell me something? I dared say I said to her, "You are very good."

She said, "What are you talking about?"

How coincidental, I say, old chap. But you know what? I stood my ground because when I think of what I have with Zora, it is just not worth the risk. Indeed, I was surprised with myself. The unseen power of love has simply taken its toll.

The End

My dear friends, I do hope that you have enjoyed the read. If this story have any impact on you personally, or you simply want to talk to me on a one-to-one basis, don't' hesitate to communicate.

You may contact me via e-mail at rayanfra@aol.com